Thomas Woodbine Hinchliff

Over the sea and far away

Being a narrative of wanderings round the world

Thomas Woodbine Hinchliff

Over the sea and far away
Being a narrative of wanderings round the world

ISBN/EAN: 9783337197346

Printed in Europe, USA, Canada, Australia, Japan

Cover: Foto ©Andreas Hilbeck / pixelio.de

More available books at **www.hansebooks.com**

BRIDAL VEIL FALL, YOSEMITÉ

Frontispiece.

OVER THE SEA AND FAR AWAY

BEING A NARRATIVE OF

WANDERINGS ROUND THE WORLD

BY

THOMAS WOODBINE HINCHLIFF, M.A., F.R.G.S.

PRESIDENT OF THE ALPINE CLUB

AUTHOR OF 'SUMMER MONTHS AMONG THE ALPS' 'SOUTH AMERICAN SKETCHES' ETC.

'PER DIES FESTOS IN REMOTO GRAMINE'—*Horace*

WITH FOURTEEN ILLUSTRATIONS

ENGRAVED ON WOOD BY G. PEARSON FROM PHOTOGRAPHS AND SKETCHES

LONDON
LONGMANS, GREEN, AND CO.
1876

TO

WILLIAM HENRY RAWSON, ESQ.

'THE FOUNDER OF THE FEAST'

THIS RECORD OF PLEASANT AND SUCCESSFUL
WANDERINGS ROUND THE WORLD IN
COMPANY WITH HIS SON

Is Dedicated

WITH THE VERY KIND REGARDS OF
THEIR SINCERE FRIEND

THE AUTHOR

PREFACE.

IN THE AUTUMN of 1873 I had a very welcome opportunity of starting upon a journey round the world in company with Mr. W. H. RAWSON; and we took so erratic a course that, though the world is generally supposed to be only about 24,000 miles in circumference, we succeeded in traversing nearly 36,000 miles of ocean, in addition to spending about six months in sojourns and expeditions among the terrestrial regions of the earth.

Two principal reasons have induced me to venture upon publishing an account of our travels. Former visits had made me familiar with the forest-depths of the country about the beautiful Organ Mountains of Brazil, with the palm-crowned rolling hills of the Banda Oriental, and with all the delights of shooting and galloping over the boundless Pampas of the Argentine Republic. I had, however, never before seen the wonders of the Straits of Magellan, with glaciers falling into the sea; I had neither seen nor imagined the stupendous peaks of the Andes looking down upon the plains of Chile and Peru; nor had I any sufficient idea of the wonders and curiosities of the whole Pacific coast, its multitudinous fish and birds, its arid hills and earthquake-smitten cities. After having seen all these things, and been enabled to compare the Pacific with the Atlantic side of a neglected continent, I felt irresistibly tempted to say something concerning it, with the view of, if possible, persuading others to see what I myself intensely enjoyed, and to avoid following the example of the great majority of modern travellers, who, for some unknown reasons, appear almost unanimously to exclude South America from their programme.

My other reason is, that there appeared to me to be abundant room for a further and more detailed account of the natural aspect of many of the countries which we were fortunate enough to visit, especially with regard to their scenery, their flowers, ferns, and forests. The taste for these matters is, I hope and believe, advancing rapidly; and, though I have refrained from giving long and perhaps wearisome catalogues of plants, yet I have endeavoured from time to time to call attention to some of the most remarkable of those which give a distinct tone and individuality to the countries in which they are found. Moreover, having convinced myself in these and in many other wanderings of every variety, from the tops of lofty mountains to the recesses of the Tropical forest, that even a slight knowledge of plants doubles the pleasure of travelling, I gladly impress the fact upon others. It adds a new charm to every delightful scramble, and gives continual interest even to what might otherwise be considered a dull walk.

I enjoyed our Spring rambles in California even more than I could have expected. The wonders of the Yosemité Valley, the sublimity of the forests, the shining snows of the Sierra Nevada, the lovely hills of the Coast ranges, and the vast regions of park-like land clothed in sheets of innumerable flowers, all combine to form a picture of beauty and magnificence which can never fade from the memory of the fortunate beholder.

In the short time which has passed since our visit to Japan, many changes are already reported to have taken place; and I understand that greater facilities are given to those who wish to travel in the interior. There are, however, many other changes in full operation, which will be far less acceptable to lovers of the curious and the picturesque. Fortunately, nothing can take away the exquisite charm and beauty of the country itself, and I hope that nothing will impair the amiable simplicity of the masses of the people. Nevertheless, if anybody contemplates a journey to Japan, he may be very sure that the sooner he goes the better he will like it. Let him take his strong boots, and say if he ever enjoyed anything more than a walking tour in the hilly region which we visited.

The Illustrations are chiefly taken from photographs, which have been carefully engraved by Mr. George Pearson; but I am indebted for the mountain view from Santiago in Chile to the well-known pencil of my friend, Mr. WILLIAM SIMPSON, who made the drawing from a pen-and-ink sketch taken by myself upon the spot; and the engraving of the Bridal Veil Fall is taken from a picture painted by the same artist, and kindly lent by Mr. WILLIAM LONGMAN for the purpose.

T. W. HINCHLIFF.

LINCOLN'S INN FIELDS:
March 1876.

CONTENTS.

CHAPTER I.

A Start for Brazil—Teneriffe and the Grand Canary—St. Vincent—Pernambuco—Bahia—Rio de Janeiro—The Royal Palms—The Imperador Moth—Off to Petropolis—The Organ Mountains—A Delightful Garden—Vegetation of the Hills—Fern-hunting—Road to Juiz da Fora—Agassiz and Glacial Action—Speed of the Mules—Rough Method of breaking them in—Humming-birds—Araucarias and Gigantic Aloes . . . . Page 1

CHAPTER II.

Valley of the Retiro—A direful Spider—Evening—Entrerios and Palmeiras—Ferns and Palmitos—Feather-flowers—Sail in the 'Neva'—Storm at night—Arrival at Buenos Ayres—Great changes—Railway progress—The 'Camp' revisited—Owls and biscachas—Reports of Cholera—The magnificent 'Luxor'—Arrival of the 'Eothen'—Excursions to Ensenada and Chascomus—A brilliant shot . . . . Page 26

CHAPTER III.

Quarantine—The *Deus ex machinâ*—The Pampero at night—Start in the 'Eothen'—'Seeing the New Year in' at sea—Cruelty in hoisting cattle—The Straits of Magellan—Sea-birds and wonders of the Kelp—The tragedy of Sandy Point—Snow Mountains and Glaciers—Cape Pillar—Albatrosses and bad weather—Coronel—The Gardens and Smelting Works of Lota—Arrival at Valparaiso . . . . Page 47

CHAPTER IV.

The Cochrane statue—'Earthquakis'—The suburbs of Valparaiso—Building materials—Fox-hunting—Chacabuco revels—Delightful climate—Railway to Santiago—Fruit—The bell of Quillota—Llai-Llai—Moonlight effects—The highest station—The plain of Santiago—Arrival by night—The Grand Hotel Santa Lucia and view of the Cordillera—Aconcagua and Tupungato—Will they ever be ascended? . . . . Page 72

CHAPTER V.

The Alameda of Santiago—Precautions against fire—What became of the Jesuit Church—Remains of the dead—Bismarck in South America—A model farm in Chile—Climate and Irrigation—Baths of Cauquenes—Thrashing wheat—Refreshments at Rancagua—A strange coach-and-four—The Hot Springs—Golden Adiantum—A view in the hills—Great Aconcagua—Return to Valparaiso . . . . Page 95

CHAPTER VI.

On board the 'Santa Rosa'—A Floating Fair—Porpoises on St. Valentine's Day—Coquimbo and Serena—Huasco Grapes—Mountains of Melons—Countless Pelicans—Luminous Fish—A 'Little Revolution' in Bolivia—Iquique and Arica—Arica Mummies—Mollendo and Islay—Scorpion-fight—Peruvian Soldiers—Remarkable situation of Quilca—Astonished Whales—The Chincha Islands—Callao . . . . . . Page 119

CHAPTER VII.

First view of Lima—The Cathedral—Thoughts of Pizarro—Origin of the name of Lima—Climate of Lima—The Watershed of Peru—Breakfast at Chorillos—Fruits and Flowers—The Exhibition Building—Fair Ladies—The Alameda Nueva—Return of Rosito—Payta and bad news from Panama—Crossing the Equator again—'Old Boots'—A Haunt of the Buccaneers—Arrival at Panama . . . . Page 147

CHAPTER VIII.

Great Fire at Panama—Difficult boating—The effect of Judge Lynch—The miseries of the 'Arizona'—'Dipping'—The Barber's Shop on board—St. José de Guatemala—Champorico not to be found—Acapulco—Rubbed with a Jelly-fish—Mexican atrocities—The Whale and the 'Thrasher'—Doings of Brigands—Mazatlan—Sharp change of Climate—Cape St. Lucas—A lonely Post-office—Towing the 'Colima' to San Francisco—The Golden Gate . . . . Page 169

CHAPTER IX.

Good living at San Francisco—'Oldest Inhabitants'—Living by Bears—Progress of Good Taste—Splendid Lupines—Cliff House and the Sea-lions—The Redwood Tree—Wild Flowers—Berkely University—Buildings in Earthquakia—The 'Heathen Chinee'—A Chinese Theatre—The Chinese Immigration—The Mission Church of Dolores—Detestable Tramways—Californian Hospitality . . . . Page 196

CHAPTER X.

A good pace over the Bay—Calistoga—The 'dare-devil' Coachman of California—Corn and Wine—Poison-oak—Pine Flat and a Tragedy—A long jolting to the Geysers—Close to Gehenna—Nothing to eat—White Sulphur Springs—A Happy Valley—Californian Quail—The Poison-oak again—Return to San Francisco . . . . Page 220

CHAPTER XI.

Geographical comparison of Chile with California—Start for the Yosemité—Judging distances—Deserted Diggings—Lonely Chinamen near Mariposa—Skelton's—A lively Mule in the Forest—The 'Devil's Gulch' and the 'Bishop's Creek'—Hite's Cove and the Miners—The Demi-john defunct—A Miners' Inn—The Mule beaten—Fallen Rocks—Arrival in Yosemité Valley . . . . Page 242

CHAPTER XII.

The Yosemité Valley—Its discovery—Indians—Size of the Valley—Inspiration Point and the Domes—Theories of formation—Erosion or Subsidence—The 'Bridal Veil'—El Capitan—Leidig's Hotel—The great Yosemité Fall—The Sentinel Rock—The work of ancient Ice—The Mirror Lake—Avalanche Snow—Comparative Scenery—Return to Mariposa and Merced . Page 267

CHAPTER XIII.

Stockton and Milton—Fine drive to Murphy's—'Trap-door' Spiders—'Shakes'—The Big Trees of Calaveras—Cutting down a Giant—The 'Mother of the Forest'—The Prairie Owl—The Rising Generation—Sacramento City—Farewell to California—The Farallon Islands—Sea-lions and countless Birds—A Flying Escort across the Pacific—John Chinaman on board—'Perdidi Diem'—Our Escort departs—Arrival at Yokohama . . . Page 293

CHAPTER XIV.

First view of Yokohama—Substitutes for Cabs—Lilium Auratum—Start for the Interior—Our Head Coolie—Pelted with Blossoms—The 'Plains of Heaven'—Kanasawa—Kamakura, and the Temple of Hachiman—Daibootz——Disestablishment of Buddhism—What the Priests thought of it—Popular Religion—Will they break their toys?—The Holy Island of Inoshima—Race into Fuji-sawa—A break-down—The Treaty Limit—Town of Odawarra—Abundance of Ferns—Destruction of Hata—A Native Gentleman—View of Hakoni . . . . Page 317

CHAPTER XV.

The Lake of Hakoni—Running Postmen—Sulphur Baths—Meauoshita—Apparition of Mat—The 'Good Gardener'—The Baths—Two-man Ginrikishas—Native Curiosity—Tattooing—A touch of Earthquake—A dangerous Bridge—Excursion to Totska—Caves and Tumblers—Japanese Executions—The Tomb of Will Adams—His story—A Tattoo-Professor—Railway to Yeddo—Temples of Shiba—The 'Hundred Steps'—New Fashions—The Invisible Prince—Tombs of the Shōguns—Temple at Asakusa—The merciful Kuanon—Binzuru—A Japanese Tussaud—Miracles of Kuanon . . Page 346

CHAPTER XVI.

Departure from Yokohama—Waterfall at Hiogo—The Inland Sea—Countless Fishing-boats—Straits of Simonosaki—The Cathedral Rock—Nagasaki—Cruel method of Coaling a Ship—Farewell to Japan—A Japanese Pilot—His Powers of Drinking—Arrival at Shanghae—Chinese Heat at Midsummer—A Boat at Midnight—Voyage to Hong Kong, and View of Formosa—Flora of Hong Kong—The 'Happy Valley'—Fresh Ferns—Crossing the Island to Little Hong Kong—A Hot Beach—Wild Pine-apples—Lychees and Mangosteens—Expected Typhoon—Visit to Canton—Chinese Gardens—Catastrophe of the 'Spark' . . . . Page 373

CHAPTER THE LAST.

Sights in Canton—Temple of the Five Genii—Temple of the Five Hundred Gods—Chinese Shopkeepers—Goldsmiths—'Dogmeat' and 'Oatmeat'—A Broken Bottle—The City Walls—Chinese Cleverness—Farewell to Hong Kong—Thoughts of Cambodia—Singapore—Divers—Botanical Gardens—A Mixed Crew—Penang—Myriads of Cocoa-nuts—The Atchinese—The Monsoon—Ceylon—The Cinnamon-Gardens—Great Rascals—Homeward-bound—The Milky Sea—Heat in the Red Sea—The Suez Canal—Alexandria—Home Again . . . . Page 395

LIST OF ILLUSTRATIONS

BRIDAL VEIL FALL, YOSEMITÉ		*Frontispiece*
(From a Picture by WILLIAM SIMPSON, Esq.)		
SUMMER PALACE AT PETROPOLIS, BRAZIL	*to face p.*	19
THE TUPUNGATO GROUP, FROM SANTIAGO, IN CHILE		90
(From a Drawing by WILLIAM SIMPSON, Esq.)		
THE BATHS OF CAUQUENÉS, IN CHILE	,,	112
SEA BIRDS, ON THE COAST OF PERU		125
SEA-LIONS, NEAR SAN FRANCISCO	,,	204
THE DOME AND HALF DOME, YOSEMITÉ VALLEY	,,	272
THE YOSEMITÉ VALLEY AND SENTINEL ROCK	,,	279
THE FOOT OF A 'BIG TREE'	,,	302
FUJIYAMA, JAPAN	,,	316
DAIBOOTZ AT KAMAKURA, JAPAN	,,	331
VIEW ON THE WAY TO HAKONI, JAPAN	,,	342
THE 'GOOD GARDENER' OF JAPAN AT HOME	,,	351
THE CINNAMON-GARDENS IN CEYLON	,,	411

OVER THE SEA AND FAR AWAY.

CHAPTER I.

A Start for Brazil—Teneriffe and the Grand Canary—St. Vincent—Pernambuco—Bahia—Rio de Janeiro—The Royal Palms—The Imperador Moth—Off to Petropolis—The Organ Mountains—A Delightful Garden—Vegetation of the Hills—Fern-hunting—Road to Juiz da Fora—Agassiz and Glacial Action—Speed of the Mules—Rough Method of breaking them in—Humming-birds—Araucarias and Gigantic Aloes.

'OVER THE SEA! Over the sea!' What words of magic charm to those who love the sea as I do in all its moods and fancies, and who never enjoy any prospect with more unmixed satisfaction than that of a run to Southampton with a couple of portmanteaus, and the purpose of starting next day across the Ocean! The Royal Mail ship 'Douro' was already an old friend when we stepped on board her on October 9, 1873, for I was one of a party who had two years previously made a voyage in her to Rio de Janeiro; and I hoped this might be a favourable omen for a successful journey round the world.

It is impossible to mention a pleasanter route with which to begin such a journey, but yet there seems an astonishing prejudice in the popular mind against having anything to do with South America. The ordinary Englishman seems disposed to confuse all the different States of the whole continent in one mass of danger, and imagines that, if he does not get his throat cut, he is bound to die of the yellow fever. Owing to these, and perhaps other equally ridiculous delusions, the fact remains that very few people go there, except those who are bound by commercial or professional ties; and, as far as my own experience goes, I may say that I have been ten times into and out of Rio harbour, from north and south, in various years, and, excepting my own companions, I never had a fellow-passenger who was travelling for pleasure only. So much the better for those who do go to those beautiful regions; there is no appearance at present of that crowd of tourists which is gradually destroying the pleasure of seeing some of the fairest regions of the earth.

Outside the Isle of Wight we ran into a very heavy swell, left behind by a gale of wind, and for the first two days the 'Douro' danced a lively measure, which thinned the ranks of the passengers at feeding-time; at night there were sounds as if all the glass and crockery were being smashed, but the casualties were found to be very slight when morning came. I had an after cabin near the screw, where, of course, the motion was rather violent, and the captain told me a story of a man very fond of hunting, who once had the same berth in similar weather, and who, on being asked next day if he had managed to sleep there, replied, 'Oh yes, first-rate, and I dreamt all night that I was jumping over hedges and ditches.' After this, a glassy sea bore us into Lisbon, where we wandered about for a few hours, and said goodbye to Europe in the afternoon. Two or three days afterwards, in the early morning, we passed between

Teneriffe, about twenty-five miles distant on the starboard, and the Grand Canary Island much nearer on the port side. As the sun rose, the Peak came out splendidly clear of clouds, and clothed in snow towards the summit, while the Grand Canary presented a very remarkable sight. The lofty and fantastic forms of the central volcanic mountains were draped in the gloomy blackness of a storm cloud, discharging deluges of rain, from the very edge of which a long headland, ending in a steep precipice to the sea, was shining serene and golden in the morning sun.

After three days more of violet seas, just broken into crests by the sweet breath of the north-east trade wind, with frightened flying-fish skimming over the waves in all directions, whales rolling like barges turned topsy-turvy, and merry porpoises running races as if for dear life against the ship, we found ourselves at St. Vincent, in the Cape de Verde Islands, on the tenth day from England. This island is frequently without rain for two or three years together, and I had always seen it looking like a red, burnt-up mass of hills, culminating in rough and irregular volcanic rocks. I could hardly believe my eyes when I saw a good deal of it touched with a delicate green, as the result of unwonted showers. We went on shore at the invitation of Mr. Miller, the late Consul there, and practical king of the island, who kindly showed us over his factories and vast coal-stores, which, together with the security of the harbour, form the sole *raison d'être* of St. Vincent. It is, in fact, a harbour combined with a gigantic coal-cellar, for all the steamers that run up and down the Atlantic. The dirty operation of coaling went on all day, while the ship was surrounded by boats full of young niggers and half-breeds, who spend their lives in diving for sixpences and shillings, in water which is so clear that a plate can be seen at fifty feet below the surface. The love of gain even overcame the fear of sharks, which must have been near, for two half-grown ones were caught from the deck in the course of the day. As a proof of the advance of the English language, I observed that one of the darkies, who probably called himself John Brown, had painted JOHN BROON SBOTE on the stern of 'his own canoe.'

Four days later we crossed the Equator in the coolest weather I ever knew in the same position. A fresh easterly breeze just capped with foam the deep violet sea, and nothing could on this occasion have been less applicable to the equatorial belt than the usual sailor's sobriquet of the 'doldrums.' We passed the island of Fernando Noronha, a Portuguese convict settlement, on the 25th, and saw its wonderful obelisk of rock, which rises up exactly in the form of a lighthouse to such a height that I have seen it from fifty miles across the sea. This is the scene of a recent picture in the 'Illustrated News,' which showed us the sea serpent rising out of the water and taking a 'double turn' round a whale, which he then dragged down to the bottom of the ocean. *Credat Judæus!* The next morning found us at Pernambuco, with its exquisitely green cocoa-nut palms coming down to the edge of the sea. This place is renowned for its pine-apples, which are among the finest in the world, and happened on this occasion to be even cheaper than usual. We got very good ones, weighing about six pounds, for half a milrei, or one shilling apiece; but I have seen them very much larger, and have heard on good authority of their being sometimes grown at Pará and Pernambuco to the weight of fifteen or twenty pounds.

Three days more brought us to Bahia, where we went on shore in time for breakfast, and then walked up the hill to smoke a cigar under the dense shade of mangoes and jack-fruit trees at a point which commanded a view of the city and shipping below us and the magnificent bay around. It is scarcely possible to pass Bahia without laying in a stock of humming-birds and beetles, and it is the best place to buy them. Everyone who is not much afraid of evil smells should walk through the markets and amuse himself by bargaining for mangoes, oranges, or marmoset monkeys with the laughing negresses, who in the most brilliant coloured dresses and turbans preside over the stalls and chatter merrily. I suppose it was the wrong season for the navel-oranges which I had always been accustomed to find at Bahia, and which are such a *specialité* of the place that they deserve a word in passing. They are almost as large as pomeloes, and the pips are collected in an excrescence on the outside, so that the inside is simply a mass of delicious juicy flesh without any of the leathery divisions which form the only drawback to the delights of an ordinary orange.

Very early in the morning of the 31st we passed between the fort and the Sugarloaf Mountain and went into Rio de Janeiro, after heavy rains which had not yet cleared the sky of vapours dense enough to spoil the beauty of the view. I must not dwell here too much on the charms of Rio scenery, as I endeavoured to describe the Atlantic side of South America more fully some years ago ;[1] and must merely confine myself to matters not then described or more recently changed. One remark, however, I must make now as I did then, though it does not come under either of these definitions. The miserable want of decent hotel accommodation I found just as conspicuous as it was a dozen years before; and it is hard to believe that in a city of four or five hundred thousand inhabitants, with immense commercial interests, there is only one hotel, the 'Estrangeros,' that is in any way worthy of the name ; and that the others are hardly equal to a third-rate inn in any provincial town of Europe. The 'Estrangeros' even is far away from the business centres, and is yet in such demand that there is generally very little chance of getting a room there without engaging it about a fortnight beforehand. We took up our quarters at the 'Nova York,' which is the remains of McDowall's original establishment, and we had hardly been a quarter of an hour in the house before I had the pleasure of seeing Dr. Gunning, one of our best Rio friends in 1871, and the ablest *cicerone* for the whole neighbourhood.

Under his guidance we had then ascended the strange peak of the Corcovado, which, though only 2,400 feet above the sea, commands an astonishing view, and is the best point for comprehending the whole surrounding country. From the city and from the sea it looks perfectly inaccessible, and yet we took two ladies to the top without fatigue, and horses can go safely to within a short distance of the summit. The upper half of the mountain is a perpendicular precipice of granite, except on one side, where a

[1] 'South American Sketches.' 1863.

very good path winds upwards through a shady forest. Here I saw what, for a moment, I mistook for a bird coming right at me with something like the jerky flight of a woodcock just flushed; but it proved to be only a very large Imperador moth. This species of moth is the largest of any I have seen, either alive or in collections, some specimens being from ten to twelve inches across their spotted pale brown wings. A great variety of ferns ornament the sides of the road, amongst which were two lovely species of *Lindsæa*, which were quite new to me, but the fern collector has to be careful about snakes, for we saw several, and killed two in a very short time.

The Botanical Garden is near the base of the Corcovado, and its famous avenue of royal palms is a truly magnificent sight. One of the many tramways lately established for the convenience of the city, runs thither in little more than an hour. The change made by these institutions has been very great indeed. When I knew Rio formerly, carriages were excessively expensive; and as the place is too hot for much walking, people seldom moved more than they were obliged to move: now the tram-cars are full all day with people going in every direction, and numbers of clerks and men of business are enabled to sleep in the lovely suburbs, amidst groves of oranges and gardens full of brilliant flowers, instead of being cooped up in the city itself. The receipts of the companies must be very large and the expenses small. Their tickets serve as small change, which is a great convenience in a country where there is nothing but paper money, with the exception of copper dumps, a cumbrous exaggeration of our extinct cartwheel penny-pieces.

The car stops at the very gate of the garden, where a startling effect is always awaiting a visitor for the first time. An avenue of one-third of a mile in length is formed by a double row of cabbage-palms (*Oreodoxa regia*) lining the broad path which intersects the garden. These noble palms are a hundred feet high, and have grown with such marvellous regularity that their crowns meet in a continuous arch, as if composed of glorified Corinthian capitals. There is a shorter similar avenue at right angles to the first; and in clear weather it is a charming sight to look up those tall pearl-grey stems to the shining green of leaves gently rustling under the 'central blue.' I was making notes one day at the foot of one of these giants, when I heard a swishing sort of noise overhead, like that of heavy rain, though the sky was cloudless; and a bystander had just time to warn me from the spot, when a dead leaf about twenty feet long, with a stem as thick as my arm, fell exactly where I had been sitting. It was just as if the royal palm had thrown down a leaf to enable the stranger to form some notion of his noble proportions.

Right and left are broad lawns planted with trees from various tropical regions, varied by flower-beds and artificial pools of water, gay with lilies, and shaded by overhanging masses of bamboos. Here were palms and screw-pines, camphor trees, immense aloes, sago-palms (*Cycas circinalis*), mangoes, and plantains: but the handsomest foliage is that of the breadfruit tree (*Artocarpus incisa*), to which my attention was first called by one of its fruits falling on the path close by us, with so heavy a thud as to leave no doubt about a headache at all events for anyone upon whom it might have chanced to drop. At the back of the gardens, cultivation blends gradually with primitive simplicity, and they are only separated by a narrow ditch from the tangled jungle and confused masses of rocks which surround the base of the Corcovado, and other mountains in the neighbourhood. Here among deep-shaded nooks are lovely *Adiantums* of several species; and here, more in perfection than elsewhere, are beds of that exquisite fern, *Doryopteris palmata*, in stooping for which you may, as I did, lose the chance of catching a huge blue butterfly that dazzled me with its lustre as it mockingly rose beyond my reach.

Few people, however, would wish to remain long in Rio itself, where the sights are soon exhausted; especially when they know of the delightful retreats which tempt them to homes among the surrounding mountains. Tijuca, with its admirably managed hotel, its shady gardens, its cool bathing places and dashing streams, is but a few miles from the capital, and forms an abode of bliss after a hot day's work; but we wanted to go into more distant quarters at Petropolis, on the other side of the bay, and up in the heart of the Organ Mountains. This distance of about forty miles is performed every day, up and down, by the combined aid of steamboat, railway, and coach, under the command of an Englishman, Mr. George Land, whose name will be gladly welcomed by those of his countrymen who know anything of Rio de Janeiro. Day after day, in all weathers, he has for years been at his post, managing everything, never forgetting anything, and never making a mistake. I was truly glad to see his jolly face once more, and to shake hands over the fact that we were going up to Petropolis immediately. He bustled the negroes about, everything was soon on board the steamer, and at two o'clock punctually we started for the run of fifteen or sixteen miles across the harbour. This gives some idea of its size, for it is hard to believe, as we pass through the narrow entrance by the side of the Sugarloaf, that we are really entering a harbour of about fifteen by eighteen miles in extent.

In an hour and a half we had threaded the maze of islands and reached a pier where a railway train was waiting to start for the eleven miles to the base of the Sierra, through a low and often swampy region, where the only reason for wishing to stop was the desire to see more of the wonderful ferns and flowers which seemed to fly past the rushing train. Seven or eight light coaches with four or five mules apiece were waiting at the terminus, and the number on each passenger's ticket told him which coach to take. George Land stayed behind to bring up the heavy baggage in a more substantial vehicle, and in about two minutes we were already rattling up the first slopes of a sort of tropical Simplon or St. Gotthard. In scarce a hundred yards from the railway platform the road dives into the shade of a forest, which formerly completely covered the mountain side over which it has been carried in about eleven miles of zigzag to its highest point at about three thousand feet above the sea. The alternations of sun and shadow on this road are peculiarly striking. Sometimes it passes under the overhanging branches of gigantic evergreen trees, whose tall stems are decked with orchids and gay epiphytes, or masses of drooping ferns and crimson parasites, which climb to the utmost boughs to clothe them with blossoms not their own. Sometimes a sudden turn leads to a more open part of the road, and reveals the astonishing view of the bay of Rio with its countless islands already far below and stretching away to its gateway from the Atlantic, where the Sugarloaf appears reduced by distance to the dimensions of a pigmy.

Throughout the distance the banks are loaded with masses of ferns, conspicuous among which the *Adiantum cuneatum* (our hothouse Maidenhair) often grew in such thick beds that it might have been mown like a crop of grass. Several noble species of *Lomaria* and *Blechnum* were frequently in company with *Begonias*, throwing up flower-stems of six feet in height. On the whole, however, there was a greater lack of flowers in the hot month of November than in the Brazilian winter of May and June, which we spent there a few years before. At that season the forest-clad hills in all directions were dotted about with large *Cassia* trees, whose myriad yellow blossoms made them look like clumps of pure gold among the shining evergreens; and two species of *Melastoma* in great abundance were equally thickly covered with the large and splendid purple flowers which place them in the very highest class of vegetable beauties. If our carriage had been in any way like a Swiss *diligence* we should have had ample time to walk on ahead to examine the road-side treasures; but the pace of the Brazilian mules is a very different affair. The team was changed about half-way up the mountain, but with this exception they never stopped, and generally succeeded in keeping up a trot which would soon have left a pedestrian in a hot climate considerably in the lurch.

From the top of the pass the road declines a little to Petropolis, and the driver brought his team in at topspeed, till we pulled up at McDowall's hotel, exactly four hours after leaving Rio, now about forty miles behind us and nearly 3,000 feet beneath.

Those who have enjoyed themselves vastly in distant regions, and find themselves unexpectedly returned to their beloved haunts, will understand the joy I felt at seeing myself once more at home in Petropolis, with my former host, Mr. Mills, coming down the garden-steps with a smiling welcome. Nearly every plant in the garden was an old friend, and I was installed in the same room which I had formerly occupied for two or three months. The house is large and comfortable, with all the rooms on the ground-floor; and ours were part of a set which opened out upon a broad marble-floored verandah, from which a flight of stone steps led down into the garden. One corner of this was set aside for camellias grown into small trees of about fifteen feet high, and strong enough to climb into when we wanted to pick the topmost blossoms. They were so full of flower in June, that after a gust of rain the black gardener, old Matteo, had to carry off the fallen bloom by the barrowful, reminding me of the puff attributed to George Robins when, in describing the place he was selling, he added, 'The only drawback to this charming residence is, that it requires an extra man to sweep up the rose-leaves from the garden walks.'

Here, too, were *Pointsettias*, not in little plants like those which often ornament a London dinner-table, but grown into very large bushes, on which I have found the

crimson stars of their floral bracts to be two feet in
diameter. The mauve-coloured *Bougainvillea* ran along a
trellis in a sheet of beauty. The clove-tree, *Metrosideros*,
spread its flowers like crimson bottle-brushes; and
double *Altheas* of many colours hung down a profusion of
blossoms which might at a little distance be mistaken for
large carnations. The huge arms of a giant *Cereus* were
in November covered with its large white flowers, and the
Gardenias, or Cape Jasmines, in plants of eight or ten feet
high, perfumed the whole place with a thousand blossoms.
Amongst all these were beds of roses, Neapolitan violets,
with other native and European flowers, and an immense
scarlet *Salvia* of the species which we have in greenhouses, the honeyed blossoms of which were being perpetually probed by the beaks of dark green humming-
birds with a tinge of gold. Such was the flower garden,
from which steps led down into a vegetable garden,
bounded on one side by a stone wall, covered from end to
end with ferns of many kinds, including the exquisite
silver fern, which in the Brazilian hills grows to such
perfection, that I have gathered fronds from three to four
feet in length, with stems almost as thick as a lead-pencil.
At the end of this again came a plantation of bananas,
which furnish the house with a perennial supply of
that delicious fruit; and lastly, a small grove of figs,
peaches, and oranges. A steep hill-side was the boundary
in this direction, from which *Gleichenias* spread their
tangled mass of fronds which branch down like stag's
horns almost to the roots of the orange-trees. To complete the picture, it should be said that near a corner
of the orange-grove there is a bath room, where every

morning may be found a supply of pure cold water, which, even in the tropics, is abundantly supplied at an elevation of a few thousand feet above the sea.

Petropolis itself is a German colony, which was founded by the present Emperor, a man whose high intelligence is never failing to meet the best interests of his country. It is built among lovely hills, separated by as many valleys, through each of which the traveller finds small hamlets and lonely houses, where the proprietors of little plots of land cultivate fruits and vegetables for the market, and from time to time clear spaces in the forests, where blazing trees, frightened snakes, and bamboos bursting like bombshells under the influence of fire, make way for patches of the rich strong grass which is cut four or five times a year as food for the necessary sheep or cattle. The space is too small to allow these useful animals to trample and feed at their leisure; they are pastured under cover, and only allowed to eat the rations which are served out to them after being cut by their masters. On the edges of these cultivated spots the forest reigns in its primitive beauty; creepers, climbers, trailers, fasten themselves to the boughs of the monarchs of the forest, about the feet of which are dark jungles filled with choice ferns and flowers, where every now and then, rising out of the mass, may be seen a fuschia of fifty or sixty feet in height, blooming from top to bottom, by the side of a group of lofty tree-ferns forming natural umbrellas with their green and lace-like fronds.

Above the limits of thick forest are seen the great bald peaks of granite, which attain their greatest height and most fantastic forms in the summits of the true Organ mountains between Petropolis and Theresopolis, where they reach the height of about 8,000 feet, and shine out with inexpressible glory far above the dark regions of trees, all lustrous in the golden haze which veils the details of their blue magnificence. Mixed with the other vegetation of the forest-paths are bamboos of every size, and of several species, from the smaller ones which droop right and left like exquisite green fountains, to the larger kinds, which rise more stiffly to the height of eighty feet, and, when they fall, leave stems as thick as a man's thigh across the track. But who shall describe the charms which await a botanist even of the meanest capacity, when he makes up his mind to discard bodily comfort and cleanliness for a few hours while he dives into the heart of any one of the valleys that lie embosomed among the Organ Mountains of Brazil? In some of them the *Cobæa scandens* hangs its purple bells from bush to bush; in some, the common passion-flower roams at its own sweet will over everything it comes in contact with, and here and there I have seen the scarlet passion-flower of our hothouses twining its brilliant blossoms round the shining green stem of a bamboo. By the sides of sweet streams, among the woods, may be seen large bushes of the *Abutilon venosum*, hanging its orange bells and crimson streaks over the placid water, close to huge *Daturas*, with their hundreds of white trumpet-like and sweet-scented blossoms, some of which I have found to be sixteen inches in length.

Of all regions that I have as yet seen in the world there is nothing comparable to this Brazilian hill-country, as a field for the fern-hunter. At various times my companions and myself have collected about 250 distinct species within a day's walk or ride from Petropolis or Palmeiras. Most of these were found in 1871, when, apart from the arborescent ferns and others too large for our apparatus, Mr. Frederick Longman succeeded in drying about 200 of them, which, on being forwarded to Dr. Hooker at Kew, were found to contain a few species new to science. But, to the last day of our three months' sojourn, I believe we never once went into the woods without finding some hitherto unnoticed treasure, and there would be work for several months more before any one could pretend to have exhausted all the haunts within easy reach.

No sportsman ever enjoyed the pursuit of game more thoroughly than we enjoyed our daily fern-hunts. Armed with our tin vasculums, we used to scramble up any convenient bank and push our way as best we could through the jungle and up into the dark depths of the forest. I suppose we ought properly to have been afraid of snakes, tarantulas, jiggers, and all kinds of noxious insects, which were certainly there, but no notion of the kind ever checked us in our favourite pursuit. What true lover of it would allow himself to be stopped by anything short of a Bengal tiger, when he has good reason to expect fresh discoveries at every step? Strong hobnailed boots that had been christened on the Alps were, however, absolutely necessary on the wet and slippery slopes where a dense vegetation often prevented us from seeing our footing, and where we were sometimes startled by putting a leg up to the knee in the rotten trunk of a fallen and invisible monarch of the forest. Then we divided the ground between us, occasionally shouting to each other, partly with a view to prevent losing ourselves entirely and partly to announce a new and precious 'find.'

Sometimes it was a new species of *Trichomanes* that had chosen to climb twenty or thirty feet up the trunk of a tree in the dark damp shade or along the face of a huge rock, where its fronds extended right and left across the dark brown surface, and stretched upwards to meet the rosy blossoms of a cactus which peeped down over its head from a somewhat sunnier position. Sometimes it was a new *Acrostichum*, the fronds of which were almost as dark and shining as a branch of Portugal laurel; and then again, upon another tree-stem might be found, rarest of the rare and loveliest of the lovely, the pendent fronds of *Asplenium mucronatum*. This exquisite plant fixes its slender root in the bark of a tree, whence droops a cluster of narrow pale green fronds tapering through a length of from two to four feet, beautifully indented, and so light and delicate in structure that when held by the root and waved in the air they seem to float as if they were strips of gauze. Another remarkable fern is the *Trichomanes Prieurii*, which was also very rare, but generally to be found in a dark and moist wood near a place called the Presidencia. A fine frond of it is about fifteen inches long and very finely divided; it grows in such dark places that it cannot be appreciated till brought out into full daylight; but its colour then appears as something truly marvellous. The green is that of the deepest emerald, but it has a metallic lustre which seems scarcely 'canny' in a vegetable, though its beauty is exquisite.

Its beauty is also, unhappily, evanescent. The lustre departs from it immediately like the hues of a captured mackerel, and all the care in the world will hardly suffice to carry it home without shrivelling up in the vasculum. Though dried in the most painstaking fashion, every frond turns perfectly black and looks as if it were made of fine black lace.

In these scrambles and tusslings in the forests it was often difficult, and sometimes impossible, to avoid a tumble among the trailing plants which were generally ready to trip up our feet; and we used to present a very shabby appearance when, dishevelled, covered with moss, and bathed in perspiration, we emerged upon the paths of daylight, and had the intense pleasure of sitting down to compare discoveries under the soothing influence of the pipe of tranquillity. But I must not let this hobby run away with me any further; it would fill a book by itself. My excuse for saying thus much must be, that there are now so many thousands of people who delight in similar pursuits in Europe that I was anxious to give them a hint of what an infinitely grander field awaits them if they like to go to the Brazilian hills, where, without any difficulty, and with luxurious quarters to live in, they may ramble and botanize to their hearts' content till they come home hungry to dinner. They will find the coverts full of floral game from one end of the year to the other, and a three months' holiday from England will give them six or seven weeks for the *chasse*.

Before the Emperor founded the German colony of Petropolis and built a summer palace in the middle of it, the site was only represented by a filthy little hamlet on

Summer Palace at Petropolis, Brazil.

the line of the old mule-road to the important province of Minas Geraes, which contains the most valuable of the mines in the interior. Some of the most intelligent men of the country, and notably the Count Mariano Lage, who had seen the advantage of good roads in Europe, resolved to make a magnificent one into Minas, instead of the miserable track by which all produce was brought down to the coast on the backs of long trains of mules floundering slowly over the muddy and irregular soil. Granite mountains were on both sides of it in endless quantity: a company was formed, and at a very great expense a macadamized road was made for 100 miles to the northward of Petropolis. They induced Mr. Morritt, an experienced Yorkshireman, to come out and inaugurate all that was needed in the way of coaches for passengers, and the whole arrangements required for an extensive traffic.

No one could possibly have done the work more thoroughly, and no one who has been fortunate enough to enjoy the kindness and hospitality of his family and himself will be ever likely to forget them, or the pleasant days spent in their society. I have been many times over this road to Juiz da Fora, and in these degenerate days of railways and demons, as Mr. Ruskin would call them, I can safely recommend the journey to anyone still fond of good driving. A coach, built exactly after the English pattern, starts every day at six A.M. from opposite to the Emperor's palace at Petropolis, and deposits its passengers at six P.M. at the door of a comfortable hotel at Juiz da Fora. In this time it not only gets over 100 miles of road, but it stops a good hour for dinner in the middle of the day, and stays more than another hour at he various stations. The work is entirely done by active and elegant little mules, who, when once started, seem to enjoy the fun of going as fast as they can. The pace would be impossible for horses in such a hot climate, but I have timed the four little mules over a stage of ten English miles in less than fifty minutes: and, on one occasion, they took us for a short stage of six miles in twenty minutes, or at the rate of eighteen miles an hour. And yet they never seem to be hot or tired. When Mr. Rawson and I travelled over this road at the end of 1873, I found the coachmen to be the same two German brothers that drove me over the same road a dozen years before, which says something for the climate in which, in spite of its heat, such daily work should for so long be possible. But in Brazil people harden themselves to the climate instead of giving way to it.

Agassiz travelled over this beautiful road only a few years before his lamented death, and easily convinced himself that this rich and luxuriant country had in bygone ages been swept by glacial action. He even found that the most successful coffee-plantations were exactly where the movements of ice had most enriched the soil by the transportation and mixture of its component elements. A great part of this famous Minas road runs through the heart of the coffee-plantations, which clothe the hill-sides on both sides of the way; and I fancy that the general public, who do not hear much of Brazilian coffee, have little notion of the quantity grown in that country. The managing partner of one of the chief firms in Rio told me that their house alone had exported no less than 400,000 bags in the preceding year. Each bag of coffee contains five arrobas, or 160 lbs., so that the total amount shipped by this one firm was 64,000,000 lbs. in a single year! The anti-slavery sentimentalists of fifty years ago used to groan over the amount of human misery represented by a lump of sugar in their tea-cup. From a rather different point of view, I hope I may be permitted to lament over the awful destruction of vegetable life which is involved in the production of a few pounds of coffee. It is a pitiful sight to see the burning of the virgin forest and the blackened stumps which alone remain to mark what on the day before had been a scene of indescribable beauty.

A French botanist at Rio once told me that it would take a fortnight to properly botanize one of the huge trees which from time to time fall without the aid of fire. For in truth each of them is not only a tree but a garden. The whole stem is clothed with other plants and flowers, and so is each wide-spreading bough. In this way a vast variety of orchids and ferns, huge arums with shield-like leaves large enough to cover a man, brilliant red and yellow *Bromelias* and *Tillandsias*, epiphytes and parasites of all descriptions, rope-plants, creepers, trailers, climbers, mosses, all live together like a happy family, far beyond the reach of man. So luxuriant is the vegetation that every seed appears to grow wherever it is deposited; and I have even seen a species of tall white Amaryllis in full blossom growing on the boughs of a *Jiquitibá*, nearly a hundred feet above the ground! Such are the beauties which are doomed to crackle in wholesale conflagration to make way for the coffee-planter.

The first station is a place called Padre Correa, ten

miles from Petropolis, where we were often tempted to spend a day, walking there in the morning and coming home by the evening coach. One day Mr. Morritt drove us thither to see the curious operation of breaking in some new mules which had just arrived and had never yet felt the hand of man. A troop of them is brought up in the company of a quiet mare, called the *madrina*, whom they will follow anywhere, though they will submit to no other guidance. When we arrived they were feeding close at hand, but the *madrina* was soon driven into a corral, and the thirty or forty mules followed her without hesitation, though they looked rather scared when the gate was closed behind them and they found themselves in prison. To them entered one of the stalwart Germans and a couple of strong Portuguese with their *lazos*. Mr. Morritt looked over the troop and selected two handsome mouse-coloured mules as the animals to be operated upon. By a little skilful management these two were seduced into a corner and kept there; the gate was opened, the *madrina* was driven out, and the rest of the mules galloped out after her to finish their dinner.

The two victims began to run violently round the corral, the men standing in the middle, but the second throw of the lazo caught the foremost round the neck and one of his fore-legs, and brought him heavily to the ground, where he rolled and kicked furiously. Dexterously contriving to avoid his heels, the men extricated his leg from the noose and allowed him to get on his feet again, and do his worst while they held the other end of the lazo. He plunged and struggled like an eel landed on the grass; but all his efforts were of no avail against his powerful captors, who by sheer strength dragged him to a strong post, jammed his head close to it, and made him fast there. After a few moments' rest they approached him again, when he contrived to fling himself down, kicking out wildly; but they forced him up and made his head faster than ever. Then one of them managed to blindfold him with a broad bandage to prevent him from seeing where to strike with his vicious teeth; another man holding a bit before his nose waited till he opened his mouth, and then forced it in, while the other two fixed on the rest of the head-gear and harness, in spite of his maddest struggles. He was dragged outside the corral and fastened to another post, where he again threw himself on the ground in a paroxysm of rage and terror. At last he became perfectly still, and I thought he had really died of a broken heart.

Mr. Morritt, however, said that he was only shamming, and he was left motionless on the ground while the other unhappy beast was caught; and after being treated in the same ruthless fashion was tied to an adjoining post. A spare coach was drawn out into the road, and two thoroughly tame mules stood by ready harnessed. The two captives were, after another tremendous battle, forced by main strength up to the pole and made to take the position of wheelers. One of them instantly threw himself in the dust and the other was jumping upon him, when the tame mules were brought up and harnessed as leaders, looking perfectly unconcerned at the frenzied antics of the novices. Meanwhile two strong men jumped on the box to manage the whip and reins between them. The leaders began to pull at the first crack of the whip and forced the others forward; the one that was rolling in the dust did not at all approve of being dragged along the ground, and after a few yards of it he jumped upon his feet. Encouraged by wild shouts and whipping, the leaders broke into a mad gallop, and the victims soon found themselves obliged to do the same. The whole team dashed off at a run-away speed; they were splendidly driven, and after about half an hour were brought home covered with foam. The new ones were bleeding rather freely from the bit, but they seemed thoroughly subdued, and in a very few days afterwards they took their places regularly in the coach, looking none the worse for the cruel treatment they had undergone in what must have been a terribly *mauvais quart d'heure* to them. I pitied them sincerely at the time, but my pity was afterwards merged in complete astonishment at the result.

This corral is close to the banks of the Piabanha river which flows near the road all the way from Petropolis, sometimes gliding smoothly among the woods, sometimes rushing wildly among rocks and then tumbling headlong over the beautiful waterfalls of the Cascatinas. The former Emperor, Dom Pedro I., was extremely fond of this retired little spot, where he could enjoy himself in his own fashion with a few favourites 'far from the madding crowd.' Opposite to his place of abode is an enormous wild fig-tree of unknown antiquity; it has been sadly shorn of its magnificence in the last dozen years, but when I first saw it its huge and lofty boughs spread out to a circumference of 480 feet. Under its beneficent shade we often used to lunch in the heat of the day, and try in vain to count the humming-birds as they sucked the rosy blossom of the air-plants which grew on every part of the branches. At a short distance is a delicious pool among the rocks in the river, which is still called the 'Emperor's Bath,' and part of the way to it is planted with Araucarias.

The Araucaria at maturity in its own country is a very different thing in appearance to what we are accustomed to see upon an English lawn. Those of Brazil are not of the same species as the hardy *Araucaria imbricata* which we have imported from Chile. Both species, however, lose all beauty when they get old and reach the height of sixty or eighty feet, when the foliage consists of nothing but dark tufts set on the end of rigid boughs as bare as so many scaffold-poles. The finest aloes that I have ever seen grow in great profusion near Correa. The species is *Fourcroya gigantea*, some plants of which we found with leaves twelve feet in length and flower-stems like splendid candelabra rising to the height of forty feet. I think it would be no exaggeration to say that, when we were last there, there were many hundreds of them all blooming as close as they could grow to one another on a few acres of the sloping hill-side, close to a grove of Araucarias on the other side of the river. A man feels exceedingly small by the side of these monsters, with their vast and shining leaves ending in spines strong enough to run him through the body. As with other species of aloes, each plant dies when it blooms. Their pith is highly esteemed for making razor-strops, and is considered better than cork for the lining of collectors' insect-boxes.

CHAPTER II.

Valley of the Retiro—A direful Spider—Evening—Entrerios and Palmeiras—Ferns and Palmitos—Feather-flowers—Sail in the 'Neva'—Storm at night—Arrival at Buenos Ayres—Great changes—Railway progress—The 'camp' revisited—Owls and biscachas—Reports of cholera—The magnificent 'Luxor'—Arrival of the 'Eothen'—Excursions to Ensenada and Chascomus—A brilliant shot.

IT IS IMPOSSIBLE here to give any idea of the number and variety of the excursions to be made on foot or on horseback in the neighbourhood of Petropolis. The configuration of the land, with its countless hills and rich wooded valleys, offers something new for every day. One of the most interesting walks was to a point about four miles along the main road, from which a path leads up the valley of the Retiro to the left till it loses itself in the depths of the forest. Here, almost in darkness from the overhanging trees, a stream of pure water dances down among mossy rocks from the hills, inviting cool repose among the palms, while through the gaps in the dense foliage overhead the specks of deep blue sky give a hint of how the sun is blazing on the outside of our mighty forest-umbrella. This forest clothes the base of three mountains which shut in the head of the valley; the one on the left presenting a surface of nearly perpendicular granite which rises at an angle of 70° or 80° to the height of about 2,500 feet above the tops of the trees which grow to its very base. The surface of granite disintegrates very easily in a climate which combines considerable heat and great moisture; and every crack or minute hollow is seized upon as a place of habitation by *Bromelias* and other epiphytic plants. From top to bottom this awful and inaccessible precipice was bristling with their rigid forms, and here and there ornamented by their tall spikes of flower.

The beautiful falls of Itamarity, in the heart of the woods, are a constant source of delight for a day's walk in one direction; and the view from the Alto do Imperador over all the island-studded bay of Rio, is an equal attraction in the other. Everywhere is an infinitely changing variety of ferns and flowers, palms and forest-trees; and an entomologist will find plenty of employment amongst brilliant butterflies and beetles, moths, and mantises, to say nothing of the direful spiders which are occasionally to be met with. I shall never forget one of them which was brought to us by a negro who had captured it by putting a box over the log of wood upon which it was found. The beast was black, with a body about an inch in diameter, and immensely long hairy legs, so thick and strong that when we coaxed him under a large tumbler he kicked inside with such force that we thought he would upset it. However, while one of us held the tumbler with one side slightly raised, the other introduced a little chloroform. The monster executed a savage dance, kicking out in all directions; but in a few moments he suddenly collapsed, the body tumbled down in the middle of his hideous legs, and he was 'as dead as Julius Cæsar.' The people are very much afraid of these creatures, even when dead, and we were warned that a touch upon the hairy deceased would cause a poisonous irritation.

The climate of these hills is exceedingly healthy, which is probably owing to the frequent and refreshing changes of weather. After a few days of rather excessive heat, everybody knows that a thunderstorm is coming, and it is a grand sight when it does come. Sometimes it is heralded by dense clouds settling down upon the ground, playing among the plants in the garden, and rolling along the streets, black and bodily, under the influence of the accompanying storm-wind. The lightning leaps out of the darkness, the thunder crashes among the surrounding hills, the rain comes down in torrents; but the storm soon passes; the thermometer goes down twenty degrees; and a deliciously cool evening follows. And ah! what pleasant evenings have I passed, sitting with a few friends under the broad verandah, chatting about friends at home, listening to the distant cries of the monkeys in the forest or the clattering rattle of the great blacksmith-frogs by the river, watching the glory of the southern heavens, and trying to follow the dances of a thousand fireflies, themselves like stars endowed with locomotion!

But the day came at last when we must bid a long farewell to the quiet pleasures of Petropolis. In a week we were to sail from Rio southwards, and we meant to get there by a new and more roundabout way. I was more sorry than ever to leave a place where I had so often lived alone with Dame Nature and a few other quiet friends, entirely out of reach of Kursaals and crowds, operas, picture-galleries, and all other distractions of Art.

We sent all heavy baggage down to Rio, under the charge of George Land; and in very light marching order we climbed to the roof of the coach at six o'clock in the morning. It was a great comfort to have a parting look at all the favourite spots by the way, the mountains of the Retiro, the rapids of the Piabanha, and the aloes and Araucarias of Padre Correa. About eleven o'clock, the iron bridge over the Parahiba and the clusters of waving bamboos on both sides of the road gave the familiar notice that we were not far from Entrerios on the Parahiba river, fifty miles from Petropolis. Here the road is intersected by the Pedro II. railway, by which we were going westward to Palmeiras to spend a few days in Dr. Gunning's part of the Sierra. Entrerios being half-way to Juiz da Fora, the coaches arrive from both sides at the same time; and as the train comes in soon after, everybody wanting to eat and drink at the same time, the little place is rather lively about noon.

Two years before this our party slept there for a night, which gave us a day for exploring the neighbourhood. Here we found a great quantity of *Gymnogramma tomentosa*, a choice and very peculiar fern; and, pushing up by the first track that we could find into the upper forest, we were soon in the midst of magnificent trees and jungle, taking care to mark our way back to the trail which we had left. We found many ferns here, different from those at Petropolis; but the one which I must especially mention is the very rare and exquisite *Adiantum lunulatum*. This curious form of Maidenhair is simply pinnate and does not branch: the rachis is almost as fine as a hair, and when it is about a foot long it droops down to the ground and takes root from the end like a strawberry-runner, repeating the process perpetually. We only found three or four specimens of it in a long search ; but while I was peering on the ground to look for it in the gloom of the forest, I suddenly came upon what appeared to be a pair of brilliant eyes glaring at me from just beyond the toe of my boot. Stooping lower I found that the eyes were the bright round spots on the wings of a superb moth, apparently just emerged, and stupified by the new state of life to which it had pleased Providence to call him.

The train started at 12.30, so we said good-bye to the German representatives of Mr. Weller in Brazil, and were fortunate enough to get a parting shake of the hand with our kind friend Mr. Morritt, who was returning from Juiz da Fora. For about a couple of hours the line passes through comparatively tame scenery near the side of the Parahiba river, which it crosses by a fine bridge before it begins to run down the Sierra on the south. Lower down it turns and twists among the mountains like a gigantic eel; now running over ground cleared through the glories of the virgin forest, now diving into cool tunnels, and again emerging among the luxuriant vegetation all glowing in the tropical sun. Immediately after coming out of one of the tunnels the train stopped early in the evening at the little station of Palmeiras, made for the convenience of the colony established by Dr. Gunning among the mountains; and we walked up to the neat and comfortable hotel, built by him, about 200 feet above the level of the railway.

With the exception of the occasional trains, nothing on wheels comes near this blissful retreat. Dr. Gunning has built himself a house on the hill-side near the station, and there are three or four other houses near at hand occupied by a few people who prefer the fresh air of a mountain-garden to anything they can find in city life. A good deal of ground has been cleared for coffee and mandioca; and the negro slaves who cultivate it live in a small settlement by themselves. A philanthropic effort was made to provide a scheme by which these people might free themselves by a very moderate amount of work. Every piece of work done was credited to them in a book as money due to them at a rate agreed upon: when the money thus apparently due amounted to the price at which each slave was valued, he was to be allowed to go free. Not one of them attempted to avail himself of it, and they could hardly be induced to do anything, for fear of being turned adrift in a state of freedom, where they would have to work hard, instead of leading a nearly idle life at the expense of a kind master. I am afraid that some of our compassion is sadly wasted.

Palmeiras is hotter than Petropolis, as it is not nearly so high above the sea, but it commands a much more extensive view, being on the side of the Sierra itself, with the forests sloping down into the open country in front, beyond which again are seen the blue forms of far-distant mountains in the south.

The hospitality of Dr. and Mrs. Gunning generally fills their spare-rooms, and we found our friends Captain and Mrs. Brooker, of H.M.S. 'Egmont,' already established there. But the delightful little hotel which he has built, within a hundred yards of his own house, affords everything necessary. There are not many rooms, but they are scrupulously clean and very comfortable, the best of them opening out upon a wide covered balcony, where we could sit out of doors in any weather, and enjoy the glorious views of mountain and forest. The Doctor has installed a capital Englishwoman, Mrs. Williams, as the landlady, and I have little doubt that the beauty of the scenery, and the utter tranquillity of this most charming but generally unknown spot, will soon attract a larger supply of visitors from Rio.

A path into the forest runs from the very door, and we soon found considerable differences in the vegetation. There is a far larger proportion of palms than at Petropolis, and a great quantity of the *Palmito*, or eatable palm, may be seen in all directions. When we dined with Dr. Gunning he introduced us to this vegetable and showed us how it is procured. Unfortunately the production of a good dish of it involves the destruction of several palm-trees. When the tree is cut down, the growing top-shoot is taken off and stripped of all its coatings till the heart is reached; it is scarcely an inch in thickness, and though delicate it has not any very special flavour to justify the murder of an exquisite palm-tree in the heyday of youth.

We found an immense variety of ferns, many of which we had never seen on the other side of the mountains. Palmeiras is a perfect treasure-house of choice Adiantums, and those who know anything of our stove-ferns will sympathise with the intense delight I experienced at finding in their native beauty and perfection such ferns as *Adiantum trapeziforme, cuneatum, St. Catarinæ, cultratum*, and *subcordatum*, a joy which perhaps reached its maximum when we came upon a moist and hot corner in the lower forest, where was a solitary colony of *Adiantum macrophyllum*, the tender rose-colour of the young fronds mingling with the green elegance of the older ones. Here also were two species of *Lygodium*, twining like hops round the stems of palms or any other convenient support to the height of about twenty feet, their fronds fringed with the delicate characteristic tassels which contain the spores.

One of the greatest curiosities was what we called 'the jointed fern,' till the authorities afterwards gave us its true name of *Danæa elliptica*. Instead of the tough and more or less woody rachis of almost all other ferns, this *Danæa* has a very juicy one, divided like the shoot of a geranium by joints, at each of which it breaks with a light touch and gives forth a liquid drop. It is a large and handsome plant, but very difficult to dry on account of the tendencies described. Palmeiras is the only place in the world where I have found in its native state that remarkable fern the *Hemidictyon marginatum*, of which there are some very humble specimens at Kew. Not more than a quarter of a mile from the house was a plant of it, which in July had pale green fronds eleven feet high with broad pinnæ as delicate as silver paper.

In the last days of November it was almost too hot for mid-day rambles, especially as we had thus far continued to wear nothing lighter than ordinary English shooting-clothes. I was so nearly roasted one day by the blazing sun, that on reaching a shady place with a trickling stream I was compelled to sit with my feet in the water and bathe my head for a quarter of an hour with a wet handkerchief. While I was in this position a purple fresh-water crab walked across my toes, and the largest blue butterfly that I had ever seen was fluttering in the sunshine just outside my dark retreat. On getting back to our quarters about two o'clock that afternoon, I found for the first time in my life that the ferns in the vasculum had dried like hay; my clothes were dripping as if I had been cast into the sea, and we were both very glad to apply the best remedy that I know for over-heating or over-exertion in a hot climate. It consists of simply drinking a bottle of Guinness's stout before doing anything else. The cure is instantaneous.

That evening we dined at Dr. Gunning's, and the heat was so great that his wife kindly supplied us with thin white Chinese jackets in place of coats and waistcoats 'allowed to retire.' But our reward was at hand. A tremendous thunderstorm burst over our heads during dinner and was followed by a divinely tranquil night. The moon and stars came in fullest beauty to illuminate a scene which appeared to belong to some other world. The whole extent of the lower ground before us was covered by a vast sheet of mist as white as snow, over which rose up the mountains bathed in moonlight and looking like islands rising out of a sea of glass. There was almost an unearthly beauty in the sight, and it was hard to tear ourselves from the cane chairs in the verandah long past midnight, though at five o'clock in the morning we had to make a last start from the hill regions of Brazil.

Early as was the hour, the kind-hearted and faithful Doctor came down to the station to see us off and give a few useful hints for our convenience. Rushing down the hills, charging through tunnels and twisting round strange corners among the mountains, the train reached Belem or Bethlehem, and ran into the station at Rio about ten o'clock. Not far from the city we passed near the Emperor's palace of St. Cristovão ; and nearer still to the station is the singular quarter of the *abattoirs*, or public slaughter-houses. Every wall and every roof in their immediate neighbourhood was black with the small vultures called *Urubus*, which form themselves into an unusually useful board of health by devouring and assimilating every particle of the garbage which might affect the sanitary condition of the city over which they so worthily preside. As we went into Rio another violent thunderstorm burst upon us with deluges of rain, and turned the streets of the capital into rivers, often up to the knees of the horses, and considerably spoiling the effect of a state visit of the Emperor and Empress to the large church in the Rua Direita.

There was little more to be done at Rio and still less time to do it in. There was a certain amount of shopping to get through, the most notable feature of which was the customary visit to Mdlle. Natté in the Rua do Ouvidor, who has a splendid collection of ornaments made from the feathers of Brazilian birds. Let no man think he knows anything about feather-flowers till he has been to Rio. The gay imitations which may be picked up in any quantity at Madeira or St. Vincent are rough, vulgar things made of painted feathers: those in Brazil are made of genuine feathers in all their naturally splendid colours. The wreaths formed of the breasts of humming-birds, the pure white fans edged with the flamingo feathers of scarlet, tipped with black, are beautiful beyond description, and Mr. Rawson took home some exquisite specimens. With regard to the birds themselves, it is surprising to find how few of them, except the many-coloured humming-birds, are visible in the ordinary rides and walks. Now and then a grand kingfisher may be seen on a river-side rock; and here and there a brilliant toucan darts across the road in all the splendour of crimson, blue, and yellow; but as a rule they remain in the depths of the forests, where they are very difficult to see amongst the multitudinous branches and leaves. Three of us once tried a day's shooting at a place about twenty miles from Petropolis, but we only shot a few small birds, most of which fell into impenetrable jungle, and the largest of those picked up was a quaint little kingfisher scarce three inches in length. The butterflies and moths everywhere were simply magnificent, but the audible and visible birds were far more scarce than I should have expected.

We spent our last evening very pleasantly in dining on board the 'Egmont,' with Captain and Mrs. Brooker; and, as the weather turned out so bad that the captain did not like sending away a boat's crew with us, we settled down to a comfortable rubber of whist, with a shake-down on board at the end of it. In the afternoon of the next day, December 3, we fairly started in the Royal Mail ship 'Neva,' where we spent a pleasant week under the charge of Captain Bax, and in company with several of my old friends who were returning from England to Buenos Ayres. Heavy rain once more spoiled the famous view of the Organ Mountains as we steamed out of the bay, and the Sugarloaf was, as it were, draped in a shower-bath; but the sky cleared soon after we got outside, and we were favoured with a full moon and a lovely evening.

After three days of charming weather, I was saying to Captain Bax that I thought matters must have greatly changed of late years, for in four voyages I had made over the same course in the branch steamer 'Mersey,' we used always to have violent winds and storms from every side of the compass. He laughed, and said that I must have been a particular Jonah to the 'Mersey.' But that night the Pampero, the great south-west wind from the Pampas, burst upon us in all its fury. The lightning blazed almost incessantly, lighting up the masts and rigging, and leaving us at intervals in a darkness that might be felt. Amid deluges of rain, the wind roared through the rigging with the peculiar sound which it only makes when in its most savage humour; and the lightning revealed a sea of hissing scud, chopped down by the very force of the storm. The captain stopped the ship, and lay-to for several hours about midnight: everybody else had long turned into bed, except the watch; but the wildness of the scene had an irresistible attraction for me, and I remained chatting with him at the open door of his own cabin on deck, where we could see everything that was going on, and now and then making sallies out into the tempest to look for any signs of a change. Truly it was a sight worth seeing; but at last, towards morning, I turned in like the rest of the world, and when I woke up the storm had departed, and we were running merrily in towards Montevideo. The captain said that it was, while it lasted, the hardest blow he had ever known upon the coast.

Early in the morning of December 9 the ship was anchored in the outer roads of Buenos Ayres, and it is impossible to think of any city in the world by the side of the water that is so difficult to get at in a large vessel. We had to take up our position at a distance of about seven miles, which formerly involved a very disagreeable passage in a whale-boat. Small steamers are now in this respect a great improvement, and one of them soon came out to take us on shore. It is to be devoutly hoped that the Buenos Ayreans will soon be able to carry out one or other[1] of the grand projects submitted to them for the purpose of facilitating the approach to their city; either by deepening the channel, or making a new entrance in connection with the Ensenada railway. We had no trouble with the Custom house, and soon found ourselves settled in the Hotel de la Paix, an astonishing improvement upon the hotels of a few years ago.

A dozen years, however, have made more changes in this city than a century would have effected in many places. Instead of one little railway then going to the west of the city, important lines are now running north and south, while the Western system will some day be extended to the Pacific. Tramways are established in every part of the city and suburbs, and the suburbs themselves may be said to have been created in the time. An immense stimulus was given to the new Buenos Ayres by a calamity which at one time threatened almost to destroy it. The city of 'Fresh Breezes,' famous for its healthiness, was in the beginning of 1871 attacked with the pestilence of a deadly fever. No one could understand it: some attributed it to local uncleanliness, others attributed it to the water of the river bringing down the poison from thousands upon thousands of men and horses that perished in the

[1] I hear that Mr. Bateman's plan is being rapidly carried out.

Paraguayan war, and were thrown into the Paraná or left to rot where they lay. The latter opinion has in its favour the facts that the disease showed itself at Corrientes and other towns up the river before it arrived at Buenos Ayres; and that, though no systematic reform of the sewerage was attempted, yet the disease did not show itself in the succeeding years.

Whatever may have been the cause, the effects were appalling. Men, women, and children died in hundreds and thousands. So great a panic prevailed, that all who could leave the city did so. Only a quarter of a population of nearly 200,000 remained, and among these at one time there were a thousand deaths daily from the pestilence. Some of the low crowded houses of the Italians were said to be left full of corpses which no one ventured to touch. In the midst of these scenes, some who were compelled to remain there contrived to take it all very coolly in much the same way as that which the Decameron introduces us to during the great plague of Florence. Business was of course nearly suspended, and those who left their families in the country for a few hours' work in town knew that it was by no means improbable that they should never see them again. It was found that the disease never spread beyond the limits of the city, and the result of this was that everybody wished to provide himself with a country house.

Land buying became a brilliant speculation for good judges who saw their way to making their money over and again, and the plague was at all events one very important element in the great extension of the city. Trains now come in from all sides loaded with men of business who live at Flores, or Belgrano, or some other new suburb, where houses and gardens and railway stations cover the ground over which we galloped with our guns a dozen years ago. At the same time great changes have been made in the buildings of the city itself. Great shops and cafés in the French style have been opened, and I was told that the rent of one of the largest of these shops was equal to 2,000*l.* a year of English money. Latterly it is said there has been too much speculation in land and building; but that is a matter which always rights itself in time, though no doubt some 'go to the wall' in the course of the process.

I believe, however, that nothing can prevent a great increase in the demand for property in the territories of the River Plate. If their public men can only be persuaded to continue in the ways of peace and common sense, instead of plunging into the constant hubbub of revolutions, and calling out the citizens to cut each other's throats, to the screaming tune of 'Viva la Libertad,' there can be little doubt of a rapid increase in the natural prosperity of the country. Happily there are symptoms of a diminution of this revolutionary element, the main curse of the countries which Mr. Canning declared that he had called out in the new world to redress the old. The last attempt at a revolution in Buenos Ayres was headed by one of the most popular men in the country, but it soon died out like the snuff of a candle; and we may now, perhaps, hope that a good many of the national and political 'wild oats' have been sown. If General Mitré could not make a successful insurrection against the Government, it is hard to believe that anybody else could.

Railways, telegraphs, and steamboats are working a revolution of a different kind, and thousands of people now find honest employment instead of indulging in the mischief which 'Satan finds for idle hands to do.' Some of the railways have already made a great success, and there is little doubt that the others will. The Great Southern Company, finding they could make a better dividend for themselves than the Government guarantee of, I believe, seven per cent., paid a fine to the Government and cast off their swaddling clothes. It is feeling its way through the great plains of the south, while the Central Argentine with its branches must soon bring down the productions of half a continent from the Andes to the Paraná.

One of the first days after our arrival an old friend took us out by railway to his country place at Lomas. The whole neighbourhood had been so changed and built over that I did not know the once familiar district; and the planting of Eucalyptus, the Australian gum-tree, in all directions, contributed a good deal to the general disguise, for these trees grow so fast that there were groves of fifty or sixty feet in height where there had been not so much as a bush. He had an open carriage ready to take us for a drive to see something of the open country, which is familiarly called 'the camp.' Here, passing the limits of regular road, we found ourselves out at Santa Catalina, the adjoining property to the Monte Grande, where I formerly spent many happy days riding over the plains with gun on saddle, and hobbling our horses to stalk snipe and wild ducks in the marshes. I was quite taken by surprise, as I had no idea that we should now be taken out to my favourite old shooting-grounds in a carriage. The surprise was one of unmitigated joy as I recognised the well-known forms. Here were the little owls sitting as of yore near the holes of the biscachas, who wait till sunset to come out; here were the *tiru-teros*, or horned plovers, wheeling about with their peculiar cry; and the *chamangos*, a kind of small hawk that never feared coming close to a gun. Here on one side were the thickets of Santa Catalina where we used to shoot doves for pies; and there, right before us, was the smooth broad lagoon where I shot my first flamingo and rode home with him tied to my saddle.

On the present occasion, however, we had no intention of staying long in the River Plate. It was only a passing visit on our way to Chile, for which we were bound in all haste. To enjoy Buenos Ayres properly requires ample time for making long expeditions up the Paranà and Uruguay, with intervals of town life and agreeable society between them. On the palm-crowned hills of the Banda Oriental the large and small partridges rise from almost under your horse's feet, and you may gallop after ostriches over beds of scarlet verbenas and petunias; you may see the trees full of parrots, and dig up megatheriums on the banks of the Uruguay. In the vast plains of Buenos Ayres and Entrerios the freshness of the air and the free life of shooting and riding in a land of sunshine fill the mind and body with delight, which returns even now in only calling up the remembrance of them.

Our plan was to go down to Montevideo before long and wait for the arrival of the first ship of the Liverpool Pacific Steam Navigation Company to take us through the Straits of Magellan to Valparaiso ; but one fine day came a dismal report that the Montevidean Government had had the audacity to put the Buenos Ayrean steamer in quarantine on the pretence of cholera. She was released next day, and we hoped to hear no more of the matter. However, it was the time of peaches ; the weather was hot, and in a country where anybody could lay his boat against the banks of the Paraná and stuff it with peaches as long as he cared to pick them, it is not unnatural that a few of the people in a vast city should die of eating a superfluity of fruit. This, coupled with the fact of a few deaths on board a dirty quarantine pontoon at Ensenada, was made the most of by the Montevideans, who returned to the charge and imposed three days' quarantine on every vessel going down the river. Presently after, they increased it to ten, and then to twenty days. This promised us very serious trouble, as we could not meet a Pacific steamer without going to Montevideo, and we dared not go far from Buenos Ayres for fear of losing some chance which might be the only one.

At last we made up our minds to go by what was advertised as the 'Magnifico Vapor, Luxor,' of 3,000 tons, from Hamburg. She was telegraphed from Montevideo, and the agent offered to take us in a steam launch if we liked to look at her, at six o'clock next morning. We took the offer, and met the ship just as she came up to her anchorage. We thought she looked much more like 1,200 tons than 3,000, and when we got on board we found that she only had a few exceedingly nasty little cabins, and they were all taken. I never saw such a detestable-looking ocean-going steamer in any port of the world. We were considerably disappointed by this breakdown of our hopes, but we had to remain there for an hour or two before the launch returned. I cannot imagine what would happen to the magnificent 'Luxor' when at sea, for in the ripple of a breeze on the river she rolled at her anchorage so that a great part of her passengers were pouring their sorrows, not into the ocean, but into the River Plate.

Meanwhile we had an abundance of kind friends who loaded us with hospitalities. A good boat-club established at the Tigre, a short ride by railway, was a great attraction to my companion; and near the boat-house I once more saw an old acquaintance in the brilliant blossom of the *seibo* (*Erythrina*), which in some places higher up the Paraná transforms miles of its banks into seeming walls of deep carmine. Some other pleasant expeditions were arranged about this time by my old friends, Mr. Coghlan and Mr. Crawford, two well-known engineers. Mr. Ashbury, of yachting fame, had lately arrived with his beautiful steam yacht 'Eothen,' and it was determined to show him the works of the Ensenada and Great Southern railways.

The Ensenada day came off first. Mr. Sackville West, the British Minister, with Mr. St. John, his Secretary of Legation, and a few other friends besides ourselves, were invited to join the party. It was an unusually hot day when the little special train started out of the Buenos Ayres station, and we had a cloudless blaze till the sun sank below the horizon. The thermometer, in the coolest verandah that could be found, and entirely out of the reach of the sun, rose to 97°, but there is nothing oppressive even in this amount of heat in the glorious climate of the Rio de la Plata. A strong fresh breeze blew all day, and though we were walking about for a considerable time, I don't think anybody was inconvenienced by the heat. We inspected a large *saladero*, and saw some magnificent Basques at work upon the bone-ash. These men are considerably better paid than if they were serving Don Carlos in Spain; they are the best workmen in Buenos Ayres, and many of them are immensely powerful and very handsome. Care was taken to refresh the company from time to time with iced champagne in the railway carriage, and Mr. Simpson, the manager, provided a delicious cold collation at his own house in the middle of the day.

The Great Southern day was a somewhat longer affair, as we went to Chascomus, about seventy-five miles to the south of Buenos Ayres. This took us through the wild scenes of the Pampas, as effectively as if the distance had been hundreds of miles. We had nearly the same party as before, but Mr. West and Mr. St. John now brought rifles for the chance of a shot near the lake of Chascomus. These railways are unprotected by anything in the shape of fences, so that the herds of wild horses and cattle stray upon them as much as they please, and the 'cow-catcher' in front of the engine dashed several of them dead or dying to the right and left of the line, which is marked by carcases and skeletons. It is also marked by empty bottles thrown in great quantities out of window by the passengers; and if the Pampas sink below the sea, and rise again in some future geological period, the course of the Great Southern railway will be easily traced by a continuous line of bones and wine-bottles.

Whilst a goodly feast was being prepared by Mr. Grant at Chascomus, we walked to the edge of the lake, very much dried up by the hot weather. A gigantic crane was standing in the water up to the top of his long legs, about a quarter of a mile from us. Mr. Sackville West fired at him, but only frightened him into moving another fifty yards. Mr. St. John then fired, judging the distance as best he could; and the first shot, to our astonishment, went exactly through him, breaking both wings close to the body, as we found when a mounted man returned with the dead body. The next day was Christmas, and though the thermometer was about 90° in the shade, full justice was done to a splendid turkey and a blazing plum-pudding, with the toast of 'Absent friends.'

CHAPTER III.

Quarantine—The *Deus ex machina*—The Pampero at night—Start in the 'Eothen'—'Seeing the New Year in' at sea—Cruelty in hoisting cattle—The Straits of Magellan—Sea-birds and wonders of the Kelp—The tragedy of Sandy Point—Snow Mountains and Glaciers—Cape Pillar—Albatrosses and bad weather—Coronel—The Gardens and Smelting Works of Lota—Arrival at Valparaiso.

How were we to get away from Buenos Ayres? That was the question. Day by day we found ourselves more and more entangled in the toils of quarantine. The 'magnificent' steamer 'Luxor' had proved a delusion and a snare; and the agents of the Pacific Steam Navigation Company admitted that they had no means of putting passengers on board their own ships calling at Montevideo. We discussed the alternative of going to Rosario and Cordova, or Rio Quarto, with the view of crossing the Pampas and the Cordillera of the Andes to Santiago and Valparaiso. But this would rob us of the famous Straits of Magellan, which we were particularly anxious to see; and while the idea was in course of discussion, the news came that, so to speak, our own familiar friend had lifted up his heel against us, and that the provincial towns on the Paraná were themselves imposing quarantine on the inhabitants of the supposed-to-be-plague-stricken metropolis. Last of all we found, that even if we 'escaped to the mountains,' the Chilian outposts on the passes of the

Andes would prevent the entrance of anything unclean into their Republic. What was to be done, without the misery and humiliation of enduring three weeks in a quarantine establishment, full of Spanish and Italian emigrants whose overcrowding was in itself a natural stimulus to disease?

The *Deus ex machinâ* appeared in the person of Mr. Ashbury, who was still at Buenos Ayres with the 'Eothen.' Being anxious to return quickly to England, he determined to go home by the 'Sorata,' and leave the yacht in charge of his sailing master. The 'Sorata' was due at Montevideo on the following Monday; and Mr. Ashbury very kindly offered to take us with him down to the outside anchorage of Montevideo, and wait for her arrival. If a steamer bound for the Straits arrived first, he would put us on board her; but if not, we agreed to go back to Rio, and take a fresh departure. Thus should we defeat the demon of quarantine; and in such a journey as that which we were undertaking, the loss of ten days, and going 2,500 miles out of our way, appeared very insignificant matters. On Saturday, the 27th, Mr. Ashbury gave a luncheon on board the yacht, and the heat was so great that the coolest of champagne cups could not enable any of the party to sit down with his coat on. Late in the afternoon a steam launch came off to take the other visitors on shore, and it ought to have brought the steward, pilot, and baggage from the hotel. There was nothing, however, and we made up our minds to go back with Mr. Coles, the doctor of the yacht, and look after everything for ourselves. About half-past seven we got on shore, and found the beginning of troubles: it was unluckily Saturday evening, and not a cart or a peon could be found to do anything for love or money. We had the additional bad news that the hour was too late for getting the 'permit' from the captain of the port, without which we could not go on board again. There was, however, a very active and intelligent man in the service of one of our friends, who thought he could surmount all these obstacles if we gave him *carte blanche* to make the best bargains he could. Meanwhile we went back to the house of a hospitable friend, and for my own part I must confess that I heartily hoped that our ambassador would fail in his negotiations, and leave us in peace for the rest of the night.

No such luck, however. About 9.30 he returned, and said that everything was ready. How he had managed to get the 'permit' I know not, but there it was; and he had also hired a crowd of peons and a couple of boats to take us and our baggage. The great heat of the day had been followed by a dark and rather threatening night, and the prospect of rowing for an hour and a half was far from pleasant; but we felt bound to try it after so much trouble had been taken. The peons, bribed by double pay, took all the baggage down to the end of the mole, and a few of the articles were already in one of the boats when the boatmen suddenly declared that a storm was at hand, and nothing would induce them to start. Looking up to the moonless but starry sky, we saw to our astonishment a black wall of cloud rising swiftly over all the west and south. We were in the midst of perfect calm, and yet this awful cloud was seen dashing and surging towards us with the speed of a hurricane. In another moment it smote us in the face with all its fury. The *avant courier* of the storm was dense and almost blinding dust carried by the roaring blast, in the midst of which we contrived to get all our traps together again, and made a vain attempt to persuade the *guardia* to shelter us in their guard-room at the extremity of the mole. There was nothing left for us but to go 'bock again;' and in the howling of the storm we had to pay an outrageous price to the peons for carrying our things back to where they had come from. The first heavy drops of rain came pelting through the dust-storm; and in another moment a very deluge burst upon us with continuous crashes of thunder and lightning, and a wind which seemed trying to blow us into the river. Amidst the uproar of the elements the Custom-house people made us understand that we could take nothing with us from the pier till the next morning, but they put our goods under the shelter of their office; and perhaps this was all for the best, as the peons were saved from the temptation of running away with some of them in the darkness. Then we ran for the Café de Paris through deserted streets, which were suddenly turned into rivers, into one of which I plunged nearly up to my knees. A scrap of hasty supper was very necessary after this, and then in pitiable plight, covered with a kind of mud, caused by the rain coming upon a thick coating of dust, we returned to be welcomed by the good friends who, when they had recovered from laughing at our ridiculous and crest-fallen appearance, provided us with clean clothes while our own were drying. After some vigorous washing we were tolerably fit to join the social band, and forgot the sorrow of the evening in a nocturnal tobacco-parliament, and a comfortable shake-down on the floor.

A little before 5 A.M. we shook hands with our kind host in bed, and slipped out of the house to the *rendezvous* on the mole. The weather was once more splendid; we collected the pilot and the steward, got all our traps out of the clutches of the Custom-house, and started for the distant anchorage of the yacht. We got on board in time for an early breakfast, after which I was very glad to take off coat and waistcoat and lie down for a few hours. The heat of the previous day, the vexation and excitement about the baggage, the uncertainties of the evening, the difficulty of doing anything, the terrific appearance of the storm, and the short rest after it, all combined to make me feel unusually tired.

About noon we slipped down the river with a rather sulky pilot in charge; the water was rough enough to compel closing the ports, and the heat below was intense. Very early next morning we dropped the pilot at the lightship, went on and came to anchor some miles out from Montevideo, wondering whether the outward or homeward Pacific steamer would arrive first. In a couple of hours the problem was solved by the arrival of the magnificent 'Sorata' on her way from Valparaiso to England, and as soon as she anchored, the yacht moved on and anchored about three hundred yards from her. Our yellow flag would have compromised her seriously, so we waited patiently for the next morning, when she was to sail for Rio. All day we endured a series of thunderstorms with tremendous lightning and deluges of rain, which made the deck untenable, but in the morning all was fair. We had all the baggage ready in one of the yacht's boats, while another was to take the party; and the moment the last Montevidean boat, full of officials, left the side of the 'Sorata,' we pushed off and stood on her deck just as she finished weighing anchor. We waved a farewell to the beautiful 'Eothen,' which weighed anchor at the same time, and started for her voyage home under command of the sailing master.

It was with an indescribable feeling of relief and deliverance that we found ourselves once more at sea and clear of the clutches of Montevideo. The recent thunderstorms and rain had somewhat cooled the air, and nothing could be pleasanter than the voyage of four days and a half to Rio, during which we did our best to bury the old year properly and to welcome the new one. Our small company of passengers assembled on deck at midnight, and under the broad light of the moon shining over a calm sea we drank the health of the new year, while the sailors rang the ship's bells with all the vigour they were capable of. With 2,500 tons of copper on board we did not travel particularly fast, but in the afternoon of January 3 we were running past the Sugarloaf into the ever-beautiful harbour of Rio. Never, perhaps, did its now familiar scenery appear to greater advantage, but as it was no part of our plan to stay there longer than necessary on the present occasion, our pleasure was greatly increased by finding that the Company's ship 'Cotopaxi' had not yet left for the south, and would be ready to take us back as soon as she could complete taking in her 600 tons of coal. The 'Sorata' wanted a similar supply, and the coaling of two such ships at once made a hard day for the people at the wharf in the intense heat of an extra-hot Brazilian sunshine. Next day we were transferred to the 'Cotopaxi,' where I found an old friend in her commander, Captain Bax, the brother of our late captain of the 'Neva;' and in the afternoon of the 5th, still with perfectly fine weather, we once more said farewell to Rio de Janeiro. We had a very fine and fast passage of only three days and a half to Montevideo, doing one day 338 knots in the twenty-four hours, or rather more than fourteen knots an hour throughout; and here I may as well say a few words in praise of the splendid vessels of the Pacific Steam Navigation Company. To anyone who does not particularly dislike the sea, and wishes for three months' change of scene, combined with repose of mind and comfort of body, I could not recommend anything better than a voyage from Liverpool to Callao and back in one of them. Many of them, of about 4,000 tons burthen and considerably more than 400 feet in length, are from end to end like the finest yachts, combining the elements of speed, beauty, and stability. They carry their ports high out of the water; some of them have the admirable arrangement of a nearly square saloon in the middle of the ship, and they have libraries of such well-chosen books that it is difficult to know which to begin with.

Such was the 'Cotopaxi,' which brought us back to Montevideo on the tenth day after leaving it; and sweet was the feeling of triumph over the worthy people of that place as we looked at it from our anchorage, and thought of the pleasant days we had been spending at sea instead of in their hateful quarantine establishments. I suppose they were pleased with the result of that system, for we now found that it had been extended, and ships from

Brazil also were condemned to eight days' quarantine in consequence of a few cases of fever on the coast. As Montevideo therefore for a second time prevented us from having a chance of shaking off her dust from our feet, we spent the day chiefly in watching cargo and cattle coming on board in lighters during a pretty fresh breeze. The cattle were lifted in a very primitive fashion by fastening a nooze round their horns, and applying the steam-winch at the other end of the rope. Under the pressure of this irrepressible 'demon,' as Mr. Ruskin would call it, their necks were drawn out to a length which I could hardly have believed possible before their ponderous bodies were lifted from the deck of the barge. There was something ludicrous in the appearance of a bullock in mid-air with his tail hanging down and his neck stretched upwards to a preternatural length; but the cruelty of the proceeding soon overcame the idea of mirth. I asked why they were not brought up properly in slings; and the answer was, that the Montevidean cattle are so wild that if they were brought on board in any such gentle fashion, they would make a furious disturbance as soon as they touched the deck; whereas by the rougher process of stretching and straining they were frightened into a state of tranquillity. Whether the end justified the means we must leave to the casuists; at all events it was successful, and when the rope was cast off, each beast allowed itself to be led away by one horn as quietly as a tame lamb. The sheep had even worse treatment, if possible. They were piled in the barge one upon the other, each with its four feet tied tightly together; the rope from the winch was passed through the fastenings of eight sheep at a time, and they were thus hauled up by the feet like bales of goods, and deposited anyhow on the deck. Once upon a time I was remonstrating with the rough mate of a Scotch steamer about the cruelty of taking sheep from Leith to the London market without giving them a particle of food or water for the two days and nights; the surly answer I received was, 'What's the good o' giving them anything to eat? they'll be eat theirselves o' Tuesday.' I suppose the Montevidean purveyors would have agreed with him.

Next morning the wind and sea had gone down, and all was calm sunshine. The departing officials consented to take letters on shore after sprinkling them with a touch of carbolic acid; there was a very grave question as to the necessity of quarantining an old donkey brought by a passenger from Spain; and among other discrepancies, the health officers allowed a box of specie to pass when duly sprinkled, while a case of jewellery was not to be purged so lightly from its contagious impurity. At last we weighed anchor, and went down in an hour and a quarter to Flores Island, where we left our Montevidean passengers to languish for a week in the lazaretto; and as we steamed off grandly on our way, we could see some of them sadly waving handkerchiefs and waiting their turn to be fumigated with all their effects. We hear of International Congresses about peace, labour, socialism, and other matters: those who travel much about the big world, and know how often lazarettos are made conducive to the revenue of individuals, as well as how often quarantine is established on the most frivolous pretences, would like to see a Congress assembled to put a strong curb upon such absurdities. The Flores Island establishment is not so bad a prison as it might be, but it is a prison; and those who come out to work in a new world find it remarkably unpleasant to be 'cribbed, cabined, and confined,' and made to pay for it too, when they are eagerly longing to make money instead of spending the small savings they may have brought from Europe. But I must dismiss the subject for the present, and remember that we are going at the rate of 300 miles a day towards the famous Straits of Magellan.

Soon after crossing the extreme mouth of the estuary of La Plata we found the sea for a considerable distance varied by large patches of a brownish colour, caused by shoals of countless small fish which were affording a royal feast to innumerable gulls and other sea-birds. Screaming and darting down with a splash upon their victims, they seemed to be vying with one another as to who should eat the most, while a school of porpoises, tumbling merrily, seemed to enjoy their share of the fun. Next day, with perfectly calm weather, the sea presented an appearance which I have never seen elsewhere. It was divided into broad, irregular belts, with well-defined lines of foam, much as if caused by water rippling against a muddy shoal or bank. The seeming shoals were represented by sheets of glassy water, while the intermediate belts were ruffled by a fresh breeze into a rippling sea. There was nothing of the passing cat's-paw phenomenon in this, for the dividing belts of foam showed clearly that these parallel belts of alternate breeze and dead calm must have maintained much the same position for some time. As we ran to the southwards, the sea at about 100 fathoms deep was only moderately blue, and looked as if it were mixed with a solution of chalk or skim-milk. The whole appearance of the sky and the tints of the clouds changed very rapidly in a couple of days ; the warm glow and lustre of the tropical regions vanished like a dream, and the hard chalky clouds looked more like what may be seen on a fairly bright day in the European spring.

What strange events have sprung from small causes ! That invaluable treasury of geography, the book of 'Purchas his Pilgrimes,' tells us that 'Fernandus Magalianes, a Portugal,' after serving with great distinction in the Portuguese navy, under Albuquerque in the East Indies, thought that his services were not sufficiently appreciated by his royal master; and, on being refused an addition to his stipend of 'halfe a duckat a moneth,' he went over to the Court of Castile, and told the Emperor that the Spice Islands of the Moluccas properly belonged to Spain as being to the westward of the meridian, which the Pope had fixed as the boundary between the possessions of Spain and Portugal in the new world. He went further, and offered to go by the west and secure those 'Islands of Spicerie' for the Spanish Crown. The Emperor listened to the enticing proposal, and Magalianes, or Magellan, started on August 10, 1519, with five ships and 236 men under his command. After a fair share of the troubles which usually disturbed the navigators of that period, he and his expedition discovered the Straits which bear his name, and sailed through them to the Pacific Ocean, which he also named. They were much astonished by the 'giants' whom they found in Patagonia, and who appeared to them so good-humoured in spite of their size that they resolved to capture some specimens.

They induced a few of them to come on board, and delighted the giants by filling their hands so full of presents that they could not use them without dropping their treasures; and they then succeeded in putting steel fetters on the feet of two of them. The fetters looked very pretty and bright, and the giants were more pleased than ever till they found they could not move. Then they 'roared like bulls,' but all their roaring was useless. The ship that contained one of them deserted for home, and the luckless giant died when he felt the heat of the equatorial regions. The other died amidst the sickness which semi-starvation brought on the expedition when crossing the Pacific ; and however lovely they may have been in their lives, the Patagonian giants in their death were very far divided.

What would not poor Fernandus Magalianes have given for the 'Cotopaxi' that on the fifth day took us round the Virgins Cape and into the eastern entrance of is famous Straits? We were there before 4 A.M., which was long after daylight at that high latitude in the middle of January. The land on both sides was flat, and almost as low as the banks of the Scheldt at Antwerp ; the sea was smooth as glass in that tranquil morning, and patches of gigantic sea-weed afforded floating sofas to countless gulls, divers, ducks, cormorants, and penguins. There they sat in luxurious ease till every now and then it suited one or other of them to take a header after one of the fish which rejoice in these beds of kelp: he returned in a moment, shook his head as he bolted his victim, and quietly sat down to digest it while his friends followed his example. This sea-weed, the *Macrocystis pyrifera* is, in a marine fashion, the most successful rival of the 'big trees' of California, which are the largest upon *terra firma*. Mr. Darwin [1] says that 'it grows on every rock from low-water mark to a great depth, both on the outer coast and in the channels.' It has been found growing up to, and spreading over, the surface of the water from a depth of forty-five fathoms, which, when added to the angular slant given to it by currents, was probably equal to a height of 400 feet. Its branches serve as buoys over sunken rocks, and at the mouths of harbours have a very considerable effect in breaking up the force of the waves. In addition to this, Mr. Darwin remarks that the number of living creatures of all orders that depend on the kelp for existence is wonderful. He 'never recurred to a branch of the kelp without discovering new creatures.' Shells, corallines, crustacea, &c., made it white below the surface of the sea; among its leaves live numerous species of fish, which nowhere else could find food or shelter. Upon these in turn depend the fishing-birds, seals, otters, and porpoises; and, lastly, without these, 'the Fuegian savage, the miserable lord of this miserable land, would redouble his cannibal feast, decrease in numbers, and perhaps cease to exist.' As I have elsewhere said that a forest monarch of Brazil, covered with ferns, orchids, and all kinds of parasitic plants, is 'not only a tree but a garden,' so it would seem that the kelp stands in a somewhat similar relation to the creatures of the sea.

In a few hours we found ourselves in narrower water, with the shores rising into low hills, on the top of one of which we saw our first *guanaco*, looking about him like an

[1] Voyage of the 'Beagle.'

old chamois on guard. The long sharp bow of the 'Cotopaxi' slipped through the glassy sea almost without making a ripple to disturb the multitudinous birds as they fished comfortably from their sea-weed beds, and rose and fell lazily as the gentle swell reached them. About 2 P.M. we reached Punta Arenas, commonly called Sandy Point, and here the transformation scene may be said to begin. Thus far the temperature could hardly have been called cold, and we were still a long way from the snow mountains; but in the three hours which we spent at Sandy Point a biting wind set in off the land, and gave us a foretaste of what we might expect in the next twenty-four hours. Punta Arenas has long been a Chilian convict settlement, and was in 1853 the scene of a fearful tragedy. The convicts made a successful rising, and after murdering the governor, their guards, and everyone that came in their way, about forty of them put to sea in a small schooner which they had appropriated. Unluckily for them, they fell in with a British man-of-war cruising in the Straits. Their appearance and their story appeared remarkably unsatisfactory, so the captain took them on board and carried them to Sandy Point, where a scene of horror showed what had lately taken place there. He then took them round to Valparaiso and handed them over to the Chilian authorities, by whose orders, as I was told, they were all shot forthwith. The place is still a station for military and naval prisoners, with a Chilian guard of about eighty men.

The governor, an Anglo-Chilian, came off to pay us a visit, and embraced one of our French passengers *more Gallico* with effusion. With him came an enormously tall

Englishman, who had been travelling and shooting in the neighbourhood, and who in an Ulster coat reaching to his heels out-Patagonianed the Patagonian giants. There appeared to be very few boats, but one or two came off to trade with a few ostrich feathers, guanaco skins, &c., but they were not of very tempting excellence. The settlement is a very small one, containing as nearly as I could count about 150 houses and shanties, some of them of the smallest possible size consistent with sheltering human creatures. The land slopes up steeply from very near the beach, and it is only in the immediate neighbourhood of the settlement that a clearance has been made in the forest, which must previously have clothed the whole of the hill-side. The appearance of the trees was far finer than I could have expected. Two kinds of beech grow to a large size, and at the edge of a clearing their white stems have a charming effect against the forest depths behind them. Evergreen trees grow luxuriantly, for the climate, though on the average of the year about ten degrees lower than at a similar latitude in the Northern hemisphere, is much more equable, with almost constant wet. The immense amount of moisture covers the surface of the ground with a deep growth of mosses, film-ferns, and water-loving plants, which encroach even on the low-lying branches of the trees to such an extent that the inquisitive pedestrian, in trying to make use of these boughs, can easily slip off and find himself up to the middle in a mixture of bog-plants and rotten trees. Above this forest belt comes a region of scrub reaching nearly to the top of rough hills in form and colour very much like the Highlands of Scotland. A discovery of coal has raised the hopes of those who wish to see the advancement of the place; but, as far as I could hear, neither the quality nor the quantity was very inspiriting as yet.

We sailed about 4 P.M. through Famine Reach, Froward Reach, and English Reach, passing between mountains which were higher and more snowy as we advanced towards the west. Many of those nearest to the shores rose up to a height of probably about 3,000 feet directly from the sea, with the upper half still nearly covered with snow; and every now and then an opening in the line enabled us to look up lateral gulfs and fiords to the grand heads of the higher order of true snow mountains, with their glaciers running down to the sea. A distant glimpse of Mount Buckland revealed a peak almost exactly like the Jungfrau as seen from the Eggischhorn, and farther on we had a fine view of Mount Sarmiento, which is a noble mass of rocks and snow slopes rising to the height of nearly 7,000 feet. The ship was stopped for the few hours of a southern midsummer's night, as the captain did not like venturing on the intricacies of Crooked Reach till daylight. It was a strangely wild scene; the mountains so closed in upon us that we seemed to be only in a rather narrow lake, with snow to the left of us, snow to the right of us; and a biting wind drove great dark clouds before it, pelting us with blinding hail and sleet that chilled the very bones of those who a week before were in the hottest weather of the southern tropic. In the intervals between the squalls grand gleams of sunshine would illuminate the forests and the snowfields; and the departing sun, between the rolling away of one black mass and the attack of its successor, gave a rosy tint to the crests and warmed the mossy rocks and nearer forests with a rich lustre of golden brown.

About 3 A.M. on the 18th there was light enough to go ahead again through the turns and twists of Crooked Reach. We passed Glacier Bay on the north with splendid fields of ice sweeping down towards the sea; and with the telescope could make out the details of many other glaciers a little further removed from the main channel, and flowing down into the lateral fiords. All the well-known phenomena were distinctly visible: rocky arêtes separated by precipitous couloirs; vast fields of névé, crevasses and blue icefalls, ending with the fan-shaped structure bounded by its lateral moraines. Here and there we thought we could detect a small puff of smoke, indicating the presence of a few wretched Fuegians, but we saw no boats or any positive evidence of these houseless savages. Long Reach was a kind of exaggerated Loch Lomond, with snow mountains on both sides, the view towards its eastern extremity closing up with a magnificent group of the higher summits, chief of which was a noble mass which very closely resembled the Finsteraarhorn as seen from the Furka. It must of course be remembered, that though the highest of these Fuegian mountains are only from 6,000 to 7,000 feet high, yet the effect upon a spectator who sees them from the deck of a ship, rising straight out of the sea and covered with snow almost down to its level, is quite as surprising as the view of an Alpine giant from some lofty pass.

The wind grew stronger and colder with every hour; and those of us who faced the pitiless hailstorms that swept across the deck were glad of the thickest coats we could muster. One of the quartermasters seemed rather astonished at my evident enjoyment of the wild scene and chilling blast; but I had not seen any snow mountains for three years, and the old spirit of the Alps was upon me, in addition to the spirit of curiosity which was roused as I looked upon this untouched region of Antarctic mountains. What a field of enterprise for a Patagonian branch of the Alpine Club, with two hundred miles of untrodden 'peaks, passes, and glaciers' on each side of a strait which is regularly passed by some of the finest steamers in the world! Not only does all the charm of novelty await investigation, but in addition to all the ordinary difficulties of mountaineering they would have the excitement of feeling that at the end of an otherwise successful day, they might perhaps go to supper with some hungry Fuegians of the coast, and find themselves, like Polonius, 'not where they eat, but where they're eaten.'

About noon we passed the eastern end of the well-named Island of Desolation, and entered on broader water, where we encountered a heavy head sea, which was big enough to make the 420 feet of the 'Cotopaxi' pitch and tumble like a lively porpoise, though nothing seemed able to materially slacken her pace. Most of us heartily wished the weather to get worse, for in that case the captain would have taken the ship through the renowned Smyth's Channel to the northward. The scenery of that channel is described as wonderfully fine, and in its narrow waters ships of the largest size are sometimes moored for the night in twenty-five fathoms, so close to the shore that their bowsprits and anchors actually intrude into the surrounding trees. It is, however, considered so risky that the Pacific Steam Navigation Company's captains have orders not to attempt it unless when the state of the weather is such as to make the passage out by Cape Pillar a still greater peril. We tried in vain to induce Captain Bax to think that such was the case at present; and so we held on against an ever-increasing sea, till in the afternoon we passed the fearful rocks of Cape Pillar at the end of the Island of Desolation, where we saw the waves dashing up the cliffs and pinnacles in towers of foam such as I never elsewhere beheld. The whole force of the Pacific beats against these tremendous precipices under the influence of perpetual gales from the west; and I can fully agree with Mr. Darwin, who, when taking leave of Tierra del Fuego, remarks that 'one sight of such a coast is enough to make a landsman dream for a week about shipwrecks and peril and death.'

As we passed into the open ocean and saw the fierce sea with which we were battling, a French passenger pointing to it, said to me, 'Et voilà, monsieur, ce qu'on appelle la mer Pacifique!' He seemed to think he had been swindled. The sudden transition from a very hot climate in its hottest season to the cold and bitter winds of the Straits caused a good many very severe sorethroats, some of which required the use of caustic daily, and prevented the sufferers from swallowing anything but slops for the rest of the voyage to Valparaiso. A considerable number of albatrosses were waiting to escort us when we got clear of the Straits, and it was a constant amusement to watch them hovering close over the deck with their keen eyes ever on the watch for waifs and strays from the food department, or sweeping backwards and forwards with irresistible but seemingly motionless wings. There is no flapping movement to renew the speed; with wings rigidly extended to a breadth of twelve feet and upwards, and moving only as the body moves, they look like wonderful machines wound up for the day, or perhaps endowed with perpetual motion. They were the only creatures that appeared to enjoy the weather of the next two days. A strong north-west wind and driving rain made life on deck miserable, and the rolling of the ship in a heavy cross sea set things flying in all directions in the cabin; but the albatrosses seemed as serene as ever, and though they often came within close pistol-shot we remembered the fate of the 'ancient mariner,' and no one ventured to pull a trigger on them. In the neighbourhood of Chiloe we had a dose of the rain which almost always falls there and nourishes a dense vegetation. Soon after this we began to feel warm again. The sea subsided into a long swell, and with sail and steam we went northwards at our best speed. The increasing heat did not at all suit the constitution of our friends the albatrosses, who tailed off one by one; the last of them deserted the day before reaching Valparaiso, and went back to cool himself in the more congenial blasts of the Southern Ocean.

Early in the morning of the 20th we passed the island of Santa Maria, and with perfectly lovely weather anchored at the coaling station of Coronel, a few miles to the south of Concepcion. Here, close to the low sandy beaches, were the familiar forms of coal-shafts, reminding us of the north of England, and showing how the discovery of a new source of wealth can in a few years transform the wilderness, even if it does not make it to blossom like the rose. The fortune of this neighbourhood was made by the discovery of coal in 1849, and the subsequent establishment of the great copper smelting works at Lota, about seven miles from Coronel. The coal has a very indifferent appearance, looking more like slaty rubbish, but it does good work; and while the 'Cotopaxi' spent the day in replenishing her bunkers we had a singularly happy chance of seeing another application of it. We were fortunate in having for a fellow passenger an English merchant of Valparaiso who was well acquainted with the chief proprietors of Lota, and very kindly offered to escort us over the works. There was some uncertainty about horses, and we agreed to make a party of four and go by boat.

A bargain was soon made with four sturdy Chilenos to take us there and back for eight dollars, waiting at Lota as long as we wished. They had a capital whale-boat and rowed well, getting over the seven miles in an hour, and passing round the rocks of a projecting point into a snug bay, which is furnished with a pier for ships to load and discharge at. In a few minutes more we found ourselves in the hospitable charge of the authorities, who led us through vast rows of buildings, crowned with a forest of chimneys vomiting smoke. Here, in addition to the natural heat of the day, we were brought almost up to melting-point by wandering amongst endless furnaces and rivers of molten copper, some fresh and red-hot, and others treacherously concealing their real condition by a newly-assumed shade of external blackness. Here were vast piles of ore brought from the northern ports; ponderous machines in haunts of darkness crushing it to powder; tough Indians and many-coloured demons of the alternate gloom and glare carrying it hither and thither, and watering the ground with their sweat; foul smells, sulphureous and abominable; and then came the excitement of opening a fresh furnace and the outpouring of a new river of hell. We were introduced to the mysteries of variously valued ores and regulus, to mountains of slag and rubbish, and to the arcana of the scientific German who tests and certifies to the quality of all the specimens that pass through his hands. At length we emerged into the comparative coolness of a blazing sun, where I saw men using brooms made of myrtle-boughs, blossom and all, to sweep the grimy floors of some outlying sheds. It seemed a cruel outrage on that divine flower, and made me think of the surprise with which Voltaire's Candide saw the children of the Incas playing at marbles with nuggets of gold. Here, too, we were in comparative absence of noise, and could listen to statistics about Lota and its works. The coal mines and smelting establishment are said to employ 2,500 hands; and the little town contains about 7,000 people, more or less dependent upon the works. The furnaces turn out about 1,000 tons of copper monthly, and could make more if pressed; and the value of the metal at the lower figure would be not much under 1,000,000*l*. sterling a year. In addition to the vast quantities of coal required for the smelting works, I was told that the company also sell coals to the extent of 400,000*l*. a year: and some idea may thus be formed of the vast business which is now being carried on at what was lately a desolate corner of the Chilian coast. The land formed part of the estates of the Cousiño family, who have, of course, made an immense fortune, and who out of their abundance have lately given a large public park and garden to the good people of Santiago.

Half a dozen saddled horses[1] were ready to take us up the hill that rises from the valley, at the end of which the works are placed. And here a wonderful change of scene presented itself. The fumes of preparing and smelting the ore have destroyed nearly every kind of vegetation in the line of the valley up which they are carried by the prevailing westerly winds ; but, on turning a few yards to the left when we reached the high ground, which is about 300 feet above the sea, we found ourselves among the brilliant gardens of Madame Cousiño. Long winding walks made of pounded shells, some bordered with thick rows of Neapolitan violets, and others with hedges of scarlet geraniums, led in every direction to and from a handsome English-looking house, which commands the view to the Pacific. Here were all the best native plants, aided by fresh supplies from Veitch's stores at Chelsea, all under the care of highly-paid European gardeners, with a good supply of water at their disposal. In some parts there were green sloping lawns decked with groups of the large yellow broom in full blossom, and scarlet geraniums eight or ten feet high, the combined effect of which was brilliant beyond description. In another direction paths had been cut out of the hill-side among the dense shade of the Chilian evergreen oaks, between the stems and branches of

---

[1] One of these horses had carried one of the managers 90 miles the day before our arrival, and won a race when near the end of the journey.

which we looked down upon the blue and shining ocean. The rose garden contained many of the choicest sorts, and the scarlet *Calosanthus coccineus* bloomed marvellously. The blue spiked veronica of our greenhouses was like a weed, growing into bushes of twelve or fifteen feet high, loaded with flowers from top to bottom. Bright calceolarias and verbenas clustered round immense heliotropes; and many-coloured dahlias, backed by thick evergreens, added their share of brilliance to the scene. From the gardens the land slopes gently towards the sea in park-like fashion, studded with groups of dark ilex, till it terminates in the undulating line of coast, with ferny caves and sunny headlands, which, in their warm tints of red and brown and yellow, reminded me of many a view on the coasts of Greece. Among them are the haunts of the Copigue, or *Lapageria rosea*, which with its long rose-coloured, wax-like bells is one of the most beautiful twining plants in the world. In spite of its exquisite beauty and seeming delicacy, it is said to be almost the only plant of any kind that can exist under the influence of the sulphureous smoke of the smelting houses; and Dr. Cunningham mentions having seen it 'in a flourishing condition winding round the skeletons of shrubs killed by the smoke.'

After paying some well-deserved compliments to the gardener we were invited to a very welcome luncheon by the manager, and after another walk in the garden we turned away from this floral paradise of Chile, and walked down the hill to the Gehenna of the smelting works. Here, as we stepped into our boat, we found that the gardener had appreciated praise, and kindly sent us down four magnificent bouquets, about the size of beehives.

A strong breeze blowing on shore made it hard work for our boat's crew to pull out round the first headland; but when that was done, we set sail and had a merry run back to the 'Cotopaxi.' From the sea we looked for the last time upon the splendid colours of that gay garden on the hill, and bade farewell to a place that will never be forgotten. A visit to Lota was a delightful first introduction to the West Coast of South America. We sailed early next morning, and at sunset buried a poor fellow who had fallen down dead in the stoke-hole. On the 22nd, about breakfast time, we anchored in the bay of Valparaiso.

CHAPTER IV.

The Cochrane statue—' Earthquakia '—The suburbs of Valparaiso—Building materials—Fox-hunting—Chacabuso revels—Delightful climate—Railway to Santiago—Fruit—The bell of Quillota—Llai-Llai—Moonlight effects—The highest station—The plain of Santiago—Arrival by night—The Grand Hotel Santa Lucia and view of the Cordillera—Aconcagua and Tupungato—Will they ever be ascended?

COMING ON DECK, after the usual bustle of packing and paying stewards, I had the pleasure of finding that an English friend, Mr. Hennedy, had come off to look for us and carry us through the clamours of a legion of contending boatmen, and other human sharks and alligators, all anxious to have the first spoiling of a new arrival in a foreign land. Ridiculous claims were soon brought within the bounds of reason; and we presently found ourselves installed with all our goods in the Hotel de l'Union, kept by a remarkably pleasant and agreeable French couple, who always enjoyed a chat about France and the glories of their native Pyrenees. Rooms were scarce, however, for it was the season when the fashionable world of Santiago finds itself constrained by excessive heat to come down to Valparaiso, and enjoy the luxuries of sea-air and bathing. Almost every spare room in the town was let, and prices had risen, as they do all over the world in fashionable places, ' during the season.'

The name of Valparaiso, Vale of Paradise, sounds

very charming; but however justly it may be applied to Quillota and the country a little way inland, yet, as far as the city is concerned, it is assuredly a misnomer. It is not in a valley at all, nor is there anything in its outside appearance likely to suggest thoughts of Paradise to an ordinary spectator. It is a long, narrow, scrambling city, extending along the whole length of a nearly semi-circular bay, and walled in by a nearly parallel chain of hills rising to about 1,500 feet above the sea, with *quebradas* or ravines partially dividing them. Landing at the mole and entering the Plaza adjoining, we found ourselves face to face with a statue of Lord Cochrane; and the street to the left where our hotel stands is also named after the British hero to whom South America was so much indebted, and whose ghost seems now the presiding genius of the place. The next thing that I particularly noticed was the abundance of large cracks and recently filled patches in the handsome buildings all round, testifying to the violence of a July earthquake six months before. We were in truth now committed to what might properly be called 'Earthquakia,' a region which, regardless of all political boundaries, extends through about ninety degrees of latitude, and more than 7,000 miles of coast from Southern Chile to the north of California. Throughout the whole of this vast extent the earthquake-power flourishes the sword of Damocles over the inhabitants, and they know not who will first be struck. There is scarcely a place along the whole coast which has not been fearfully shaken, if not wholly destroyed, within the memory of man. Concepcion, Valparaiso, and Santiago have been shaken to the ground over and over again within the last three centuries; and if anyone wishes to see the catalogue of disasters in Chile alone during that period, I would refer him to the valuable work[1] of Lieutenant Gilliss, of the American navy, who was in charge of their Astronomical expedition from 1849 to 1852. Nowhere have I read a more admirable account of what a courageous man could do under circumstances which drove all the inhabitants into panic-stricken flight. He remained watching his instruments and calculating how long the parting ceiling would be supported by the opening walls; and only seizing his watch and hiding under the shelter of the lintel of the door whilst all the rest of the building came down about his ears in a blinding crowd of rubbish. But, even since the date of his work, a still more terrible catastrophe happened in 1861, at Mendoza on the Argentine side of the Cordillera, when the whole of that city was destroyed, and three-quarters of a population of about 20,000 perished in five minutes. On that occasion the shock was so far felt at Buenos Ayres, 900 miles distant, that the chief watchmaker there told me that his pendulum clocks were at once left ten seconds behind his chronometers. A special peculiarity about the phenomena of 'Earthquakia' is this. Soldiers and sailors will tell you that they soon get accustomed to be shot at, and I have no doubt that they speak truthfully: the merely close probability of being killed in that way is comparatively nothing. They have at all events the satisfaction of feeling that they have a chance of shooting somebody else; but when the solid earth shakes under the feet, the feeling is quite otherwise.

[1] 'The United States Naval Astronomical Expedition to the Southern Hemisphere.' Washington, 1855.

All human computations fail: the most experienced are the first to run out in their night-shirts, and they say with trembling that 'the more they look at it the less they like it.' Nevertheless, they live near the gaunt terror as happily as most people; those who are not killed rebuild their houses on the same spot if they can find it; laugh at the past misfortune, and forget the future probabilities of a similar scene. Mr. Gilliss speaks of a man who had heard of the crust of the earth surrounding sempiternal fires, but graphically remarked that he never realized the fact of its being something like mere pie-crust till he tried by standing tiptoe on the opening earth to delay his precipitation into the realms of Pluto.

The docks, wharves, storehouses, &c., are chiefly at the southern end of the crescent-shaped bay; the railway station is near the opposite extremity, and between them run nearly parallel streets which are traversed by an abundance of tramcars at the smallest of small fares. There are many good shops with all the latest useful and pretty things from London and Paris; but everything seemed excessively dear with the exception of tramcars and photographs of Chilian scenery, which were well worth a dollar each. But a dollar for hair-cutting seemed an extortionate charge, though we afterwards found it was the regular thing all the way to San Francisco and China; and one might fairly hesitate before giving 2*l*. 10*s*. for a white hat, or sixteen shillings for a bottle of ordinary champagne; but such were the prices. The houses at the back of the city are built almost close to the rocks, much like the situation of Hastings under the castle; and steep flights of steps and zigzag roads lead at different points to the upper part of the town. Here is the English Church and the Cerro Alegre, where many of the leading men of business have pretty houses and gardens ornamented with good Norfolk Island pines, *Araucaria excelsa*, huge bushes of scarlet geraniums and yellow broom, passion-flowers, fuchsias, heliotropes, calceolarias, and roses of all descriptions. In front of these there is a kind of terrace road, commanding a fine view of Aconcagua, the highest mountain in the world with the exception of some of the chief Himalayas. It is 23,600 feet above the sea, and even at this distance of about 120 miles its vast and solitary mass of snow and precipice presents a most magnificent appearance. It is quite alone in its glory, and being more than half as high again as Mont Blanc it appears to rise farther into the sky than one would think possible.

Wandering past this comparatively aristocratic quarter we soon found ourselves exploring a still higher region of suburbs, wherein are to be seen the dwellings of peons, water-carriers, and labourers of all sorts and grades, tapering down to the domesticated Indians. Here the style of architecture also tapers off till it arrives at the primitive simplicity of mud huts; and little bits of land separated by curiously varied fences which, in a region where timber is scarce, are made by the poorer classes of anything but wood. 'Nothing in matter is lost,' and nothing in the way of flotsam and jetsam seems to be lost sight of by the industrious *chiffonniers* of Valparaiso. A very popular kind of fence consists of broken tea-chests, beaten-out biscuit tins, old sardine-boxes, scraps of corrugated iron, and perhaps a cactus here and there to help in keeping the strange mixture together. A good many of the inhabitants of this quarter occupy themselves with the washing of clothes for the city, and through the open doors of their small houses many a picturesque group of half-Indian women off duty may be seen squatting on the ground in their own fashion, playing with their babies and chattering over a feast of figs and melons while the clothes are drying in the brilliant sunshine of a country where it scarcely ever rains except in one short season of the year. Yet a little farther on and higher up the last straggling hut is left behind, and the burnt-up ground is taken possession of by happy donkeys, who roll themselves in dust and rubbish among the half-dead remains of calceolarias and antirrhinums till they are carried off to be again loaded with water-casks for the city.

Beyond this come long successions of undulating hills, which were for the most part burnt brown, except where cactus and evergreen bushes took possession of the ground and offered some protection to innumerable blossoms of orange-coloured *Alstrœmeria* lilies. The rough roads and hill-sides were so steep and hard under our horses' feet that it was difficult to believe all we heard about the delights of fox-hunting in such a country; but it appears that if, instead of being in the hottest season of the year, we had seen Chile after the rains of winter, the country would have been green to the eye and soft to the foot, and we should have seen young England in full pursuit of Reynard. As it was, we rode on to see the cricket-ground, close to which football was going on, with preparations for a hurdle race. Another favourite hobby with the young men is their volunteer fire brigade, which is kept up in great style. Conflagrations in these countries are almost as much dreaded as earthquakes, and great attention is given by the volunteers to their system of organisation and drill. Their uniform is very handsome, and with jack-boots, white breeches, scarlet coats, and helmets they looked almost as imposing as our Life Guards.

An English visitor to Valparaiso, furnished with a few introductions, will feel himself quite at home before the first day is over; he will find abundance of pleasant friends who spare no pains to entertain him; and the foreign community in general, so far as I could see or hear, are on very sociable terms with each other. We were immediately made members of the club, which is an institution worthy of all praise. Throughout the middle of the day men of various countries meet here for luncheon, and all find something to their taste. Speaking as an Englishman, I am bound to say that the draught beer was admirable, and the cold roast-beef was as good as could be found in London itself, which is more than I can say for it in any other country that I have seen. The Chilians are making great progress in breeding good stock, and both their horses and their cattle are better than those on the other side of the Cordillera. The reading-rooms of the club contained the chief newspapers of the world, and all our favourite reviews and magazines were ready to tempt us into idleness. Excellent dinners were always ready in the evening, after which we sometimes went to the opera in the Plaza Victoria, where 'Norma' and 'Lucrezia Borgia' were being given by an Italian company with considerable success. There was a specially grand performance one evening before we left in honour of the anniversary of the battle of Chacabuco. I am sorry to say I do not know who was the great hero on that occasion, but it was evident that the Chilians have an extremely grateful remembrance of the affair. As the audience came out from the opera they found the whole of the Plaza filled with a dense crowd assembled to see a display of fireworks in front of the theatre, which was carried out in true South American fashion: grand set pieces showing illuminated sentences, such as 'Viva Chile,' alternated with showers of rockets and every species of explosion, with a recklessness as to the close proximity of the crowd which made me rather surprised next day at not hearing of anybody being killed. Suppers and various festivities followed, which among the lower classes caused an unnecessary amount of drunkenness, and gave rather more work than usual to the 'vigilantes,' or policemen, who parade the streets at night with whistles which make a hideous noise, and have the effect of keeping honest folks awake while giving rogues a very liberal warning that they had better get out of the way of justice. On the day after the Chacabuco revels we were very much surprised at finding we could get nothing for breakfast in the hotel, and the only waiters who appeared at all were manifestly obfuscated. Resolved to appeal to head-quarters, I went in search of our bright-eyed hostess, who explained that five of the staff had not come on duty, and probably would not come for a day or two. She added that she dared not complain to them, because they would leave her at once for the service of some one who would make more allowance for accidents connected with the glorious battle of Chacabuco; and she wound up by saying, 'Ah! Monsieur, il faut beaucoup souffrir dans ce pays-ci!' By degrees they dropped into their places again, looking as if nothing had happened, and evidently thought that it was 'dulce et decorum' not only to fight for their country, but also to get drunk for it.

The climate was delightful for true lovers of sunshine and clean dry heat. Clouds were very rare and never came to anything. There had only been one shower in the last six months, and even that was, as I heard, considered quite an exceptional phenomenon. June, July, and August are the rainy months; September is the spring, and by Christmas most of the fruits and flowers are in perfection, and the wheat harvest is complete. When we were there, in January and February, the country was already pretty nearly dried up, in all places not assisted by artificial irrigation; and the hills round Valparaiso, being too steep for such a process, were entirely burnt up. There are no trees upon them, and hardy bushes and huge cacti presented almost the only fresh vegetation among the withered remains of the summer flowers; we could see by the countless stalks how gay the yellow calceolaria must have been, but it was only in shady nooks that we ever found a tolerable bunch of bloom. One afternoon, clouds gathered so gloomily and so low that I remarked to a friend, 'In any other part of the world that sky would certainly bring rain in half an hour;' to which he replied, 'Ah! but it won't here.' I was so far right that an almost imperceptible drizzle did fall for a few minutes; but I could hardly have claimed the stakes if we had made a bet about the matter. Lieutenant Gilliss says that the result of three years' observations at the Valparaiso Exchange gave 62° as the maximum at 8 A.M., 78° as the maximum at 4 P.M., and 70° 8' as the mean of all the observations, but he does not appear to be satisfied as to their perfect accuracy. Santiago is hotter in summer, being away from the influence of the sea. What appeared to me especially delightful, was the almost constant brilliance of the sun, with the absence of anything like oppressive heat. A light fresh air kept everything cool, except in the full sunshine, and the temperature at night was all that could be desired. The bright and exhilarating air of Chile frequently made me think of that glorious chorus in the Medea of Euripides, beginning with—

> Ἐρεχθείδαι τὸ παλαιὸν ὄλβιοι,
> καὶ θεῶν παῖδες μακάρων . .
> . . . ἀεὶ διὰ λαμπροτάτου
> βαίνοντες ἁβρῶς αἰθέρος . .

It was an air to rejoice in; and although it may not seem to have quite such an ennobling effect upon the Chilians as upon the ancient Athenians, yet the Chilian spirit of progress, industry, honesty, and activity may at all events contrast very favourably with the doings of modern Greece.

In spite, however, of the attractions afforded by hospitable friends at Valparaiso, the fresh breezes from the sea, and the ever-to-be-remembered roast beef at the club, we became anxious to go into the interior of the country, to see the famous Santiago, and the great chain of the snowy Cordillera. On January 28, leaving most of our baggage in charge of our landlady, we drove to the railway station and started by the afternoon train at 5.15 P.M. for Santiago, which is 184 kilomètres, or about 115 miles, from Valparaiso. The railway runs close to the sea for a short time, and then dives through a tunnel under the precipitous headland, which forms the northern end of the semicircular bay. The change of scene was wonderful before we had even left Viña del Mar, the first station on the line. We had been living in a city where treeless and barren burnt-up hills look down upon the dusty roofs of houses : we were now entering upon a valley where the busy hand of man, aided by water from the Aconcagua river, has turned a desert into cornfields and fruit gardens. Pretty country houses and inns were frequent, standing in gardens full of fruit and flowers to tempt the worthy citizens to come from Valparaiso dust for a refreshing holiday in the country, whence they may return loaded with bouquets and fruit baskets for friends in town. On the platforms were dozens of picturesque women and Murillo-like boys with baskets of peaches, nectarines, apricots, plums, figs, grapes, and melons. Figs are both abundant and admirable in Chile, and a ration of them is in some districts given to the miners as part of their wages; but the melon is, I should say, the national fruit *par excellence*. They are to be seen everywhere in hundreds and thousands, and the common water-melons are almost equalled in number by some of the finer sorts, the flavour of which can hardly be surpassed. A common peon thinks nothing of eating an enormous melon in great hunches at a single sitting, and washing it down with a drink of water. At many of the stations on the line they were lying piled up near the roadway in vast heaps like the coals in a gas factory, and waiting to be sent down to Valparaiso, where the consumption is prodigious.

The gradual rise of the railway soon extended our view over the richly-cultivated plains, where corn stubbles, gardens, and orchards stretched away to the foot of the hills which culminate in the famous Campana, or Bell, of Quillota, which at a height of 6,400 feet above the sea affords a good landmark for vessels, and is a fine point for viewing the surrounding scenery. Here it was that Mr. Darwin had an opportunity of testing the astonishing purity of the Chilian atmosphere by finding that he could see the masts of ships lying in Valparaiso Bay, though the distance is twenty-six miles in a straight line. Long rows of Lombardy poplars line the road-sides and water-courses; and though I believe that the original stock only came in the shape of a bundle of twigs from Mendoza about forty years ago, they now form an important feature in all the culivated parts of the country, and have grown almost as high as any I have seen in Europe. Very many of them were ornamented by patches of crimson, which afterwards proved to be the blossom of a brilliant parasite, which, mixing with the rich green of the poplar leaves, had almost as charming an effect upon the eye as a branch of our holly well garnished with berries. As we approached Quillota, an old native gentleman became rather voluble and excited about its charms. He was a very goodhumoured and sociable companion all through the journey to Santiago, but at Quillota we passed through some of his own country property, and he was justly proud of its condition. Here, besides the usual groves of peaches, apricots, figs, cherries, &c., were orchards of walnuts rich in foliage and loaded with fruit; and here, as elsewhere in Chile generally, I could see no trace of blights or imperfections upon any of the various kinds of fruit-trees. Every leaf was perfect, and almost every shoot produced its fair share of spotless fruit. All the chief European vegetables flourish well, and I believe we sustained a serious loss by being too late for the strawberry season. The half-way station is Llai-Llai, pronounced Yai-yai, and, as there is only a single line of rails, the trains are so timed as to arrive there at the same hour from both ends of the line, and wait there a quarter of an hour for refreshments.

The accommodation for this purpose was creditable, though in rather a simple fashion. However, there was plenty of the national soup, called *casuela*, with the usual allowance of chicken and mutton, and the inevitable lump of Indian corn floating about in it; and we secured some very respectable tongue with a first-rate bottle of Guinness's stout. We had time enough to look about us and see the motley groups of people who had emerged from the two trains, crowding round the fruit vendors, and almost covering the ground with peach-stones, grape-stalks, and the débris of a very varied collection, while bargaining with half-Indian girls for a fresh supply. Amidst all this bustling scene of gay dresses and swarthy skins we found the English engine-drivers having a quiet chat, and not sorry to find fellow-countrymen. They seemed to like their lot in Chile well enough, and have the honour of taking supreme command of the trains: the conductor is a mere ticket-taking official, and none of the natives have anything to do with the progress or control of the company's trains. There are many parts of the line requiring prudent management of powerful brakes, and the sure steadiness of highly experienced men. From Llai-Llai a branch line goes to St. Felipe, near the base of Aconcagua and the Uspallata pass to Mendoza; but leaving this on the left, the main line begins a long steady ascent to cross the mountain ridge which separates the valley of Aconcagua from the Santiago plain, and is obliged to follow such a winding course, that though Valparaiso is only seventy miles in a straight line from the capital, yet the railway takes 115 miles to accomplish the distance.

The sun set in the usual cloudless sky as we began the ascent from the Aconcagua valley, but the last golden glow had hardly left the orchards and gardens and poplar avenues in the rich plain below, when the nearly full moon came out to lend a new kind of enchantment to the scene. The train curled itself higher and higher up the hill-side, groaning through tunnels and dashing out among chaotic masses of rock, but still every now and then we could see all the plain below bathed in silvery light and distinct in all its details. By degrees, however, we seemed to get lost in wilder and wilder scenes. The moon looked upon nothing but awful rocks and weird cactus plants, throwing up their pillar-like arms against the sky-line; then more tunnels, more rattling reverberations from adjoining precipices, and at last we reached the Montenegro station, the highest on the line. The moonlight that shed such a charm on comparatively near objects failed to give us any idea of the distant objects to be seen at this part of the route; but as the train rushed down into the plain of Santiago before us, we made up our minds to choose daylight for our return and fill up the missing links in the scenery. It was nearly 10.30 P.M. when we reached Santiago, and found ourselves in the difficulties attendant on arriving at night in an entirely strange city with no knowledge of the ways of its inhabitants. However, our old friend helped to start us; we got a comfortable carriage and successfully carried off our goods from the crowd of contending peons who do duty for regularly constituted porters. The driver lost no time, as we went at full speed through the long avenues of poplars which line the Alameda, and which looked doubly imposing in the broad light of the moon shining between them. Presently we turned into a large square and were installed in the luxurious quarters of the Grand Hotel, looking for the morning to show us what manner of place Santiago might be.

I was more delighted with it than I could have expected, when I was roused from sleep by the noise and bustle of an early-rising people. Our windows looked into the principal square, the Plaza *par excellence*, facing the north—*i.e.* facing the sun in the southern hemisphere. The opposite side of the Plaza is occupied by the post-office and various public buildings; the western side is devoted to the Cathedral and the Archbishop's Palace, and the eastern to shops and stores with a colonnade in front of each of its two floors. It was not till we came out of the house that we had any notion of what a magnificent hotel we were inhabiting. It occupies the whole length of the south side of the square, and is built in a style which calls back the memory of the Tuileries. After the confined and crowded space at Valparaiso, the airy well-furnished bedrooms and lofty-vaulted *salle à manger* afforded a most agreeable change. The centre of the square is occupied by an octagonal enclosure with a circular garden in the middle of it. Four basins and fountains surround a central fountain with a sculptured group, apparently representing Christianity baptizing the Indians; but, thank Heaven, there are not as yet strangers enough in Santiago to produce a demand for guide-books, so people may interpret these things for themselves and be happy. The garden was brilliant with petunias and verbenas, pinks, stocks, *Phlox Drummondii*, and the deep blue *Convolvulus minor*. Acacias and Australian gum-trees are planted round about them, mixed with fine magnolias and a beautiful shrub whose name I do not know, having exactly the appearance at a short distance of our purple lilac in full bloom. Though it was the hottest part of the year and five months after the latest rain, all these were maintained in perfection by constant and abundant watering. Here in the evening a gay crowd, with a large proportion of very elegant and charmingly handsome ladies, walk happily and listen to the music of a military band, as the sinking of the sun gives coolness to the air, and the snowy crest of Tupungato looks down 'sunset flushed' from its throne in the distant heavens.

The city of Santiago is nearly in the middle of a plain, at the height of about 2,000 feet above the sea; and it contains one feature that is admirably adapted for showing off the whole place and the mountain panorama which surrounds it. Scarcely ten minutes' walk from the hotel stands the small rocky hill of Santa Lucia, rising about 200 feet above the surrounding streets, and eminently dear to the hearts of the Santiaguenos. The view is certainly superb, and the place has so long been popular that at last some spirited people have taken upon themselves to turn it into a more perfect triumph of Cockney genius than anything of the kind, even in Europe. It is easy to think of places where we should be reminded of some one or other of its details, but for a grand combination of gimcracks, the hill of Santa Lucia must carry off the palm. In some places they have blasted the rocks to make caves and staircases, and in others they have built up wondrous edifices of brick, representing gateways and towers, through and among which the visitors ascend hotly and tortuously. They have shown their regard for the good national love of flowers, and planted shrubs also, wherever they could get a spot of earth large enough for them. Near the entrance is a Grotto of Neptune, as we are informed in large letters; and soon after there is a Cascada de Moises, or waterfall of Moses, with a solitary bust of the late L. Cousiño, looking at nothing in particular. He was so good a benefactor to the city that he ought not to have been placed in such an uncomfortable position. A little farther is the Enchanted Cave, and a stone slab entitled Sofa de Don Diego. A statue of a black horse, with no apparent object, stands across the skyline, looking almost as awful as the monster at Hyde Park Corner, save that there is no Duke of Wellington on his back. Some very steep stairs cut in the rock lead to an exceedingly hot corner, called, for some incomprehensible reason, the Campos Eliseos, or Elysian fields; after which the pilgrim passes a Calvary and gets to the top of the hill, where he is invited to pay twenty cents for looking through a telescope. Part of the hill-side was devoted to gymnastics, swings, merry-go-rounds, flags, music, fireworks, refreshments, and all the stock-in-trade of a tea-garden. 'Persons of taste,' to use a last-century phrase, would hardly admire such an incongruous mixture, but nevertheless the place is an infinite source of delight to the inhabitants ; and the little Frenchman who cut my hair assured me that he had been all over the world, but had never seen anything so beautiful as the Santa Lucia of Santiago.

The officers of the United States astronomical party of about twenty years ago fixed their temporary observatory on this summit, and have recorded the effects of the astonishingly pure and clear atmosphere in enabling them to perfect their observations. The view from it is magnificent as well as interesting in a high degree, and explanatory of the main geographical system of central Chile. Looking beyond the great city spread out around our feet, we see towards the north the comparatively low range which we crossed in the railway at Montenegro, and which bars in the rich plain on that side. It connects the inferior Cordillera of the coast with the main Cordillera of the high Andes, each of which runs, generally speaking, parallel to the other, down to the latitude of Chiloe, where at about 41° 30′ S. the coast Cordillera vanishes, unless perhaps the island of Chiloe itself, separated only by a narrow strait at San Carlos, may be considered practically as an extension of it for a hundred miles farther to the south. The space between these two chains is the great plain of Chile, which extends with few interruptions for about 500 miles to the south from the neighbourhood of Santiago. Looking therefore southwards from Santa Lucia, we see on the right hand the long undulations of the coast range; while on the left hand the eye loses itself in following the mighty chain of mountains, clad in perpetual snow, which extends southwards to the Straits of Magellan. The greater part of this appears rather like an irregular snow-capped wall, with only occasional summits like towers entirely dominating the rest, the sublime point of culmination in the view from Santiago being Tupungato. This truly magnificent mountain is 22,500 feet above the sea; and, when seen from the city, though at a distance of nearly fifty miles, its crest of snow has a sublime appearance, being more than 20,000 feet above the plain. Day by day, as the sun sank to its western bed in the Pacific, and the coast range of hills threw its dark shadows over the plain of Santiago, the summit of Tupungato clothed itself in that ineffably lovely rose-colour which speaks of heaven illuminating the dead. Afternoon clouds would often fold themselves round the mighty sides of the mountain, only to disappear in the evening and leave the whole scene in unbroken splendour. And what nights were those at Santiago, when the full moon shone out between 'Great Orion' and the Southern Cross to keep watch over these stupendous glories, till the sun rose again to claim them for himself!

Lover of mountains as I am, and familiar with such summits as those of Mont Blanc, Monte Rosa, and other Alpine heights, I could not repress a strange feeling as I looked at Tupungato and Aconcagua, and reflected that endless successions of men must in all probability be for ever debarred from their lofty crests. When we used to look at the highest peaks and passes of the Alps, the only

THE USPALLATA GORGE, FROM SANTIAGO, IN CHILE
(From a Drawing by Wm. Simpson, Esq.)

question which suggested itself was, 'Which is the best way to get there?' In the presence of the huge peaks of the Andes I could but think of the great probability that no one would ever get to them at all. There they reposed in divine dignity, too great for mortal approach, and suggesting the abodes where the gods of Epicurus 'sit careless of mankind,' and careless of the tremendous calamities dealt out to men by the fires concealed beneath the feet of these glorified monsters. The Alps have been conquered, and Mont Blanc has been obliged to bow down to the monarchs of the Caucasus; but nature proclaims the existence of an impassable limit somewhere; and the latest conquerors of even Elbruz and Kasbek have been compelled to admit the effects of the rarefaction of the air. Those who, like Major Godwin Austen, have had all the advantages of experience and acclimatisation to aid them in attacks upon the higher Himalayas, agree that 21,500 feet is near the limit at which man ceases to be capable of the slightest further exertion.[1] Even this has only been attained by halting after a very few steps and lying down exhausted in the snow. Mr. Simpson, whose pictures of Himalayan scenery are so well known, tells me that he and his party suffered severely in crossing the famous Purung pass, which is 19,000 feet above the sea; and that some of the natives from the plains declared they were not only dying but dead! None could advance without more and more frequent halts. There is reason to believe that from some climatal reason this diffi-

---

[1] Since this was written, I find that Mr. Johnson, of the Himalaya Survey, has crossed a pass at 22,000 feet above the sea, but the slope was probably long and gradual.

culty of breathing, called *puna* in South America, is experienced with greater severity in the Andes than in other great ranges. When Mr. Darwin crossed the Portillo pass to Mendoza at the height of 13,000 or 14,000 feet, he found that 'the exertion of walking was extremely great, and the respiration became deep and laborious.' With their 9,000 or 10,000 feet above this, Aconcagua and Tupungato may probably defy intrusion unless through the medium of a balloon.

As the eye follows the vast snowy chain in its course towards the south, it is impossible to avoid thinking of the changes which come over it within a few degrees of latitude. Here, in the latitude of Santiago, the height of the line of perpetual snow is about 15,000 feet above the sea; in the latitude of Chiloe, only about eight degrees more to the southward, the snow-line descends to only 6,000 feet above the sea; and this marvellous change is supposed by Mr. Darwin to take place not far from the neighbourhood of Concepcion, where the region of long rainless summers and great heat begins to join the region of endless forests, rainy climate, and little heat in summer. In the Straits of Magellan the perpetual snow-line descends to 3,500 or 4,000 feet above the sea, according to Mr. Darwin; but when we passed through them I think it was certainly not so much as 2,000 feet above us. This, however, was in the latter half of January, when there were still two summer months to assist in the melting and disappearance of the snow. Where the snow-line is so low as this, true glaciers are found flowing into the sea, and almost every fiord which penetrates to the higher chain, not only in Tierra del Fuego, but on the

coast for 650 miles to the northwards, is terminated by
'tremendous and astonishing glaciers.'[1] The remarkable
difference between the temperatures of the northern and
southern hemispheres is well illustrated by the fact that
we must go a thousand miles nearer to the North Pole in
Norway to find in 70° N. lat. a snow-line as low as that
which prevails at 55° S. lat. in the neighbourhood of the
Straits of Magellan. The great glaciers on the coast for
hundreds of miles nearer to the Equator break off into
the arms of the Pacific with 'a crash reverberating like
the broadside of a man-of-war, and drive huge waves
across to the opposite shores of their lonely channels.'
Through all this region the highest mountains are not
more than 7,500 feet, whilst only about five hundred miles
to the northward we have peaks, as we have seen, of from
20,000 to nearly 24,000 feet above the sea.

In this more elevated region, however, it does not
appear that there are any true glaciers at all. I was
deceived at first by the grey colour of the water in the
mountain rivers, which resembled the produce of glaciers
like those in the Alps, but the effect is in truth caused
by the constant grinding and pounding of stones and
pebbles, which are ever moving down towards the sea
with a continuous roaring noise. The height of the
perpetual line of snow no doubt varies exceedingly in
different seasons, being determined, as Mr. Darwin says,
more by the extreme heat of the summer than by the
mean temperature of the year. This is certainly highly
probable, but when he says that he 'was assured that,
during one very long and dry summer, *all the snow disap-*

[1] Darwin's 'Voyage of the Beagle,' p. 246.

peared from Aconcagua, though it attains the prodigious height of nearly 24,000 feet,' I confess it is difficult indeed to believe the accuracy of his informant. When I remember what Aconcagua was in the middle of February, with the summer, and a very hot one too, drawing near its end; and when I recall the pure masses of snow rivalling in appearance the grandest névé of the Alps, and stretching downwards to the distant visible horizon, I should almost as easily have believed in the total disrobing of Mont Blanc and Monte Rosa as in that of this noble monarch of the Chilian Cordillera.

CHAPTER V.

The Alameda of Santiago—Precautions against fire—What became of the Jesuit Church—Remains of the dead—Bismarck in South America—A model farm in Chile—Climate and Irrigation—Baths of Cauquenes—Thrashing wheat—Refreshments at Rancagua—A strange coach-and-four—The Hot Springs—Golden Adiantum—A view in the hills—Great Aconcagua—Return to Valparaiso.

THE position of the hill of Santa Lucia naturally commands a complete view of the bright-looking city, which stretches out its long white streets till they lose themselves in the fields and gardens of the plain which extends in all directions to the base of the surrounding hills; and instead of looking down upon a forest of chimney-pots, which do not appear to exist there, we could see into the open *patios* or courtyards of the houses, many of which were shaded by huge magnolias, Norfolk Island pines and other evergreens, with a variety of creeping and climbing plants hanging in fringes from the surrounding corridors. The Alameda runs through the city from east to west. It is a very broad road divided into several parts by parallel rows of tall Lombardy poplars, which through its whole length throw a very delightful shade in the hot hours of the day. Part of it is traversed by tramways, which in most of the cities of South America have become an established institution, and the rest of the road is for all kinds of other vehicles, including even the

English style of omnibus, together with a sprinkling of Hansom cabs. We were at the season when the *beau monde* of Santiago was supposed to be refreshing itself at baths and seaside places, which greatly curtailed what was described as the normal gaiety of the Alameda; and we heard that many who could not afford to go anywhere else hide themselves strictly in their houses that they may not be supposed to be 'in town' at the unfashionable season, when the opera is closed. There was always, however, plenty to be seen of the more amusing kind of life which is not so much influenced by fashion. The fruit-stalls by the side of the road, and the mountains of melons on the ground, were always in full request among picturesque groups of peons, women, and children. Now and then a couple of horsemen, with brilliant-coloured *ponchos*, galloping in at the end of a hot ride from the country, would pull up with the sudden grip which Chilian horses are accustomed to, and spend a few minutes in discussing a melon and pitching the rind into the lively little water-course which runs down by the road-side, while a group of children were admiring the carving of their huge wooden stirrups, which are something like the newest form of the domestic coal-scuttle. More languid dandies amble gently past holding overhead a kind of umbrella made of ostrich feathers; but I am happy to say that throughout both sides of South America people generally take the sun as they find it; and no one, either native or foreigner, thinks it necessary to shelter his head under any of the monstrosities of hats and helmets which are presumed to be indispensable in the East. A common wide-awake hat, with a pocket-handkerchief in it on an extra hot day, is quite enough for a well-constituted head in the cloudless sunshine of the Pampas.

Under the front of the hotel is a colonnade which contains some of the best of the shops, and a large bar with billiard-rooms and refreshment-rooms attached to it. This covered way is wide enough to admit of very pretty stalls with their backs against the broad pillars, doing duty as a humbler kind of shop, and looking when closed like large cabinets of carved wood. A very large and handsome cruciform arcade runs through the whole block of buildings, and is certainly in much finer proportions than anything of the kind that I am acquainted with in Europe. Here, as in most parts of Santiago, the doors of many houses have a small square *grille*, which enables the police to see if any unusual light within is giving notice of fire. There is a look-out tower for a similar purpose; the city is divided into fire districts, each of which has powerful engines, and every possible precaution is taken against what is a more than usually terrible danger in an excessively dry climate. We had the honour of being made members of the two principal clubs, where all manner of good things were always to be found, and one of them was supplied with the handsomest furniture that could be sent from London. There was, however, a very great difference between the number of English-speaking people in the two cities of Santiago and Valparaiso: at the seaport they swarm in its busy streets, but in the capital they appeared to be extremely scarce. If no other proof of this could be found, it would be sufficient to say that a room in the house of an upholsterer was the only apology for an English church.

The cathedral is built very substantially, with rather low roof and no towers, with a probable view to the earthquakes of the future. It is more than usually gaudy with golden shrines and candlesticks, and the Englishman who looks at the inscription in front of the gallery may delight his national vanity in finding that the organ is the handiwork of Messrs. Flight and Son.

But the church that I most wished to see was the Jesuit church, the Iglesia de la Compania, which was the scene of the holocaust of a congregation in 1863. Here, on one of the most important festivals of the year, the church was decorated with a magnificence which drew together an immense assemblage of women and children, who compose nearly the whole bulk of the congregations in Catholic South America. Some of the ornaments took fire, and a panic-stricken rush to the door was followed by a block-up of people falling one upon the other, and making escape impossible for the rest. Some were rescued from the entangled mass by seizing the ends of lazos thrown in by people in the street, who dragged them out by sheer strength of pulling. The great majority, however, to the number of 2,000 or 3,000, perished in the flames, in a scene of horror which has probably never been surpassed. While this tragedy was being enacted, the priests were described as preventing all egress through a door which would have saved many victims, if they had not kept it for their own protection and the removal of their property in the church. Such was the indignation of the public against the clerical party that it was determined that they should not rebuild the church; so, when we went to look for it, behold it was no more! The whole of the site was levelled and dug up, and an exquisite monument has been lately erected in the centre of the space. It is, as we were told, the work of a Parisian artist, and consists of a superb female figure with outstretched arms and hands expressing the very depth of helpless and despairing agony: weeping angels in varied attitudes are placed around the pedestal, and the lamps which surround the whole monument are veiled on one side by an elegant imitation of drapery. The design is admirable, and it would be difficult to conceive a more touching memorial of such a scene of horror We afterwards crossed to the Recoleta, or burying-ground, on the north side of the city, which is separated from the chief part of it by the Mapocho river flowing down from the neighbourhood of Tupungato to join the main waters of the Maypu. The bed of the river is of considerable width, and is crossed by a long and very curious old Spanish bridge; but in February therewas so little water in the river that it would have been easy to cross on foot over the small channels flowing among the desert of pebbles and large stones which testified to the power of the stream in the rainy season. Donkeys and boys seemed to think very little of the barrier. We walked for some time between the rows of huge dark cypresses in the Recoleta before we came to a rather handsome railing which enclosed a space of ground about the size of a small room, in which was a metal cross over the remains of the victims to the conflagration to the number of 2,000, 'mas o menos' (more or less), with a tablet recording the event. Our landlord said he believed that 3,000 would be nearer the truth, but no one knew exactly; and he added that he knew of men in Santiago who had so awful a remembrance of the smell of burning flesh that they could not touch roast meat for twelve months after the catastrophe! Santiago had long enjoyed the reputation of being eminently loyal to the Catholic Church; but that loyalty must either have been sapped, possibly in part by the remembrance of the conduct of the priests on this occasion, or else it has been overweighted by other parts of the country; for the telegraph informs us that the Chilian House of Deputies have sustained by a two-thirds vote the penal clauses which impose imprisonment upon all persons, lay or ecclesiastical, who execute any orders of the Roman Curia to the detriment of the State. The Bismarckian method has crossed the Atlantic and the Pampas: in spite of violent opposition, Brazilian bishops have been arrested and punished by imprisonment, and their friends in Chile will assuredly meet with the same misfortunes if they attempt the subjection of the State by the Church.

At the British Legation I had the pleasure of finding an old friend in the person of our Minister, Mr. Rumbold, in whose company I could revive sunny memories of Greece and Switzerland, as we looked over his portfolios of familiar photographs, and forgot the distance between the Andes and the Alps. His secretary, Mr. Milner, was also a kind companion and excellent *cicerone* to us while we remained at Santiago. One morning he came by agreement to escort us to the model farm of the Cousiño family at Macul, about nine miles from the city. We drove away in a carriage with three horses, in the normal blaze of the Chilian sun, which often made me think of the Indian griffin who, day after day, saluted his chief with 'Another sunshiny morning, Colonel!' till at last he got tired of the monotony. For the greater part of the way Tupungato was in full splendour in front of us, looking 'every inch a king' of mountains; but we only now and then could see much of near objects by reason of the Cyclopean walls of *adobes* or sun-dried bricks between which the road winds through the suburbs. The dust was something inconceivable; confined within these wind-excluding barriers it rose up vertically from under the hoofs of our horses, and lazily settled down upon us like a thick raiment. Sometimes we passed herds of cattle, and then the sky was obscured for awhile as completely as in a London fog of *première qualité*. In spite of the consoling effect of cigars, I think we were all very glad when at length we entered the gates at Macul and reached our destination. Here we found Mr. Graham, a well-informed Scotch gardener, who is engaged in laying out the ornamental part of the estate, and who led us through a large extent of orchards, gardens, and rough uncompleted park. Immense quantities of melons of all sorts were growing on open plots of ground, together with most of the European vegetables; long grass paths were flanked on both sides by rows of fruit-trees in wonderfully healthy condition. The apricot trees were still loaded with good fruit, though the earth beneath them was yellow with those which had fallen; plums and pears of the best sorts were mixed with peaches and nectarines of very tempting appearance, though scarcely ripe; and beds of delicious Alpine strawberries made up for any deficiencies on the part of other fruits. Here, too, were fig-trees grown to nearly the size of forest trees, and looking something like horse-chestnuts; near which was a large piece of rough ground with the remains of huge olive-trees which must probably have been planted about three hundred years ago: their 'giant boles' had been lately pollarded, and they are fast forming new growth. Beyond these we were taken to an enclosed piece of land with scattered trees, surrounded by a high bamboo fence, in which we found a herd of fallow deer, together with a few alpacas and a tame guanaco which amused us highly, capering and jumping like a young lamb, but preserving all the time that vicious expression which characterises all the animals of its class, and is quite in accordance with their habit of spitting in one's face on the smallest provocation. Afterwards we were taken to the stables, and found an Irish groom who had just come from England with the last valuable addition to the stud. One handsome stable had twenty-four stalls on each side, and had a small tramway and truck from one end to the other, which saved a great deal of labour both in bringing in and carrying out. Another Englishman, Mr. Canning, was in charge of the stock, and showed us his flock of Southdown sheep; but unfortunately his famous herd of cattle were far away at the other side of the estate, and we had not time enough to ride after them. Everything that money can do was being done to perfect the establishment of Macul; and, as Englishmen, we could not but feel a little reflected pride at seeing our countrymen at the head of every department of it, while watering-carts and agricultural machines from Ipswich and Chelmsford made us almost forget that we were in the very centre of Chile. Foreign plants are sent out from Veitch's nurseries, and Mr. Graham told me he had already sent them in return 22,000 bulbs collected by him and his peons on the neighbouring hills.

We had had rather a roasting day for our long tour of inspection, and thoroughly enjoyed a glass of his good whisky before saying good-bye to Mr. Graham and his wife, with hearty wishes for their success in the new world. The effect of exchanging beds of flowers and groves of fruit-trees in their highest perfection for the ride home through fathomless dust was anything but pleasant: the remembrance of it, however, calls up reflections upon the cause of a contrast which must strike a traveller in many parts of Chile. When Pindar dashed into his Olympian odes with the expression of ἄριστον μὲν ὕδωρ, or 'water is the best of all things,' even better than gold, he was more likely to have had an arid country in his eye than any prophetic vision of Sir Wilfrid Lawson. Any one who travels on the Chilian plains, and sees the desert made to blossom like the rose, feels himself impelled to think of the difficulties imposed upon the cultivators by the climate. They have had to do for themselves what the Nile does for the land of Egypt. The nature of the climate may be easily understood by looking at a very few figures. A register was kept at Santiago from 1824 to 1850, to record the number of minutes and hours during which rain fell throughout the twenty-seven years; and the average of a year's fall was $215\frac{1}{2}$ hours, or nine days. Seven-ninths of this fell in the four months of May, June, July, and August; while in the whole five months of November, December, January, February, and March rain fell only for seven hours and a half. The whole twenty-seven Januarys would only have given fourteen hours' rain, had there not been an unexampled fall of forty hours during the January of 1837. June and July, by far the wettest months, only gave four and a quarter days' rain between them. The American Government party kept their record of rains in the usual way of reckoning by inches, and found the average of two years to be 48 inches, this being reached by an abnormal fall of fifteen inches in June 1850. These rains have the immediate effect of producing a fresh and lively vegetation from the heated earth; but, in fact, they have very little substantial effect in a country where the plateau, being 2,000 feet above the sea, the bulk of the water is carried off by rivers rushing headlong to the Pacific; and where a grilling sun holds undisputed sovereignty for the greater part of the year. The successful and ever-increasing agriculture of Chile is produced by abundant irrigation, and the Government may take the Pindaric saying for their motto.

The everlasting snows of the Cordillera are their natural reservoirs, and of course melt most rapidly in the hot season when the inhabitants are cut off from supplies of rain; but most of this fund would naturally pass away in roaring torrents which do no work except that of driving stones towards the sea. 'Divide et Impera;' spread them, and you compel Mother Earth to give forth her richest treasures. At the time when the earlier part of the register referred to was being kept, the country round Santiago was almost a desert, and there was no mode of irrigating it till a canal was cut from the Maypu river to the Mapocho, so as to tap the waters of the former river and bring them down for the service of the plain. This was followed by leading countless small rivulets, called *acequias*, from the canal across the valley, and the land was gradually brought into cultivation. Vines and poplars, trees, gardens, and green fields, have sprung into luxuriance in every direction; and, as these in turn must give out some of the moisture they have absorbed, they, by the mere fact of their own existence, are modifying the dryness of the climate, and making vegetable existence still more and more easy for the future. Moreover, the actual moisture is not the only good brought to the land by this system of irrigation. As the slope of the land is exceedingly steep from the high-lying snow of the Andes to the level of the plain, the descending streams have a furious speed. Let anyone imagine what the river Visp would be like, if, between the village of Zermatt and its confluence with the Rhone, it fell through 5,000 feet of elevation more than it now does. The case is almost strictly parallel. The mountain torrents from the Chilian Andes fall with great impetus towards the ocean, urging forward masses of limestone and other rocks containing mineral manures, and grinding them to a fine powder which mixes with the water. The water therefore not only irrigates the land, but supplies it with a manure which, though the only one, appears perfectly sufficient and exactly calculated to repair the exhausted forces of the earth. 'Wheat fields ordinarily receive four irrigations between the cessation of the rains in September and the maturity of the grain at the end of November; on each occasion the fields remaining submerged during one night, and sometimes for twenty-four hours.' The mineral deposit left by this method of flooding 'in some years amounts to a stratum of three-quarters of an inch.' Land which a few years ago would hardly yield the planter fivefold of wheat, has, we are told, been now raised half a foot by this process without the aid of any other manure, and now produces in many parts twentyfold and even fortyfold. The wheat crops of Chile have, in fact, become amongst the most perfect in the world; and Mr. Gilliss is my authority for saying that in the province of Concepcion sixtyfold is not an uncommon return, while there are fields which give a hundred for one.

We had been strongly recommended to pay a visit to the Baños de Cauquenes, as a kind of little Wiesbaden, or rather Leukerbad, in the bosom of the Andes. On February 2 we left Santiago by the Southern Railway, which was already open as far as Curico, but will in due time be carried through the Republic to Concepcion and Valdivia. Our station was Cauquenes, about seventy miles from the city, and we were to get there in three hours. The engines and carriages on this line are of the American build instead of the English, as they are on the Valparaiso side: there were crowds of passengers, and at every station the groups of fruit vendors were in full activity to meet the wants of dusty and half-roasted folks. Passing through the most cultivated districts of the plain country we had plenty of opportunity to observe its condition. At this time of the year the wheat-fields were brown stubbles, but at several places we saw the people at work upon the concluding operations of harvest. The corn is collected into vast heaps in the open air, where, without fear of rain, it is thrashed out by the feet of horses galloping round and round; afterwards, with a dry fresh breeze blowing across the plain, it is tossed up and down in the air, the chaff and fragments of straw flying before the breeze, covering the adjoining land, and producing a ludicrous effect on the nearest row of tall poplars by making them look as if they were packed in straw. Poplars in abundance line the edges of the rivulets which keep their feet cool, and divide luxuriant fields of maize and melons, beans, and *alfalfa*, the lucern of the country, and vineyards and orchards with every kind of fruit. Every now and then, however, we were forcibly reminded of the artificial condition of everything around us. Close to the edge of verdant crops were occasional pieces of land not yet brought into subjection. where nothing was to be seen but a few dried-up weeds upon the burnt ground, and the two species of gigantic thistles which in the same way lord it over parts of the Pampas of La Plata, and terrify the horses with their formidable thorns.

We crossed the turbulent Maypu and other streams, having exactly the appearance of true glacier rivers; but the turbidity of the water is due, as I have said, to the grinding and pounding of stones by furious torrents, and not to the gradual effect of glacier ice polishing its way over the rocks. For some miles, however, the road was carried by the side of a beautiful stream of clear spring-water, where we could see fish leaping like English trout, and the natives doing their best to catch them. Not far from this, among the low hills on the western side, is the lovely lake of Aculeo, whose pure water mixes itself with the fertilizing mud of the Maypu. Near to most of the stations, and at various parts of the road, we saw groups of the most miserable huts, or fragments of huts, that could be imagined. Some of them seemed to consist of mere scraps of mats and sticks, with bunches of rushes on the top; but they were full of copper-coloured peasants who seemed living happily and even merrily in a strange medley of children, dogs, cats, pigs, poultry, and hillocks of the inevitable melons. It often occurred to me that the simple half-Indian rustics of Chile must console themselves with the reflection that the dread spirit of the earthquake is ever brooding under them, and that any day, in the twinkling of an eye, the hut-dwellers may have reason to thank Providence for not having exposed them to the risk of being buried alive in the ruins of grand hotels and crumbling cities.

At Rancagua the train stopped a few minutes 'for refreshments.' There was a large, low, and dirty room, with sundry tables garnished with peaches and melons, which rapidly disappeared before the invaders; and at one end of it was a kind of counter where flies were playing with all sorts of cakes and lollipops not suited to the substantial tastes of Englishmen. It was presided over by a comfortable-looking individual of the Sancho Panza type, aided by a cheery old woman worthy of being his wife, to whom we applied for a glass of brandy and cold water. The old lady seemed rather confused among a collection of black bottles of every shape on the shelf, and smelt them hesitatingly after removing the old corks. She could not satisfy herself, however, by the application of one sense only; and—Oh! tell it not to the fair damsels of Messrs. Spiers and Pond—she proceeded to taste them one by one, with her lips applied to the neck, freely spitting out 'her failures,' with many grimaces, on the floor, till she arrived at the right bottle, and handed it to us with a triumphant air of satisfaction. We reached the Cauquenes station about half-past five; and as the train rolled away to the south, we found ourselves in solitude upon the little platform: there were no other passengers and no officials. Two or three boys came presently to stare at us, and we told them that we wanted to go to the baths if we could find a coach and somebody to drive it. By-and-by they produced a man from the back, who rather sulkily pointed to a queer old vehicle in a shed, and said that was the coach. He demanded twelve dollars (2*l*. 10*s*.), which we remonstrated with, but in vain. He declared that if we had been four persons we should only have paid three dollars each, but that as we had the bad luck to be only two, we must pay double fare; adding, that if we did not like his arrangements, we might stop where we were, or words to that effect. We had to surrender; and whilst he very leisurely began to make preparations we looked about curiously for a chance of something to eat, as we knew that the drive of nearly twenty miles, mostly up hill, would not be finished till long after nightfall. A pleasant good-tempered woman, who had something to do with the charge of the station, offered to make us a *tortilla*, or omelette, in a few minutes. It proved first-rate; and, with the help of an admirable bottle of Bass which she brought forth from a cupboard, we were fully prepared for a start. There stood the coach at last, a wondrous vehicle with four horses abreast, like the chariots of the ancients, and all covered with dust and dirt as if the day's work was over instead of beginning; but the man added to our humiliation by refusing to start till we had paid the twelve dollars beforehand, so we supposed there must have been something suspicious about our appearance.

At last we got off at a rattling pace, and though the near horse was dead lame, he was not excused from work on that account. There were some peculiar features in our mode of progression; the driver charged at full speed through several shallow rivers which we had to cross; and, whenever we came to the base of a particularly long or steep hill, he halted the team for a few moments and then thrashed and larruped them at a gallop till they reached the very top of it, declaring that in no other way would they do it at all. If anybody likes to start a society for prevention of cruelty to animals in South America, he will have a fine field for his operations. The road rises through the valley of the Cachapual river, the head waters of which come from the snows of Maypu, an extinct volcano of 17,700 feet above the sea. The occasional force of this river is manifested by the vast wilderness of large stones and sandbanks, which are spread over the land where it enters the plain, and through which it makes a great variety of ever-changing channels. From our higher elevation we could see groups of men with horses and cattle, carefully picking their way among them and looking for the shallowest fords. But we soon left the plains far below, and found the road winding along the side of barren hills, which in the then dry season appeared to have little upon them except cactuses, aloes, ilex, and a few thorny shrubs; but I afterwards found that these burnt-up hills are not so really bare as they seem to be.

The grass, which grows abundantly in the rainy season, is simply turned to hay as it stands or lies, and cattle find plenty of food on a hill-side, which looks like a sheet of yellow ochre. Meanwhile the sun was sinking fast behind us, and in front we had exquisite views of the snowy Andes to the eastward, glowing with those sublime, rosy tints which make the crowning glory of an Alpine evening.

Somewhere about half way along the road our team was pulled up in a broad open space, with what we should call a good farmhouse on one side, and a store on the other, in which, as usual, anything and everything can be bought, from a tin pot to a bottle of champagne. We were to change horses. The driver threw his reins upon their backs, and, with the aid of a wild-looking native, took off all their harness and threw it down bodily in the two-inch dust of the road. The released animals started off according to their own sweet will, and we were left to wonder where their successors were to come from; the coachman disappeared from the scene, and the aide-de-camp had jumped bareheaded on a barebacked steed and galloped off into space. It looked like a plot to keep us where we were for the night; but after a rather *mauvais quart d'heure* and something longer, the wild man returned driving four fresh horses at full gallop before him in a cloud of dust. The old harness in wretched plight was picked out of the dirt, and fitted on the new-comers somehow or other, by dint of much pulling, jamming, and excessively bad language. We were soon off again at full speed; and, aided by the stars above and the white dust below, we kept the road safely, and soon after 9 P.M. arrived at the gateway of the baths of Cauquenes. We brought a special letter of introduction from a friend at Santiago to the proprietor of this excellent establishment in the heart of the Andes, who is a fine handsome German, named Hess, and doubtless christened Carl; but he is known familiarly in Chile as Don Carlos, and is much more to be envied than his royal namesake in the Pyrenees. Late as we were for sanitary country quarters, he bestirred himself to find us two charming rooms and a light supper, after which we closed a hot day of bustle and dust with a sweet sleep in the comparatively cool mountain air that came through the open windows.

When Mr. Darwin visited this place some forty years ago, and said that 'the buildings consist of a square of miserable little hovels, each with a single table and bench,' he had very little notion of what the development theory would do under the management of Don Carlos Hess. The establishment now consists of several quadrangles surrounded by corridors, into which the various rooms open, all being on one floor; the gardens in the middle of them are well planted, and intersected with paths shaded by thick trellised vines, while the pillars of the corridors are surrounded with passion-flowers, honeysuckles, fuchsias, and the drooping blossoms of *Abutilon venosum*. There is a large public room for meals in *table d'hôte* fashion, and those who like to pay for it can have any amount of luxurious feeding in their own apartments. The main attraction to the place is its hot mineral springs, which, as usual in these cases, are warranted to cure all the ills that flesh is heir to; fortunately we had no excuse for testing their efficacy. Hot springs in an earthquake-smitten country have an

THE BATHS OF CAUQUENES, IN CHILE.

interest peculiar to themselves; and I am quoting Mr. Darwin[1] when I say that 'the mineral springs of Cauquenes burst forth on a line of dislocation, crossing a mass of stratified rock, the whole of which betrays the action of heat. A considerable quantity of gas is continually escaping from the same orifice with the water. Though the springs are only a few yards apart, they have very different temperatures, and this appears to be the result of an unequal mixture of cold water; for those with the lowest temperatures have scarcely any mineral taste. After the great earthquake of 1822 the springs ceased, and the water did not return for nearly a year. They were also much affected by the earthquake of 1835, the temperature being suddenly changed from 118° to 92°.'

Don Carlos pays a rent of 6,000 or 7,000 dollars a year, and has built a large new bath-house at his own expense. The whole neighbourhood belongs to a family whose estate, as I was told, extends for three days' ride from north to south, and nearly as far from the west to the base of the Andes. The situation is good, and the views over the lower ranges of hills away to the snowy peaks in the distance are well worthy of a painter; the plateau on which the buildings are situated ends in a precipitous rock, the base of which is washed by the roaring Cachapual about 150 feet below; the springs flow into tanks a few yards from the edge of the rocks, and their overflow nourishes a large crop of the well-known Pampas grass which clings to every cleft. A winding path leads down to a suspension bridge, which hangs about forty feet above the furious stream. The footway consisted of sticks not

[1] 'Voyage of the Beagle,' p. 263.

stronger than those of a common sheep-hurdle, and was suspended from two ropes, one of which having stretched more than the other, caused the frail structure to slant down to one side in a most unpleasant fashion. Altogether it was the most rickety attempt at a bridge that I ever came to, and I saw a dog stand howling for half an hour before he could be induced to cross it. However, we had to go over to look for one of the rarest of rare ferns, the *Adiantum sulphureum*, which Mr. Hennedy told us was to be found among the rocks on the other side of the river. We only found some burnt-up specimens there, but on the following day, in a wild rocky glen moistened by a small stream and shaded by overhanging ilex, we found it in perfection. The upper side of the frond is almost identical with that of *A. Capillus Veneris*, the Maidenhair of Europe; but the under side is covered with a bright yellow powder like gold-dust. When I mentioned this interesting plant to Mr. Bates, the well-known 'Naturalist on the Amazon,' he said it was somewhat curious that Chile should produce a golden *Adiantum*, as it is also the home of a butterfly, which, though in other respects the same as one of the English species, has the under side of its wings apparently covered with silver.

In the same gully we also found a fern which appeared to be identical with *Lastrea oreopteris*, the mountain fern of Europe; but Mr. Rawson ascended for a considerable distance without finding any other species. He brought back, however, a very pretty red mimulus; and on the hill-side we saw the earliest flowers of a grey, thorny, narrow-leaved aloe, which throws up a tall spike of bell-shaped blossoms of an aquamarine colour with very brilliant orange stamens. Snakes were seen occasionally, and we tried to kill one in the garden close to my room, but he escaped in the long grass under the edge of the corridor. In the middle of the day the heat was certainly very great, so we made a start before breakfast one morning with a small boy as guide to the top of a hill, which was probably about 2,000 feet above the house. The greater part of the way was over a steep, rocky slope, sprinkled with pebbly grit, which gave extremely bad foothold for the nailless boots which I had unluckily trusted to; at other parts a slight track wound up amongst huge cacti, armed with spines six inches long, ready to impale anyone who slipped, mixed with ilex, aloes, and a few scrubby bushes. Amongst the trees of Cauquenes is one which is said to be found only in this part of the country and the world. I am sorry not to have succeeded in finding its botanical name, but in Chile it is called the Quillai, or soap-tree; it produces pure potash, which is used for washing, and is exported into France for cleaning woollen manufactures. The upper part of the ascent reminded me rather of the last division of the Eggischhorn, without the benefit of steps; except that the rocks were excessively hot from the sun and were garnished with the thorns of aloes and gigantic cactus. The actual top of the hill was smooth and covered with burnt-up grasses, varied with groups of ilex, under which it was possible to get a temporary shade. The view was remarkably fine, as on the one side we looked across the Chilian plain to the Cordillera of the coast, while on the other the great snow-peaks of the Andes rose serenely over the brown outlines of the intervening slopes. At our feet was the Cachapual, roaring through the ravines of the valley, charged with the meltings of those vast snow-beds, and pounding the sides of the mountains into fertilization for the plains. By the time we got down again we were very glad of some cold water and breakfast in a shady room. The regular patients and residents seemed scarcely ever to leave the protection of their corridors and trellised paths. When neither eating nor soaking in the baths, they collected in little groups, working or reading, and playing at cards, dominoes, and chess. There did not appear to be any gambling; everything was in a very peaceful, domestic style, and Cauquenes is probably the sleepiest as well as one of the most out-of-the-way bathing places in the world. The supplies are excellent; the whole place is well managed, and it is well worth the while of any traveller to pay it a visit for a short time. If, however, he wants gay society, or hankers after the joys of Homburg and Wiesbaden, I would not advise him to hope for them at the baths in the heart of the Andes.

After three or four days in these peaceful halls we said good-bye to Don Carlos, and were carried swiftly down the valley by another team of four abreast; and, after another light refection with our former friend at the station, we joined the midday train and reached Santiago in the early evening. But our days in Chile were numbered, and on the 13th we were to sail from Valparaiso for the northern ports. We stayed a very short time longer in the capital, and spent the last evening in going once more to the top of the Santa Lucia to see the glories of a farewell sunset upon the snows of Tupungato. Next morning we went back to Valparaiso; and, as the train rose gradually towards the watershed near Montenegro, we had a superb view of Aconcagua. This grand mountain not only enjoys the advantage of being nearly 24,000 feet above the sea, but it is so situated that it appears quite alone in its glory; and the eye must turn through a great many degrees before anything like a rival can be found in the form of Tupungato. After crossing the crest of the hill the train began a rapid descent to Llai-Llai, checked by powerful brakes; and we could now comprehend the wild and singular features of the country which we had only partially seen by the 'glimpses of the moon.' We turned and twisted through tunnels and cuttings in the rock; we rushed down hill between sun-burnt slopes and masses of conglomerate or plum-pudding stone, some of which looked as if the first earthquake would send them crashing down upon the railway; we passed through barren tracts which seemed to be in the exclusive possession of huge cacti and flocks of lovely little doves, with the occasional variety of bright green and sparkling beds of the ice-plant *Mesembryanthemum*: the rich valley of the Aconcagua dominated by the Campana of Quillota again opened out far beneath us and beyond; and, when we next stopped, we were amongst the figs and grapes and melons of Llai-Llai. The branch line from there to San Felipe was on the point of being opened to the more distant Los Andes, which will shorten the work of those who may wish to cross the Andes by the Cumbre pass to Mendoza in the Argentine Confederation.

In a few hours more we were welcomed back at the Hotel de l'Union at Valparaiso, and found all that we had left behind in safe charge of our excellent host and hostess. Mr. Wheatley, whom we had met first at Petropolis, was here, and arranged to accompany us to California. We had only a day left for farewell visits to all our kind friends, and an evening devoted to fireworks and the opera. On the following afternoon we went on board the 'Santa Rosa' and started for the northern ports, just after seeing our good ship the 'Cotopaxi' anchor on her return from Callao.

CHAPTER VI.

On board the 'Santa Rosa'—A Floating Fair—Porpoises on St. Valentine's Day—Coquimbo and Serena—Huasco Grapes—Mountains of Melons—Countless Pelicans—Luminous Fish—A 'Little Revolution' in Bolivia—Iquique and Arica—Arica Mummies—Mollendo and Islay—Scorpion-fight—Peruvian Soldiers—Remarkable situation of Quilca—Astonished Whales—The Chincha Islands—Callao.

I THOUGHT I had seen a tolerably large variety of ships and cargoes in different parts of the world, but the first glance round the 'Santa Rosa' showed a state of things that was new and hardly credible in a sea-going vessel. I saw not only a steamboat, but a travelling fair, a market, a cattle show, and a farmyard combined. Like all the vessels of the Liverpool Pacific Steam Navigation Company, she looked handsome on the water; it was the novel state of things on deck that produced astonishment. The saloon and first-class cabins were on the upper deck, with a broad passage round them from end to end of the ship, two thirds of which were devoted to the fair and market. Rude divisions, made with sticks and sacking, separated the stalls of the various proprietors, who—men, women, and children—brought their own mattresses, and protected their goods by sleeping upon them at night, with the occasional assistance of a small dog. Here were piled up thousands upon thousands of sweet melons and watermelons, gourds and pumpkins, peaches, figs, and grapes, wonderfully fine onions, peas and pears, beans and cabbages, together with bundles of a large seaweed, which is dried into a semblance of brown macaroni, and made into a decoction for food. Some of the stalls offered the additional attractions of hats and bonnets, boots, cigars, toys, maté-pots, and all sorts of gimcracks: one man even tried to tempt me with a small gilt clock and an image of the Virgin Mary, or some inferior saint. With the exception of the fore-part of the ship, the decks were piled with these things through their whole length, not only up to the top of the bulwarks, but higher still, with the aid of boards and other devices. So narrow was the passage left between them and the cabins down the centre of the ship that I had to remove the dirty feet of a sleeping melon-owner before I could get at my own door. Under this deck was a lower one, half of which was the farmyard, containing scores of cattle, sheep, and pigs; the other half was another market, where perhaps the salesmen paid rather less rent in consideration of their inferior situation. On the top of all, from nearly amidships over the saloon, was raised a tent-shaped awning, under which the poorest class of passengers slept on mattresses which they provided for themselves.

I remarked at the time, that under such circumstances it would seem impossible to prevent a fearful catastrophe in the event of fire or any sudden accident to the ship. Nobody could handle the boats till the melons, &c., had been one by one thrown overboard, to say nothing of the confusion that must prevail among such a motley crowd of deck passengers and a not very brilliant crew. Scarcely more than a fortnight after we left Valparaiso my anticipations were confirmed when the Company's ship 'Tacna,' piled up with top-cargo, turned gradually over, and most of the people were drowned; a circumstance which gave rise to very unpleasant proceedings between the English Government and that of Chile. Never have I seen such a field for the Board of Trade and the immortal Plimsoll. However, there is no greater mistake than that of bothering one's self about possible calamities at sea after the anchor is weighed; and I was perfectly happy as soon as I contrived to get a cabin in the forward part of the ship, where I was removed from the proximity of foreign toes and the disagreeables of squeezing between Indians and onions on my way to bed. Having attained this point of emancipation, I was quite content to move about and contemplate the natives at my leisure, and was delighted with the prospect of a new and probably very peculiar style of voyage. We had a quiet night on a sea which is usually tranquil, except under the influence of one of the occasional northers which are so much dreaded in the Bay of Valparaiso; and we began the next day with a very extraordinary sight. Going on deck after breakfast, we found ourselves passing through a belt of porpoises in such countless thousands that I should have no hesitation in saying that they far outnumbered all that I ever saw elsewhere in the world put together. They were, roughly speaking, in a line of about a quarter of a mile in width, stretching from north-east to south-west, and extending for as many miles as the eye could reach. They were evidently in an unusual state of excitement, leaping and splashing the water furiously; and, as far even as the telescope could help the eye, the otherwise calm sea was in a turmoil of agitation. It happened to be on February 14, but whether Valentine's Day had something to do with it, or whether it was a sort of opening of Parliament, I must leave to the decision of the naturalists.

Passing the headland of the Lengua de Vaca, or Cow's Tongue, we soon after went cautiously between the coast and some wild rocky prominences rising out of the sea, and throwing up the smooth swell into towers of surf. We were presently so near the coast that we could easily see a man fishing below the lighthouse, which stands on sterile tawny rocks mixed with large patches of black. Everything seemed barren and burnt up; and, with the exception of the everlasting cactus, we saw no signs of vegetation till we turned the point of Coquimbo and anchored among a few other vessels lying off the town. Coquimbo, like most of the mining ports on the coast, is of nearly the same colour as the rocks in the neighbourhood; but a little to the north of it the town of Serena has some rather green surroundings, thanks to a small river which enables the inhabitants to produce a modicum of food. Close to Coquimbo rise the chimneys of vast smelting works, throwing off their clouds of white and sulphurous smoke as they turn into copper the ores which are brought down from some of the most valuable mines in Chile. The mining interests have introduced a good deal of Cornish blood into this part of the world; and such names as Treveck or Trevethick over a store will often attract the attention of a wandering Englishman. The mines of Panulcillo and the neighbourhood gave birth to a railway connecting them with the port of Coquimbo. Mining, indeed, appears to be, directly or indirectly, the sole *raison d'être* for the existence of civilised beings upon hundreds of miles of barren coast to the north of Valparaiso, and they ought to be well paid for consenting to exist there at all.

Early on the following morning we anchored at Huasco, a very small port, at the foot of a valley traversed by the Huasco river, which contributes a little green colouring to the otherwise brown and arid landscape. The white grapes of this place are delicious, with a flavour like that of the Muscat of Alexandria. Some of the passengers passed their time in catching large horse-mackerel, of which there was a plentiful supply under the ship's side. Both here and at Carrisal, which we reached a few hours later, there are wild and savage headlands, and rocky islands rising out of the sea, white with the deposit of countless birds, and covered with cormorants sitting upon them and lazily turning their heads right and left as if they were thinking it was almost time to have another fish. On the 16th we reached Caldera, the port of Copiapo, said to be greatly deteriorating in prosperity in consequence of its mines becoming less productive. As the ship had to take in coals, we wandered on shore and among the rocks on the beach, where we found myriads of barnacles and very large star-fish, with an abundance of a pretty little *Mesembryanthemum*, but there was very little to enliven the desolate appearance of all around. Matters were rather more lively on board, where a small crowd of the inhabitants came to transact a little marketing business, taking advantage of the ship's being alongside the mole to go backwards and forwards at their leisure. At every other port on the coast we had the amusement of seeing a swarm of boats come off almost before we had had time to anchor the ship. Racing, shouting, and swearing, they came on as if they were going to attack us in earnest, so great was the anxiety to get on board and be first in the market. They scrambled up the gangways, and in a few moments the decks were covered with the invading forces; and, as no part of the ship was kept clear of them, we found it was necessary to keep our cabins locked, a precaution which I have never elsewhere been driven to adopt.

In most of these apparently Heaven-forsaken places the people condemned to live there are absolutely dependent for existence on the supplies thus brought to them: man cannot live on nothing but cactus and copper, or silver either; and the mountains of delicious fruit and vegetables in the steamboats must be visions of veritable bliss. They also bring them the fashions, and it was often amusing to see a half-Indian beauty sitting on a heap of melons and trying on a pair of dandy boots, or taking the opinion of her friends as to the effect of a hat covered with bright green ribbons upon a complexion like that of an over-roasted chestnut. Business generally seemed done quickly, and the moment the buyers had piled their purchases in the boats, they rowed ashore as fast as they could, and at once opened a retail business near the beach. If the profits on other articles are as good as they are upon the melons, they have no reason to complain. One of them frankly told me that the wholesale price of the best melons in Valparaiso was about fifteen dollars, or 3*l*., for a hundred, while his retail price was twenty pence each, thus yielding a profit of about 160 per cent.

SEA BIRDS ON THE COAST OF LABRADOR.

A monotonous chain of dreary brown hills runs parallel to the coast, sometimes broken by hollows, like the Cwms of Wales, whose steep sides are evidently swept by falling stones. In one of these near Chañaral, the top of which was probably about 3,000 feet above the sea, the sides had all the appearance of having been formerly swept by two streams of lava. One was of much darker colour than the other, and being much smaller and less powerful, would seem to have been deflected from its course exactly as a lateral glacier is turned when it encounters the main ice-stream. It may have been only an appearance, really caused by the deposition of falling stones from two kinds of rocks; but certainly the likeness was remarkable. It is impossible to conceive more complete desolation than that which prevails for many hundreds of miles along this coast. Rain is almost unknown, and there is not a symptom of vegetation visible from the adjoining sea except the gaunt branches of the irrepressible cactus, which seems to possess the astonishing faculty of assimilating juices out of red-hot rocks.

The wild headlands and jutting rocks of the coast afford all that can be desired by the millions of marine birds that inhabit them. Countless pelicans, cormorants, gannets, &c., come forth from the clefts and recesses of their whitened crags, and fish contentedly till they can hold no more, or skim along the sea in search of fresh pastures. They were a constant source of interest, as we were never far from land in this coasting voyage; and I think that nothing can exceed the solemn earnestness of a pelican's expression as he sails past the ship, skimming close to the water with his great beak well in front, in eager search of dinner. Perhaps, however, it was still more interesting to see the gratified look with which he gently shook his head after swallowing a particularly dainty morsel. Now and then, too, we passed near flocks of various kinds of sea-birds, whirling round and round in the air, high over a shoal of fish, dashing down upon their prey as if they were shot out of a gun, and striking the smooth sea with a mighty splash. Sometimes singly, and sometimes a dozen together, they flung themselves down from heaven, with a rapidity and apparent recklessness that was worthy of all admiration.

On the night after leaving Chañaral the sea provided a novel and astonishing entertainment, which I have never seen equalled in any part of the world. There was no moon visible, and the sea, as usual, was smooth as glass. The sharp bow of the 'Santa Rosa' threw off two narrow lines of phosphorescence, but the rest of the water seemed perfectly black. Under these circumstances we were looking over the ship's side, and enjoying the evening cigar after a hot day, when I was rather startled by the appearance of illuminated fish. Porpoises were racing alongside us in their own delightful fashion, and were as perfectly luminous under the dark water as if they had been under the influence of the lime-light at a theatre. We could distinctly see the movements of head and tail and fins through their whole course under water, and each one left behind him a track of brilliant sparkling light, exactly like the tail of a skyrocket with the refulgent whiteness of silver. Sometimes they fell behind out of sight, and then made another merry rush, passing close by the ship's side, and showing us that we had no chance with them if they chose to 'put the pace on.' They were like illuminated phantoms of the deep. These seas must swarm with food for the legions of marine birds which frequent them. At distances of a few hundred yards at a time we passed large patches of very faintly illuminated water which, when the ship was almost close to them, seemed to explode in all directions like a jack-in-the-box firework. These were all shoals of fish; and, when startled by the awful presence of the steam-monster, they bolted away, leaving fiery tails like a sea of squibs behind them. Seldom could be seen so curious and interesting a sight as the phenomena of that evening. The porpoises seemed never weary of the fun; and when, after watching them till midnight, I turned into my cabin, I felt very sorry to say good-night to them.

On the 17th we reached Antofagasta, an important mining station, where we found the Chilian corvette, 'General O'Higgins,' anchored in the bay and looking for an expected incursion of Bolivian revolutionists, who were reported to have taken possession of the famous Caracoles mines. Sums said to amount to 2,000,000 dollars had been deposited on board her for security, and she had a good force ready to land if necessary. The 'Lusitania' was there also, loading with 800 tons of silver ore, and we watched a lighter full of it alongside of her which had a narrow escape of sinking. Minerals might be worked to a far greater extent in this part of the country if there were not such expense and trouble in procuring fuel and water. Nature is, as usual, just, and makes her choicest treasures most difficult of attainment.

At Antofagasta we parted with a good deal of our

garden-stuff, together with a number of four-horned sheep, which were treated with a cruelty that was perfectly disgraceful. Tied together so that they could not move a limb, they were bundled into a barge and piled one above the other as they fell, till it was hard to understand how those at the bottom escaped suffocation. A little further to the north, and just on the tropic of Capricorn, we passed round a hatchet-shaped peninsula, with Monte Moreno at one end of the face towards the sea, and Monte Mejillones at the other end; after passing which we went into the port of Mejillones, close to the frontier of Bolivia. Next morning we woke up at Cobija in Bolivia, which had a more respectable appearance than any place we had called at since leaving Valparaiso, and was possessed of a decent-looking church with two towers. A few hours later we reached Tocapilla, where there were evident symptoms of something remarkable having happened. It is a wretched little place at the foot of the usual chain of brown and desolate hills, where the Bolivian flag hung half-mast high over the office of the Captain of the port.

We waited some time in vain for the appearance of that official or anybody else from the shore, but at last his deputy came, looking very mysterious as he conversed with Captain Newman in a low voice. Presently, however, we found out all about it, and, if there had not been a tragic element in it, the whole affair would have been irresistibly ludicrous. It appeared that the good people of Tocapilla had had a little revolution, *poquita revolucion*, by themselves. Taking advantage of a temporary absence of the Captain of the port, a small band of rascals had seized the Capitania, and established themselves in a little brief authority. This news was taken by a steamer going south to the Capitan, who had gone to Cobija. He started at once with fifteen men, and, marching overland by night, he crossed the hills and dropped down upon the enemy at 4 A.M. They were probably drunk, but they showed fight, so he and his men killed a colonel and another man, wounded two others grievously, and put the rest in prison. The deputy had brought off two of them as passengers by the 'Santa Rosa,' to be exiled to Iquique in Peru. These heroes were small, shabby, evil-looking *gamins*, in imitation sealskin jackets, one of whom blubbered like a child; but the other had an eye to business. They had been provided with passage-tickets, and he was caught by the captain trying to dispose of his to another intending passenger! Having completed his victory and left his enemies all dead or in prison, the gallant Captain of the port had gone back to Cobija, whence he had been so ruthlessly disturbed. There must be a great deal of mutual affection among the simple inhabitants of Tocapilla, for the deputy who brought us the two prisoners embraced them fondly as he said good-bye to the ship; and we found that the flag at half-mast high was a delicate compliment to the memory of the rebellious colonel who had been shot dead in the early morning!

Early on the 19th we reached Iquique in Peru, where the exiles were sent ashore, and we followed with the purser to spend a few hours in the town. This place is one of those which suffered most severely in the great earthquake of August 1868, and it had by no means yet recovered from the effects of it.[1] The frail structures and

[1] Since this was written, the unhappy town of Iquique has been almost

houses of wood and plaster remind one at every step of the conditions under which people exist on a coast where it may be at any moment demonstrated that, if the dread earthquake comes, it is better that light things should fall upon their heads than heavy ones. The footway of the streets consists, as at all the northern ports we visited, of hot dust, loose stones, and broken bottles, the quantity of which latter articles in all directions surprised me till I reflected that empty bottles must be both numerous and useless among the thirsty inhabitants of regions where the barren soil contributes nothing to put back in them. The especial article of Iquique commerce is nitrate of soda (*salitre*), which is brought from the district of Tamarugal in trucks, over a zigzag railway, carried down the steep sides of mountains burnt to the colour of cayenne pepper. In this district it is calculated, according to Mr. Markham, that 'the nitrate of soda grounds cover fifty square leagues, and, allowing one hundred pounds of nitrate for each square yard, this gives 63,000,000 tons, which, at the present rate of consumption, will last for 1,393 years. In 1860 the export of nitrate of soda from Iquique amounted to 1,370,248 cwts., and a good deal of borax is also exported, though its shipment is prohibited by the Government.' The Pampa of Tamarugal is from 3,000 to 3,500 feet above the sea, and is, in fact, a continuation of the desert of Atacama. It derives its name from the *tamarugo*, or tamarisk tree, which is one of the few plants that thrive

destroyed by a fire in October 1875. The slightness of the buildings, the wooden footways, and the impregnation of the soil with nitrate, combined to make the destruction rapid and overwhelming; and the damage done was estimated at 5,000,000 dollars.

without the help of rain; and it traverses the whole province of Tarapaca. At the time of our visit there were great complaints of stagnation in the *salitre* trade, in consequence of the Government having imposed a heavy export duty; and Iquique was supposed to be duller than usual. This stagnation and consequent discontent count among the chief causes of the late revolution in Southern Peru.

There was a great delay in getting the mails ready, but at last we returned to the ship, and found the contents of the market had been considerably lightened. Many of the stall-keepers had left us, and some wild-looking half-Indians had come in their place. The men wore gay-coloured ponchos, and some of the women had very battered, grey wide-awake hats, surmounting gaudy shawls and dresses. We began to notice a great change in the climate about this part of the voyage: the salt became very damp instead of perfectly dry; the dews at night were very heavy; fogs became more frequent, and, though rain hardly ever falls, the coast of Peru may in some degree be said to have a damp climate. We called in at the Peruvian Mejillones and Pisagua on the same day, and part of the way was enlivened by a pelting-match with melon-peelings between some of the cabin passengers and the native young ladies, who, entrenched under the awning above, could lower the edge of it for a peep with their bright black eyes, to be instantly followed by a shot at the first head they could discover.

On the 20th we reached Arica early in the morning, and were met by Mr. Heimann, a very pleasant young German, who had come down from Tacna with letters for

Mr. Rawson. He took us on shore with him, and we soon found ourselves in the midst of the desolation still remaining from the earthquake of 1868. The town stands upon ground only slightly raised above the sea at a point where the hill-chain recedes from the coast; but it is flanked on the south by a lofty and precipitous headland of inaccessible rock, opposite to which is a seal-beloved rocky island about 500 yards from the beach. The great earthquake battered down nearly the whole of the place; then the sea retired till the island remained as part of the mainland, and returned again in a wave of fifty or sixty feet high, tearing ships from their anchorage and driving them helplessly before it. The ruin was complete when the sea washed over the fragments left by the earthquake. An old man, who found us some horses, told me it had been his duty to look for the dead bodies, and he reported 319, but probably many more were carried out to sea or buried completely under the ruins. We landed at a still unfinished new mole, and found that while some of the town had been rebuilt in a light and perfunctory manner, a great part of it was still represented by a mass of battered and tumble-down ruins, and there was no appearance of a population adequate to the task of restoration, It would be difficult to imagine a more miserable scene, or a more violent contrast with the cities of North America, which, after the most terrible conflagrations and catastrophes, rise like a Phœnix from their ashes.

We were anxious to ride out far enough to see the remains of the two ships which were washed up far inland by the great earthquake-wave. So scanty seemed the resources of the ruined place that it was a matter of considerable difficulty to find four horses for the party. Mr. Heimann kindly lent me his own excellent steed, but we had to rummage the place for some time before we found three others with saddles to match. It was done at last, and we rode off through the still ruined districts of the town, over the usual allowance of dust and stones and broken glass, till we found ourselves on a plain of burnt-up and scanty herbage, where at a distance of three or four miles from the town we reached the carcass of the United States ship 'Wateree,' a large iron steamer whose rusty hull and huge paddle-wheels are left like the remains of some primeval monster upon the desert plain. From the configuration of the land it would appear that the sea carried her not only far across the railway where she now lies, but to a more distant point where a low range of hills must have been the first substantial obstruction to the advance of such a wave, which, as it returned, would have left her in the situation where she is now to be seen. After inspecting the huge skeleton, we galloped across the plain to the Tacna railway, by the side of which we saw the broken remains of another ship which was a victim to the same calamity. Pursuing our course we arrived at the beach, and followed it for most of the way back to Arica; we rode for a few miles close to the seaside, where were an infinite number of sharks with their nasty fins above the water, playing among the rocks and tangled masses of seaweed on the coast, and suggesting horrible ideas connected with bathing. The beach was thickly sprinkled with the remains of whales whose bones were whitening among the shingle; and every now and then we came upon groups of vultures that were fattening upon the corruption of the latest victims to marine death. When we returned to the neighbourhood of Arica we had to push the horses up a tolerably high bank, and once more reach the region of broken bottles, instead of the whale-bones, which in Bolivia and Chile are used to make foot-bridges over streams, whenever such phenomena are found to exist. A small stream creeps past the north side of Arica, by the sides of which a few hut-proprietors are enabled to cultivate small gardens and a number of fig-trees, which seem almost to rival the cactus in producing something out of next-door to nothing. It appears that the fertility of this part of Peru was much praised by the Spanish writers, one of whom, Garcilaso, went so far as to declare that in 1556 there grew a radish so large that five horses were sheltered under the shade of its leaves! But, *nous avons changé tout cela*. One of the horses got a nail in his foot near here, and showed symptoms of kicking in reply to all attempts to extract it. Luckily by the side of the stream there was a man watering a couple of mules, who goodnaturedly came to the rescue with a piece of native craft. He walked quietly up to the horse, and, taking off his own red sash-like belt, tied it firmly to the end of the flowing tail; then going behind him he used this as a kind of breeching to prevent his kicking, and gently coaxing him to lift his foot, he fastened the end of the combined tail and belt round the fetlock; then he quietly lifted the foot higher and took out the nail very cleverly.

The sun had been very hot, and when we rode back to the town we were quite prepared to lunch with Mr. Heimann at the little Hotel Morosini. We began with Bavarian beer, the first bottle of which went off like the Great Geyser the instant the cork was drawn, leaving not a drop behind. The next was more successful, but it was only a prelude to the immortal Bass, whose works are never so highly and worthily appreciated as when they have been just preceded by foreign rivals from any other country in the world. We then walked along the beach on the south side of Arica, between the attractions of seals and sharks on the one side, and legions of sea-birds clustered all over the lofty rocks and precipices on the other. They did not appear to be at all nervous about being fired at with revolvers; and, unless the ball rattled against the rock within a few inches of them, they did not even condescend to fly a few yards to another station. We scrambled into great caverns in the rocks, and found them lined with feathers and other remains of dead and living birds: we picked our way amongst the vast irregular blocks which from time to time fall upon the beach, and lie partly on land and partly in water, where they harbour gigantic seaweeds and shell-fish, and where also we found fine specimens of echinus, or sea-hedgehog. After turning the corner of a rugged point which showed us a beautiful outline of the next great headland and the smooth expanse of the bay separating us from it, we scrambled back to the town, and returned on board with an extra shade of colour communicated to our faces by a blazing sun on shore, where it always feels much hotter than at sea. The voyage by the coast gave us the opportunity of seeing a number of curious places, but there was one disadvantage in the fact that we were seldom far enough from land to look well over the range of hills about 3 000 feet high which runs almost close to the shore for the chief part of the way. In the neighbourhood of Arica, however, we had a grand view of the snowy peaks of the Tacora group, looking doubly beautiful from their contrast with the long monotony of arid browns and yellows which are the distinguishing feature of all the intervening land. The road to La Paz and Potosi winds through this group of mountains, but the easy way of getting to the Lake of Titicaca and the neighbouring country is by the Arequipa route from Islay to Puno, where steamers have at last been established to traverse this wonderful lake at the elevation of more than 12,000 feet above the sea. The railway from Arequipa to Puno reaches the amazing height of 14,660 feet above the sea at the station of Vincocaya.

On the farther side of the hill, which flanks Arica on the south, a cemetery of the ancient Peruvians was discovered, and if I had known enough about it at the time of our visit I should certainly have wished to see it, or at all events should have inquired if the mummy-crop was still as well worth seeing as it must have been a few years ago. In an interesting book,[1] which was published in 1834 by an anonymous officer of the United States Navy, there is an account of his visit to this place. He found the spot indicated by hillocks of upturned sand with numbers of human bones bleaching in the sun, and portions of bodies with the dry flesh still adhering. 'The graves,' he says, 'have been a great deal dug and many bodies carried to England by travellers. Some boys who were playing about the place told us that an " Inglez " at Tacna had a large collection of them, which he is continually increasing:

---

[1] 'Three Years in the Pacific.' By an Officer in the United States Navy.

for a pair of the mummies, when perfect, he pays a doubloon.

'We dug in several places without being able to find anything. At last we inquired of an Indian, who was fishing with a cast-net, where the graves were and how we might discover indications of them. He said that there were none, except to stamp on the ground and dig where it sounded hollow. We pursued this plan with considerable success. The surface is covered over with sand an inch or two deep, which, being removed, discovers a stratum of salt, three or four inches in thickness, that spreads all over the hill. Immediately beneath are found the bodies in graves or holes, not more than three feet in depth.

'The body was placed in a squatting posture, with the knees drawn up and the hands applied to the sides of the head. The whole was enveloped in a coarse but close fabric with stripes of red, which has wonderfully withstood the destroying effects of ages, for these interments were made before the conquest, though at what period is not known. A cord was passed about the neck on the outside of the covering, and in one case we found deposited on the breast a small bag containing five little sticks about two and a half inches long, tied in a bundle by two strings, which broke in our efforts to open the bag. A native gentleman told me that drinking-vessels, and the implements of the occupation pursued by the deceased when living, as *balsas*, paint-brushes, &c., were frequently found in these graves. Several of the bodies which we exhumed were in a perfect state of preservation. We found the brain dwindled to a crumbling mass about the size of a hen's egg; the cavity of the chest was nearly empty, and the heart contained what seemed to be indurated blood, which cut with as much facility as rich cheese. It was reddish black. The muscles cut like hard smoked beef.'

We sailed again in the latter part of the afternoon, and early next morning arrived at Mollendo, where we took on board the English Vice-Consul and the agent of the Company. Mollendo is a small town, fortunately perched at a considerable height above the sea, for this circumstance saved most of it from the ravages of the wave which followed the earthquake, but was checked by the loftiness of the rocky coast. It must have been a wonderful sight to see it rushing amongst the singularly sharp crags of the small islands which adjoin the port. An Englishman who was present told me that, when he ran out of his house and found the earth trembling visibly, and waving up and down to such an extent that he was obliged to straddle his feet apart to help him in keeping his balance; and when, in addition to the horrors of the land, he saw the awful wave coming in irresistibly from the sea, he had no doubt whatever that the day had come when 'time should be no more.' With regard to that wave, it so happened that I afterwards travelled with another fellow-countryman who had chanced to be in New Zealand at the time, and saw it arrive on that coast about thirty hours after its birth on the coast of South America. It had crossed the Pacific at the rate of about 200 miles an hour, and had been diminished during its journey of 6,000 miles to the height of, I think, twelve or fifteen feet.

We reached Islay in the morning of the 21st, and

thence we would fain have gone by railway to Arequipa and the lake of Titicaca. Other arrangements, however, tied us to reaching Panama as soon as possible, and most unfortunately we could not afford the time to wait for another mail. All we could do at Islay was to go on shore and look about us for a few hours. The captain kindly took me with him, together with the consul and the agent, preceded by another of the boats with my two companions and the purser. As we got near the pier, there were manifest signs of some great excitement on shore, and a score or two of the Peruvian army came 'at the double' down a steep slope to prevent our landing. It seemed at first rather a joke that these men should try to stop the captain of the mail steamer, with two of the best-known officials on the coast; but the little men looked very fierce, and had the decided advantage of carrying loaded muskets to support their resolution. An officer declared he had orders by telegraph to prevent any one from landing till they had searched the ship for a dangerous revolutionist supposed to be concealed on board, and I believe the man 'wanted' was Pierola, who has since given so much trouble to the Peruvian Government. The captain and the consul were naturally rather irritated at the idea that either they or their friends could be conspiring against the Government; but it was not till after a good deal of angry altercation that we were permitted to land, upon the understanding that the authorities might do anything they liked with the distinguished revolutionist, if they could catch him.

We marched up between the files of soldiers, who now looked rather like a guard of honour, though I thought some of them seemed extremely disappointed at not having been allowed to drive the gringos, or foreigners, into the sea; and our captain began with 'giving a bit of his mind' to the captain of the port for his absurd adherence to general orders; then we went up a short steep road which leads between precipitous cliffs to the town, and slopes gradually upwards till the principal street ends with a still dilapidated church.

Here for the first time during many days we found a fair supply of good water, and a real fountain in the middle of a small circle of plants. Several of the inhabitants cultivated a few flowers in boxes or pots, among which appeared the beautiful blossoms of the cotton-plant and the large crimson Hibiscus. There was another fountain at the lower end of the town, near which Mr. and Mrs. Smart received us in their house and garden, and where they had persuaded the Norfolk Island pine to grow to a tolerable size. They said that among the greatest nuisances of the place are the scorpions, which delight in a soil consisting of burning dust mixed with stones, broken bottles, and all the rubbish of a town where rain never comes to wash it away. They are known to be combative in a high degree; and Mr. Smart told me that he had tried the experiment of putting four well-grown specimens to fight it out in a soup-tureen. In six minutes they all stung each other to death. Doubtless it was a good riddance; but what were they among so many? He tried to explain to me a diabolical creature, apparently after the nature of a centipede, which crawled up walls and came down by curtains, or by any other available means, and inflicted a deadly bite. Unluckily I have been unable to arrive at any name for it which would be recognised in science.

Islay is the port of Arequipa and the surrounding districts, and is the chief place of exportation for the wool of llamas, sheep, and vicuñas, and the famous Peruvian bark from the Chinchona trees of the interior. The country around is a dreary waste, rising suddenly at the distance of a few miles into a range of hills called the Lomas, about 3,000 feet above the sea, where for a short time in the year the ground is covered with flowers; and, in the spring of 1860, Mr. Clements Markham found that an unusual rain had produced a renewed freshness in the month of March. The country is broken up into abrupt ravines, which near the foot of the hills are watered by streams of sufficient amount 'to sustain small groves of fig and olive trees, the abodes of numerous flocks of doves.' From one of these the water is conducted through pipes for the supply of Islay, under the guardianship, in Mr. Markham's time, of a useful and obliging Irishman named Juan de la Pila, or John of the Fountain, who also combined the trades of carpenter, cooper, and blacksmith.

When we returned on board we found we were to be favoured with the company of an officer and five full privates of the Peruvian army. Many of the people we had seen in the town looked at us very sulkily and suspiciously; and the Islayenos evidently thought there was something dangerous and revolutionary about the 'Santa Rosa.' To make use of the famous confusion of metaphor attributed to Sir Boyle Roche, they 'smelt a rat, they saw it floating in the air, and they resolved to nip it in the bud' by the presence of these warriors. The officer was a young dandy, who spent a good deal of time at the pianoforte; the men were very quiet little bits of fellows, who generally carried their muskets in green-baize bags like cricket-bats, to protect them from the sea, and had a small stock of percussion-caps in their ears! The ship was searched in vain for the great revolutionist, and soon after noon we sailed for Quilca with our military escort. This is an extremely curious place, and was formerly the Spanish port of approach to Arequipa. It stands on the top of a hill about 800 feet above the sea, and is only approached from the water by a remarkable cove which turns between very lofty and precipitous walls of dark rock, in such a manner that a vessel coming out from land would be invisible till it emerges suddenly from behind the rocks. It is near the mouth of the Quilca river, which brings down the melted snows from the great group of lofty mountains clustering about Arequipa, and which is sufficient in volume to make the sea muddy for several miles, a phenomenon which we had never yet seen on the west coast of South America. A sharp line divided the fresh water from the salt; of course the former was on the surface, and the stroke of an oar upon the yellow stream cut through it, and revealed the dark water of the sea below. This river does good work before it reaches its grave in the Pacific: it has with the aid of guano turned the lofty plain of Arequipa into a rich *campiña*, green with alfalfa and Indian corn, and has spread fertility in its course to the shore, where we could see emerald groves in place of the general desolation of the coast. A large quantity of olives and olive oil was put on board, to testify to one of the benefits which it has conferred.

Here we had a slight disturbance with our detachment of the Peruvian forces, who took their weapons out of their green-baize bags and made themselves disagreeable by interfering with peaceable passengers. Our captain was not the man to submit to anything of the kind, and he caused them to collapse by saying that he was master of his own ship at sea. We soon saw the green bags again, and resumed tranquillity as we once more sailed towards the north. The highlands of the coast were for many leagues hence covered with a white dust, which made them look like a region of snow, though only some few hundred feet above the sea, and not many degrees from the Equator. It consists of mica and silica with an admixture of potash, supposed by some of the scientific men to have been deposited by ancient eruptions of Misti, the great volcano of Arequipa; but it is found to be of little practical use, except as an excellent material for scrubbing paint.

There was scarcely a day on the west coast when we did not see whales blowing at various distances from the ship; but on February 22 three huge monsters came up to the surface, spouting grandly within about a hundred yards of us. They were apparently taken by surprise at finding they were so near to a leviathan much bigger than themselves; and, after taking a few moments to look about them, they one by one dipped down their heads, and turning their vast flukes perpendicularly in the air, dived back into the profundities of the ocean. All about the rocky headlands and rocks near Lomas there were constant flights of pelicans and other marine birds passing and repassing; and we entered more and more into a region of damp fogs, though the sun was intensely hot in the daytime. The night dews made every seat on deck as wet as after a rain-storm; and one evening we saw two parallel belts of milk-white mist which stretched from east to west through the zenith, and looked exactly like an auroral arch which once upon a time I saw at Cambridge. In such a climate, and upon a coast studded with rocky headlands and most dangerous rocks, it was necessary to maintain a vigilant look-out for the perils of the sea.

On the 23rd we anchored at Pisco, in four fathoms water; and in a very short time the deck was covered with people who came to buy the last remains of our stores, and brought us a magnificent stock of grapes in exchange. They have as fine a flavour as any in the world, and it is here and at the neighbouring Yca that the favourite liqueur of the west coast, called Italia, is made from them. About two centuries ago the town of Pisco stood where the sea now breaks; and the tide does not now ebb beyond the ruins of the former place, which was destroyed by an earthquake-wave in 1682. On that occasion the sea retired, and, returning, submerged the town, and remained a quarter of a league beyond its former limits. The present town is about a couple of miles from the coast, and is backed by vineyards and olive-groves, far beyond and above which shine the distant snows of the Cordillera of the Andes, the beneficent sources of moisture destined to pass into the form of olives and grapes, and to rejoice the dwellers in a thirsty land.

Leaving Pisco behind, we soon passed very near the Chincha islands, the guano from which long proved such a substantial resource to Peruvian financiers, and comfort to the bondholders. That fountain has, I believe, been exhausted, but not till the height of the principal island had been reduced by eight hundred feet, as I was informed. It seems to be almost inconceivable that such amazing deposits should ever have been made by birds, even if all the birds in the world had for ages congregated in a few particular spots; and many men have had grave doubts as to the nature of this substance. But chemical analysis has apparently confirmed the original supposition. Certain it is that the amount of sea-birds along the coasts of Bolivia and Peru is simply astounding: at every point they are passing continually in hundreds and thousands: and every headland and rocky islet is white with the deposits, which testify to the constant accumulation of guano. It is technically divided into white, grey, and red, according to the antiquity of the bed, the former being of course the latest formation. The almost total absence of rain is of course greatly in favour of such a condition of things; but, after making all allowances, the result must remain one of the wonders of the world. Perhaps, however, the most extraordinary fact of all concerning it is that, though its immensely valuable properties were appreciated in the days of the Incas, yet the Peruvians of 1839 sold the monopoly of shipping it for nine years for forty thousand dollars. It is, however, only due to their sagacity to add that they boldly rescinded their contract when they found that they had made a mistake. The amount of their mistake may be estimated from the statement of Mr. Markham, that the guano monopoly was in 1860 producing to the State an annual revenue of 14,850,000 dollars! Three-fourths of the total disbursements of the Government were raised by the sale of these marvellous deposits, left by the birds of infinite ages in the past. They acted as if they possessed resources of inexhaustible wealth: they abolished taxes, and spent a temporary possession in unnecessary armaments, and jobbing salaries and pensions, without any regard to the ruin of their successors. They set on foot 'an army of 15,000 men, for a population under two millions, with upwards of 2,000 officers;' and, when the abnormal revenue terminates, it is easy to see what tremendous difficulties must arise.

In the afternoon of the same day we drew near the large and rocky island of San Lorenzo, concerning which there is a popular fable that it rose suddenly out of the sea at the time of the total destruction of old Callao by the earthquake of 1746, and that a boat with an astonished fisherman in it was thus elevated to an uncongenial element. We passed near some small islands, one of which is perforated by a complete arch, and was literally covered with pelicans; and in the evening we anchored at Callao, in water which is said to flow over the remains of the buried city. The five little soldiers fastened up their muskets into their green-baize bags, and, like most of the passengers, went on shore; but as there was a thick fog, and it was too late to go to Lima, we preferred sleeping on board.

CHAPTER VII.

First view of Lima—The Cathedral—Thoughts of Pizarro—Origin of the name of Lima—Climate of Lima—The Watershed of Peru—Breakfast at Chorillos—Fruits and Flowers—The Exhibition Building—Fair Ladies—The Alameda Nueva—Return of Rosito—Payta and bad news from Panama—Crossing the Equator again—'Old Boots'—A Haunt of the Buccaneers—Arrival at Panama.

THE FIRST THING I saw in the morning was the head of a dark-eyed little man poking through the open window of my deck-cabin. At first I was inclined to throw my boots at him; but, as he only asked in broken English if I wanted to go on shore, I contented myself with telling him not to bother me before breakfast. He had made up his mind, however, that our party should be his prey, and watched us like a cat for the next couple of hours to see that we did not throw ourselves into the clutches of any of the rival boatmen who were hanging about the deck. The fog cleared away before long, and we had an opportunity of seeing our surroundings. There was a large amount of shipping in the port, including men-of-war belonging to various nations, and two huge Peruvian monitors, with decks nearly level with the water, and built, I presume, out of the proceeds of guano, the bountiful mother of almost everything recent in Peru. Near to us was the beautiful steamer 'Oroya,' just sent out for the Company from England, in which we were in a few days to move northwards to Panama. In front of us, and but little raised above the sea, was the dirty, dusty, busy town of Callao, one of the last places in the world that most people would choose for a residence, though, as the port of Lima, it has to be endured. There are long quays, huge storehouses, and a railway brought down to the water's edge, which tempts the visitor to start at once for Lima, away from the various nastinesses of Callao. There are castles and batteries which would be of very little use in modern warfare; and there are more haunts of vice of every description than might be expected from the number of the population. Lima is seen at a distance of about eight or nine miles from the port, with its white towers and steeples rising out of the fresh and green surroundings, which are due to the presence of the river running through it. The city stands at the height of about 500 feet above the sea, upon a plain which slopes gently up from the port and extends to the base of the low hills of Amancaes and San Cristoval; far above and beyond which rise the serene snows of the Great Cordillera.

Soon after breakfast we consigned ourselves to the dark-eyed man, who turned out to be a rather amusing fellow, called Rosito. He was one of the *fletéros*, or numbered and registered boatmen, who are under the surveillance of the captain of the port, and appear to be a well-managed institution at Callao. With the aid of a comrade, he got all our goods in his boat and rowed us first to the 'Oroya,' where we deposited most of them, only taking enough for a few days at Lima. We were assured that Rosito might be trusted to manage everything in the way of the transit to the city; so we strolled to the club to meet our kind and agreeable Captain Newman of the

'Santa Rosa,' who did the honours and introduced us to the place. The club at Callao is a very different kind of thing from the luxurious establishments of Valparaiso and Santiago, and its architecture is conspicuous for rude simplicity; but there is a large, well-shaded balcony with a good view of the shipping, and newspapers from all parts of the world. There, too, we found a good glass of wine, and the cheery voices of a few fellow-countrymen. The general appearance, however, of Callao is irregular, shabby, dirty, and confused. The population is in the highest degree miscellaneous. Besides the sailors and men of business of all nations, and the Peruvians of pure Spanish stock, there are Indians and African negroes, and every conceivable admixture of them with other races; and here too we first came in contact with the 'Heathen Chinee.' The market-women, chiefly Indians and mulattoes, are very picturesque, sitting flat on the open ground with their little heaps of fruit and vegetables spread out on mats or ponchos in front of them. Their black hair hangs down in two or three plaited tails, which form a convenient plaything for the babies, which are often slung in the gay shawls or ponchos which cover their shoulders. They seem to squat where they please, and sometimes it is not very easy to pick one's way among them without treading upon some of their stores, the tempting appearance of which is not enhanced by their close proximity to the dust raised by the feet of the bystanders. The introduction of the Chinese element was another effect of guano, large numbers of coolies having been employed in the horrible and unhealthy occupation of digging and loading ships with it.

Rosito proved himself a good courier. He got the baggage labelled after passing it through the Custom-house; he took the tickets, and jumped into the train which took us over the nine miles to the capital. There he engaged a *coche* for us and a cart for the baggage, with which he followed us to the Hotel Aubry, where we got tolerably comfortable, though rather dilapidated, rooms. He had not lost a single package, which was something to his credit considering the confusion which prevailed in the Custom-house and railway stations; but, as he contrived to wheedle twenty-five dollars, or 5*l.*, out of us, he was certainly well paid for his services. There was no room for doubting it when he asked eagerly to be permitted to take similar care of us on our return journey to the 'Oroya.'

It is impossible to enter the great square of Lima without being profoundly impressed by the historical associations of this capital of what was once the land of the Incas. Here Pizarro, who began life by keeping his father's swine and ended by conquering Peru with less than two hundred men, drew the plan of the present city, and laid the foundation-stone of the Cathedral where it now stands on the eastern side of the square. Here he, the murderer of Atahualpa, was himself assassinated by the friends of Almagro, his rival in the plunder of Peru; and in a vault under the great altar his remains are buried. What scenes has that Cathedral looked on since then! What festivities, murders, intrigues, and executions, from the days of the unhappy Incas down to only two or three years ago, when two luckless brothers made an unsuccessful revolution; and, after being hung up to the towers of the Cathedral, were burnt in the square and publicly torn to pieces! Two of the other sides of the Plaza offer cool walks under colonnades, which contain some of the best shops; while the fourth side, which occupies the former site of Pizarro's palace, seems principally devoted to small cafés and cheap rubbish of various descriptions. The Cathedral is a noble building of 186 feet in front by 320 feet deep, and contains rare specimens of carving, as well as superb organs and many treasures. In the belfry are some very large and fine-toned bells, the largest of which, called La Cantabria, is said to weigh upwards of fifteen tons. The centre of the Plaza is ornamented with a beautiful fountain, surrounded by oleanders and other flowering shrubs; but, as we cross the brilliant sunny scene, it is impossible to forget that here, since the so-called introduction of Christianity by the Spaniards, men have been torn in pieces by wild horses, and done to death in every form of the most barbarous cruelty.

Lima was founded by Pizarro in the year 1535, and called by him the Ciudad de los Reyes, or the City of the Kings, in honour of the Magi, so well known as the Trois Rois of Continental hotels. Though this origin of the name has been disputed, it would seem to be confirmed by the fact that, when Charles V. was requested by Pizarro to give a coat of arms for the new city, he included in it the star of the wise men and the three crowns due to them. The name of Lima appears to have been derived from Rimac, an Indian oracle, or the 'god who spoke' to the ancient Peruvians, who was also the godfather of the river Rimac which flows through the city. There has been, and still is, a strange confusion in many nations between the letters L and R. The Spanish *Blanco* and *Plaza* are in Portuguese *Branco* and *Praza* respectively; and, while the Chinese call an American a 'Melican man,' the Japanese exactly reverse the pronunciation of the letters in question. In some such confusion between the Spaniards and the Indians it is supposed that the word Rimac eventuated in Lima. Nothing was considered too great or too magnificent for the capital of Eldorado, when a room full of gold was demanded as the ransom of an Inca; and even as late as the year 1682, when the Duke de la Palata made his entry into Lima as viceroy of Peru, it is recorded that one of the principal streets he had to pass through was paved with ingots of silver valued at 16,000,000*l.*! Such seems to have been the past of a country which in later days has only been saved from bankruptcy by the temporary supply of manure!

In the days of the Incas, Peru was infinitely more populous and prosperous than it has been ever since. There was not only a vast population, but it was a self-supporting population. One of my friends now travelling in the interior, writes in amazement at the immense extent of land which the Inca 'terrace cultivation' covered with corn to the tops of the hills. At the present time a scanty population of about four millions of Peruvians has to buy corn from Chile to the amount of about four million dollars per annum. He thinks that in the old days Peru must have been 'one of the grandest countries in the world.' If the period of revolutions and 'playing at soldiers' comes to an end, and the resources of the interior are developed by peaceful industry, Peru may be prosperous again.

The streets of Lima have a more picturesque appearance than those of any other I have seen on either coast of South America; they look much less new and formal, and their stiffness is broken by the many large projecting balconies, the wood dark with age, and sometimes carved magnificently to the top of their sheltering roofs. They form delightful places for repose and conversation, or for enjoying a good view of all that is passing in the street; and they are especially dear to the Limenians in the revels of the Carnival. Something answering the same purposes may be found in most places on the west coast, but in a totally inferior style. All of them however, handsome or ugly, are doomed. It having been discovered that in the event of fire they carry the flames along the streets with great rapidity, and even spread them over to the opposite side in narrow places, they are no longer allowed to be added to new houses or restored in old ones. There are said to be about sixty churches of various styles in Lima, and one of them is fronted with twisted pillars, carved all over, and recalling Raphael's cartoon of the Beautiful Gate of the Temple. The better class of houses have large gates opening from the street into a *patio* or courtyard, ornamented with flowers and shrubs, through which the rise of a step or two takes the visitor into the principal rooms. In a climate which is supposed to be free from rain, and where, in fact, it is so rare as to be looked upon as a portent of evil, the flat roofs are not cared for as they would be in Europe; consequently, when a heavy storm of thunder and rain came a year or two ago to terrify the inhabitants, they found that they were not only terrified but very seriously injured. The rain poured through every gap in the roofs; and an English merchant, who had lately filled his house with the best furniture that could be sent from London, had to lament the intrusion of an almost Noachian flood.

The climate of Lima is generally delightful, and its inhabitants may be said to enjoy a perpetual spring. For the greater part of the year light morning fogs and mists prevent the sun from heating the air too early in the day; and, after the full and glorious sunshine of midday, the afternoon brings up another tender veil of thin cloud to again check its excessive ardour. The temperature is said to be never so low as 50° Fahr. in the coolest time of the short winter, and seldom rises above 80° or 82° in the fullest summer. We were there in the latter season; and, hot as the sun was, we felt no inconvenience from walking at a brisk pace at any hour of the day. There is a lightness and purity about the air which I have hardly felt the like of, except in the unsurpassable climate of central Chile; and it is impossible not to love a sunshine which bronzes the skin without impairing the activity of the limbs. July and August are the months of the heavy mists, called *gárua* by the Indians, which exactly recall the words of the book of Genesis, where the author says that 'there went up a mist from the earth which watered the whole face of the ground.'

A little farther inland the continued rise of the land towards the great mountains affords fresh changes of climate, and enables Lima to be supplied with almost every variety of useful fruits and vegetables, for the soil is prolific wherever it can be brought in contact with water. This last is of course the grand desideratum of Peru on the whole coast of the Pacific, west of the Cordilleras, from lat. 6° S. to the southern tropic. This is, however, but a narrow belt, and a remarkable feature of the country is that a journey eastward from Lima leads in less than 150 miles to the head waters of the Amazon river, which find their way through more than 3,000 miles of tropical luxuriance to their distant rest in the Atlantic. This gigantic mountain backbone of South America, comparatively close to the Pacific coast, is, as it were, the boundary between two different worlds; on the one side an arid belt producing scarcely any vegetation except in the neighbourhood of its scanty streams, or by the help of irrigation; whilst on the other side the abundant moisture supplies the greatest river system in the world, and sends its waters rejoicing through the boundless forests of Brazil. The cause of this marvellous contrast is found in the prevalence of particular winds. The easterly trade winds carry the warm vapours of the Atlantic westward till they meet the lofty barrier of the Andes, where the last of them are condensed by the surrounding cold. On the Pacific side, the prevalent winds are parallel to the coast and carry very little moisture with them. A similar example, though in a different direction, is offered by the Himalayas, which form a line of demarcation between the fertility of India and the deserts of Thibet.

Those, therefore, who from the neighbourhood of Lima see the great snowy chain rising far above the intervening ranges of dry hills, have only to indulge a very short flight of fancy to place themselves on the other side of the visible watershed, and reach the sources of the river Ucayali which joins the Amazon on its journey to Pará.

To open up communications between the narrow belt of the coast and the far larger part of the country on the farther side of the Cordillera, is naturally a matter of high importance to the Peruvian Government; and the Oroya railway is a step in that direction. Starting from Lima, it is intended to cross the chain at a point almost exactly as high as the summit of Mont Blanc! By wonderful engineering it had advanced to a great height at the time of our visit, and has extended since to 11,543 feet above the sea; but there was much talk about financial difficulties, and it has not yet reached the lofty pinnacle of its ambition.

On the first evening of our arrival we dined under the hospitable roof of an English friend, who had lately returned from a visit to the old country, and who was kind enough to ask us to breakfast with him next morning at Chorillos. This place is about seven or eight miles to the south of Lima, and its principal *raison d'être* is that it affords a charming seaside residence to those inhabitants of the capital who, when they want a change of air, judiciously object to living in the dirt of Callao, and bathing amongst the garbage of a busy seaport. It is connected by a railway, and we left by an eight o'clock train. The glorious sun had already dispersed the morning mists, and shone brilliantly over the flowers of the cultivated gardens and the gay beds of nasturtiums which ornamented the burnt-up railway banks with sheets of yellow blossom. And here I must once more mention the remarkable fact, that some of the most juicy plants in creation flourish in perfection upon a soil resembling hot brickbats. Not only most of the family of Cactus, Cereus, Opuntia, &c., but the

Mesembryanthemums, including the ice-plant, and the various kinds of Tropæolum and Nasturtium, all abounding with tender juice, seem to revel on the west coast of South America in hot and 'barren places where no water is.' The Cacti are protected by an armour-like epidermis; but how about Nasturtiums?

Our host met us at the Chorillos station, and walked with us through the little town, which, adapting itself to the curve of the bay and the irregularities of the land, offers more variety to the pedestrian than the monotonous rectangles of a normal Spanish town. We passed through the market-place walled in with mats, where groups of women, chiefly Indians, sate behind piles of fruit and flowers, vegetables and fish; and, when not actually in the middle of a bargain, they appeared to employ a good deal of time in hunting small game in each other's heads. The *granadilla* is a favourite fruit, like a large yellow egg; it is the production of a species of passion-flower, full of delicious pulp and small seeds, like those of a gooseberry. Here too, besides many of the well-known fruits, are *paltas*, or alligator pears, a name which has been corrupted from *avocados*, as the Spaniards call them. But the most esteemed fruit of Peru is the *chirimoya*, a species of *Anona*; it has been compared to all kinds of delicious things, including 'strawberries and cream,' and its flowers are beloved by the ladies for their exquisite scent. Dr. Seemann is credited with saying that, after having eaten pine-apples in South America, mangosteens in the Straits of Malacca, and chirimoyas in Peru, he would give the palm to the latter. I have also tried them all, and must vote for the mangosteens. Among flowers, the most brilliant were those of the tree Hibiscus in various colours, imported from the East; and, as representatives of delicious scents, commend me to the white bunches of tall hyacinth-like tuberoses which abound in the gardens of both Chile and Peru.

A steep slope led down to the bathing-establishment, partly sheltered from the sea by a small pier. Here are large buildings with rows of dressing-rooms, and every convenience for either walking into the sea or taking headers from stages. Here men, women, and children bathe and gossip together, clad in long bathing-dresses and Panama hats, which, in the case of some of the ladies, were gaily decorated with red ribbons. Hither resort all the beauty and fashion of Lima; and the convenience of the railway enables many men of business to keep house at Chorillos, and go into the city for their day's work after a morning bath in the sea, just as London men go backwards and forwards from Richmond or Blackheath. Some ride down the hill and keep their horses to carry them up again: these are often very pretty animals, and the easy action called 'pacing' is esteemed very highly among the indolent inhabitants of Peru.

We walked up with our host to his house near the top of the slope, and found a delicious breakfast awaiting us, in a cool sort of verandah shaded by a slanting blind. I was introduced to a dish that was new to me, fried eggs and bananas, an admirable combination; and after a succession of good things we wound up with granadillas and chirimoyas, at the proper time of day for the true enjoyment of fruit. As he had to go to Lima by the eleven train, we walked up with him to the station, and followed his indications for a ramble along the top of the high cliffs between Chorillos and Callao. These cliffs are about the height of those between Hastings and Fairlight, and fall almost perpendicularly down to the beach, where we could see the Indian women washing clothes, and pounding them with stones: and from this fact I infer that fresh water somewhere near came through the land. The high plateau we were on was for the most part bare and brown, but here and there we found the heliotrope and yellow broom, together with a very pretty *Solanum*, and a considerable quantity of a beautiful yellow sea-poppy, which I had also noticed near the beach at Arica. Strange to say, a short distance down below the edge of the cliffs we could see some fine tall ferns in clefts of the rock, but without a rope it was much too dangerous to attempt scrambling down for them. After wandering for a couple of hours we walked back to the town, and before the next train started we had time enough to be attracted by the words 'Lunch Salon,' over a small shop. Apparently there was nothing for lunch but cigars and tobacco, but when we expressed our wishes, the proprietor lifted up half the counter and let us pass into a little room, about eight or ten feet square. Still we saw no materials for eating, but he discovered a bottle with a red triangle upon it, which was refreshing after passing the hours of noon upon the hot and treeless hills. The walls displayed a few photographs of Pisa, Florence, and Milan, from which I rightly guessed that our host was an Italian. He had come from Milan; and when, as we were leaving, I told him that I had seen Milan from the highest peak of Monte Rosa, he broke out into a fit of handshaking enthusiasm, and called forth an Italian friend to see the wondrous phenomenon of a 'Señor Inglez' who had actually stood on the enchanted spot which they had been accustomed to gaze at with admiration from across the Lombard plains. It was very pleasant to see the evident delight with which they welcomed a few moments of conversation with a stray traveller, who could talk to them about the charms of the land which they had left so far behind them.

In the afternoon we were escorted by another friend to what is called 'The Exhibition,' on the outskirts of Lima. There was no exhibition of any kind going on at the time, as far as I know; but there is a beautiful building, all ready for any sort of show or entertainment, like the nail which the Irishman drove into the wall to accommodate the coat which he hoped to hang upon it. As far as good taste and elegant architecture are concerned, I should not hesitate to prefer this building to that of any of the great exhibitions I have ever seen in the last twenty years in various parts of the world. Its pure whiteness shines conspicuously among the varied trees and flowers of the garden by which it is surrounded, and among which winding paths lead in all directions between lawns and shrubberies and artificial water. Here were French roses, huge geraniums, fuchsias, lilies, &c., backed by tall shrubs of the splendid Hibiscus, with deep red blossoms six inches in diameter, or by great purple Ipomæus and other beautiful climbing plants twining over trellised arches. Oleanders and magnolias were in the full beauty of bloom; while cypresses and gum-trees, and elegant Norfolk Island pines, looked down upon them all. One part of the ground has been made into a Zoological Garden, where the animals appeared to be kept in very good style ; at another place is erected a building for the accommodation of a curious clock, the construction of which is said to have occupied the entire attention of an ingenious citizen for several years. High above the ground, and ornamented with rather gaudy painting, it exhibits an arch of dials representing in succession the hour of the day, the day of the week, the name and day of the month, the season of the year, the date of the year, and finally the number of the century ! Chinese gardeners do all the labour of the place under proper directions, and seemed, as Chinamen generally do, to be attending to their work. The whole grounds are enclosed by a handsome open railing ; and, as we followed a side path towards the gates, a considerable force of soldiers, who had been drawn up about forty yards from us to practise file-firing, began firing blank-cartridge at us all down the line with such energy that we hoped no ball-cartridge had got in by mistake. A good many spectators seemed much gratified by the display, and great fun was caused by a grey-wooled old nigger in his shirt-sleeves, with a battered chimney-pot hat on the back of his head, and apparently mad, who walked up and down in front of the line of fire, waving a thick stick, and evidently fancying that he was reviewing the army.

In the evening, a military band playing in the Plaza brought out a crowd of promenaders, and produced customers for some of the cafés in the neighbourhood. The beauty of the ladies of Lima has long been justly famed. Their black hair, brilliant eyes, and exquisitely pure complexion, are combined with elegant figures whose every movement is perfect grace. There is a serenity of beauty in their countenances; and the favourite black silk *manto*, or shawl worn like a hood, serves to enhance their fairness, if it be possible to do so. The *manto* can be worn so as to cover the whole face, excepting one eye which flashes upon the beholder, and enables the fair owner to mystify her admirers by the completeness of the mask. Judging from the short experience of a few days, I should suppose that entirely uncovered faces are much more frequent than they used to be; on the other hand, the modern ladies would seem to be more careful to conceal the famous white silk stockings and many-coloured satin shoes, covering little feet of six inches long, which used to attract the eyes of travellers. The author of 'Three Years in the Pacific' says that the extravagance of the ladies in these articles was excessive in his time, and that some years earlier, when silk stockings cost from twenty to forty dollars a pair, it was considered a matter of reproach to wear them after they had been once washed. He moreover adds, 'it is an invariable rule, and has been from time almost immemorial, to purchase new shoes every Saturday.' Lima has been called 'the paradise of women, the purgatory of men, and the hell of jackasses;' but it would seem that shoemakers ought to have been included among those who have a good time of it.

Lima is a very expensive city to live in, in proportion to the accommodation afforded. The charge of four dollars a day, or twenty francs, for a small room and a *table d'hôte* breakfast and dinner does not seem in itself excessive till we see the nature of what is supplied for it. I very much doubt if any European dealer would have given much more than a pound for the furniture of any one of our rooms, consisting as it did of a few rickety articles covered with the dust cast down by ants or other noisome insects, and peppered from the wooden ceilings on to our beds and letter-paper. A marine-store dealer would hardly have taken what were intended for locks and bolts, and the paper was very vaguely fastened to the walls. All sorts of liquors were of course extras, and the food was very indifferent. Washing of clothes was not to be obtained on any terms whatever in a limited time; and the landlord himself told me that he could not expect to get his own things returned by the *lavandera* in less than three weeks. He and all his people were perfectly civil and obliging, but the institutions of the country were too much for his own good intentions. I fully believe that he did his best for us as strangers, but it must always be understood that activity is an unknown quality in Peru, and that to seem to be in a hurry is to confess an inferiority of race.

In the course of the next day we went to several more churches, and saw more of the lovely daughters of Lima bent upon their devotions, black-veiled, and waited on by the damsels who carry the little rugs or cushions upon which they kneel. We afterwards crossed the bridge to the farther side of the city, and entered the Alameda Nueva, a long straight walk, both sides of which are planted with handsome trees and shrubs with beds of gay flowers in the foreground. Here were India-rubber trees of large size, Norfolk Island pines, magnolias and oleanders in full bloom, and grand plants of the red and yellow Hibiscus. The Chinese gardeners kept everything in excellent order, but people in general seemed too lazy to enjoy the promenade. Thence we found our way over a burnt up hill on the outskirts of the city, which gave us an excellent view of the whole place and the neighbouring plains. At our feet were some of the gardens and orchards which supply the markets with their piles of fruit, and a little way farther was the bull ring. Bull-fighting, however, is strictly a Sunday amusement, and, as we were to sail on Saturday, we lost the chance of hearing 'Bravo, Toro!' It is a most curious contrast that is presented by such a view in such a climate. The hill we were upon was almost as burnt and desolate as if it had just come out from the fire; and, as we followed its ridge to a higher point with a rather more extended view, the only result was seeing range after range of similar desolation; yet, only a very few hundred feet below us, there lay the white and shining city with its tall steeples rising over the verdure of evergreen trees and gardens maintained by the abundance of artificial irrigation. The track over these hills was very rough, and very damaging to boots, and the sun was excessively hot; so when we scrambled down again and reached the Alameda once more, we were glad to take shelter in a large and shabby restaurant kept by an Italian, who had, however, managed to cover his walls with gaudy frescoes illustrating the chief events in the history of his native country, beginning with Romulus and Remus and the wolf, and ending with one of the battles of Garibaldi. In every country where I have met Italian emigrants or colonists, I have always found them thus accompanied by some of their favourite household gods.

On Friday evening little Rosito put in an appearance

again, but we told him we should not start till the early train next morning, and dismissed him to spend the night as he liked. It is to be feared that he spent it in evil ways, on the strength of the small fortune he meant to make out of us in the morning. He did not come till long after his time, and when he did come, he seemed extremely hazy; he also displayed a tendency to poke the ribs of one of the party, and call him a *diablo*, apparently as a term of endearment; and he was so slow in getting the baggage into a cart, that we were obliged to administer the spur of indignant remonstrance. After all, however, when we reached Callao there was no Rosito: he had lost the train, and was left behind with our belongings. This was unsatisfactory, to say the least of it; but he ultimately came down by a later train with everything all right, and he assumed a highly comical look of resentment at my having ever doubted his capacity for the perfect administration of affairs. On the whole he had afforded us a good deal of amusement, and we parted very good friends. We settled down in comfortable cabins on board the beautiful 'Oroya,' and, in company with a very few other passengers, sailed about sunset for Payta, the last port of Peru, not far below the entrance of the Gulf of Guayaquil, in Ecuador. Payta was not only the last port we were to see on the coast of Peru, but it was if possible more desolate in appearance than any of them. We, however, were occupied all day in shipping a valuable cargo of cotton which had come down from the interior, and was brought off to the ship on huge rafts, made simply of the rough trunks of trees, lashed together in such a way that the least ripple on the water must damage the lower side of the bales.

Here we received the dismal news that a terrible fire had burnt down the hotel at Panama, and the best part of the place where we knew we must expect to be detained for a few days, which would probably be anything but days of pleasure. The voyage was quietly hot and dull, the seas calm and glassy, only enlivened by the presence of countless pelicans and diving-birds, and the occasional visit of a booby flying close to the ship, at the same pace with ourselves, and now and then condescending to take a seat in one of the boats, where he narrowly escaped being knocked on the head by the chief officer. The most interesting feature in the passage was a steerage passenger, an elderly Englishman, whom I could not but christen 'Old Boots.' He had handsome features, grey hair, and piercing black eyes. He would sit reading and smoking for hours together in the sun, with his back close to the hot funnel of the ship, wearing a thick beaver greatcoat over a suit of corduroys, and having his legs encased in a pair of huge fisherman's boots. Seeing him thus on the day when we crossed the Equator, under a sun almost hot enough to fry chops on the deck, I could not resist speaking to him, and politely insinuating that I should like to know what he could possibly be made of. With a goodnatured smile he said he was accustomed to a hot climate, and had spent four or five years on the Gaboon river, which lies exactly under the Equator, on the west coast of Africa. Knowing this to be the headquarters of the gorillas, I asked him about those interesting creatures, and found that he was very familiar with them. He had brought up a young one whose mother had been shot, with the aid of a black woman to suckle it, and he declared that it did everything like a child. It throve well and became a great favourite, until one day an officious friend gave it some salt pork, which was fatal to our poor young cousin. He said that the poisonous malaria which is so deadly to white men in that climate produces fungi in the lungs, as was proved by twenty-seven dissections; and he added that one house of business lost eighty-four clerks in seven years. He had lately been employed at La Paz and Lake Titicaca, in connection with two small steamers, which were sent out from Europe several years ago, to be put together and worked upon the lake. This has at last been done, after a great expenditure of time and money; but, considering that they are said to be of about 150 tons burthen, and that every bit of them, before the completion of the railway, must have been carried for long distances over mountains and on the backs of mules, perhaps the wonder is that it has been done at all.

Near Cape St. Lorenzo we passed the island of Plata, a renowned haunt of the 'bold buccaneers,' who were said to have buried vast treasures in it. Rising several hundred feet out of the sea, with scattered groups of trees and bushes varied by enormous cactus plants, it was the sort of place to recall the famous 'Gold Beetle' story of Edgar Allen Poe, and the search for hidden treasure. What hideous orgies must have been held in this now peaceful and deserted island, when pirates and robbers, stained with blood, came hither to divide and quarrel over their plunder! After this there was very little to be seen, except the sea and its inhabitants, till, early in the morning of March 6, we awoke to find ourselves anchoring at Panama, or rather at about four miles' distance from it. A steam-launch came out to take the mails and the rest of the passengers on shore; they were bound for either New York or Europe, but as we were only waiting a day or two for the San Francisco steamer, and as the hotel was burnt down, we were kindly permitted to remain in our floating home till the other ship was ready to receive us. There she lay, close beside us, the 'Arizona,' one of those huge wooden American steamers with which we were afterwards to be much better acquainted. Our captain took us on board her in his gig, to introduce us to her commander, with whom we had a pleasant chat over our first glass of the famous rye-whisky of the United States.

CHAPTER VIII.

Great Fire at Panama—Difficult boating—The effect of Judge Lynch—The miseries of the 'Arizona'—'Dipping'—The Barber's Shop on board—St. José de Guatemala—Champorico not to be found—Acapulco—Rubbed with a Jellyfish—Mexican atrocities—The Whale and the 'Thrasher'—Doings of Brigands—Mazatlan—Sharp change of Climate—Cape St. Lucas—A lonely Post-office—Towing the 'Colima' to San Francisco—The Golden Gate.

AFTER more than three thousand miles of burnt and barren coast, with hills looking like vast mounds of cayenne pepper, the scenery of Panama was a very refreshing treat. Once more at last we could see green hills of varied form, garnished with palms and other normal beauties of the tropical forest; and in general appearance the surrounding country reminded me on a small scale of the eastern side of the bay of Rio Janeiro, where there are countless prettinesses of island and of hill, without the beauty and magnificence of the Organ Mountains and the nearer peaks, which are the glory of the northern and western sides of the bay. Panama being only 9° north of the Equator is of course tolerably hot, but we did not find it very oppressive; and it enjoys a reputation for healthiness which is a very favourable contrast to that of Colon at the other side of the isthmus. Fresh and pleasant breezes seemed to prevail; and, from a register taken every fortnight some years ago, it appears that at sunrise, noon, and sunset the thermometer never went below 74°, or rose above 87° Fahr.; while the barometer never varied more than one-tenth from 30 inches.

The city, after a long period of inactivity, was roused into new life by the gold discoveries of California and the formation of the railway across the isthmus. The latter work had to be constructed through dense and unhealthy forests, where the mortality was so great that it was said that a man died for every sleeper on the line. Immense reefs prevent direct approach from the sea, and great local knowledge is required to know by what course to take a boat in at different times of tide. Captain Hall took us on shore in his own boat the first time we went there; but on another occasion, with a native boat, we had to take a much longer route to avoid the reefs visible at low water. The old walls of the town have a very rickety look about them, and the roots of trees and bushes are continually pushing the stones into the sea. The ruined walls and towers of old churches and monasteries are also decked to the top with trees and plants, which are thus making the ruin more complete than ever. We had no opportunity of judging of the best quarters of the place, as the fire had made a clean sweep of whole streets and squares of lofty houses and stores, which burnt so quickly that scarcely anything was saved. Though this fearful conflagration had only happened about a fortnight since, I was surprised to see how little the people seemed to care about it. Business was going on in temporary places; and one man, who told us that he had lost 50,000 dollars, was quite merry as he pointed to the signboard with his name upon it, which was the first and almost the only thing that he had succeeded in saving: he was evidently satisfied that this would bring him 'better luck next time.' A group of people were examining two iron safes which were left out for inspection: they had been backed in with cement, and, though they had been subjected to twenty-six hours of terrific fire, they were hardly the worse for it, and in one of them the thin wooden drawers and partitions were not even singed.

The wind saved the cathedral, though it was in all the confusion of repairs going on, and full of planks and shavings. Near it I saw a negro carrying on his shoulder a new and splendid image of the Virgin Mary. The dress was painted sky-blue; the head was adorned with long and splendidly curling locks, and shaded by a lace veil crowned by a wreath of gorgeous red roses. As she thus went through the dirty street, sloped on the negro's shoulder, with her hands stuck out, and an inane smile on what was meant for a divine countenance, I thought I had never seen such a *reductio ad absurdum* in the matter of a divinity. Set up in the corner of a cathedral shrine I daresay it would have looked more dignified, but in such a position, and in the garish light of a Panama sunshine, the effect was too ludicrous for contemplation. A little beyond the cathedral were many unrestored ruins of another great fire in 1870; so that, while the city has been badly used of late, the church has had its lucky escapes. The upper parts of the cathedral are studded with sparkling mother-of-pearl shells, which form an important feature of commerce at Panama. Mr. Bollaert some few years ago saw the pearl-stores of a leading merchant there, who showed him a beautiful pear-shaped pearl nearly an inch and a half long, and an inch broad in the thickest part: he was hoping to get one to match it, that he might offer the pair to the Queen of England for 4,000*l*.

Life in the bay of Panama was dull enough, and I had to get through a good part of the day in reading and writing, or dosing under the awning, and lazily watching the pelicans that were constantly passing and repassing in a very business-like search for food. This, too, was the only place where I have ever seen the birds which sailors call 'man-of-war hawks.' They were ever whirling round and round in large flights, at a great height above the sea. They appeared nearly black, with great spread of wing and very long forked tails, and nothing could be more graceful than their rapid movements. One marked drawback to Panama is the difficulty of getting ashore. Owing to the dangers of the reefs and the distance at which large ships are obliged to anchor, the ordinary class of boatmen seemed to be almost unknown; and, when on the last day we were obliged to go and look for a parting chance of letters and papers, there was some little excitement in doing so on board an infinitely small flat-bottomed coble, rowed by one man with an apology for a pair of sculls. Our swarthy Charon did his best against a fresh breeze which increased steadily, and which, if it had increased a shade more, would have infallibly filled us with water, as it was already beginning to come in. Some skill was required to get through the reefs, and two hours were consumed in reaching a filthy beach, more covered with broken bottles and nastiness of every description than any bit of seashore that I am acquainted with. On the way back we hoisted a sail, and my companion Mr. Rawson, well-skilled in such matters, handled the sheet while our native laboured between the dangerous reefs with his oars. Once through them, we ran merrily under sail before the wind and safely reached the 'Arizona' in half an hour. On our way we passed close by a large three-masted canoe under full sail, slashing through the water, and heeling over to the breeze at such an angle that a quantity of cocks and hens on the top of her roof-like covered deck had hard work to hold on, and looked marvellously puzzled at the strange attitudes thus enforced upon birds which were intended by Providence to walk upright. Sometimes my companions rowed themselves in the ship's dingy to the neighbouring island and stalked pelicans; but on the whole I think that a residence at Panama must be one of the dullest affairs possible in these degenerate days. In the heroic days of gold-diggers, gamblers, hell-keepers, and drunken rowdies, ever ready to 'commence shooting,' the place was no doubt lively enough to please the most fastidious. As it was, we were very glad to leave it behind us; but in justice it must be added that, if we had found the heroic age still prevailing, we should probably have been still more eager to depart.

Apropos of those glorious days, I heard a Californian story worth repeating. It was the rule that anyone coming in to the bar for a drink should invite all present to drink with him; but one day a gentleman of the period walked in and asked for a glass of brandy for himself without taking the least notice of those about him. Whether he was ignorant of the etiquette, or whether he merely wished to break through a vexatious and expensive custom, I know not; but the result was that, as he raised the tumbler to his lips, there was a sound of Bang! ping! showing that a neat shot had taken the bottom out of his glass and spilt the liquor. Nothing daunted, he asked for another glass; but, as he lifted it to his mouth, a man from the other side of the room repeated the performance with equal dexterity, and another glass of good liquor was wasted. Then the stranger drew his revolver, and with a rapid movement, right and left, shot dead the two men who had interfered with his tranquillity, and simply asked 'How much for two glasses?' He paid his money and walked out, master of the situation, until he fell into the hands of Judge Lynch and a Vigilance Committee. It was the fashion on this side of the water to laugh at, or seem shocked by, the proceedings of Lynch; but the institution did its work well in times and places where no other law could have had any effect at all, and where it would have been impossible to detain a prisoner for ordinary trial. The result has been successful; and an informal system for the suppression of crime has been evolved into a permanent maintenance of order.

When we said good-bye to the 'Oroya' and went on board the American Company's ship, we soon found that we were in the beginning of sorrows. Instead of the beauty and cleanliness of the 'Oroya,' which was kept more like a royal yacht than an ordinary passenger ship, we had to deal with dirt and disorder in every respect. I am far from intending to make a general charge against the American Company, for the management of their ships across the Pacific to China and Japan leaves nothing to be desired; but between Panama and San Francisco the service has become detestable under the influence of the 'cheap and nasty' principles called forth by competition. The great railway system, as is well known, takes passengers from New York across the continent to San Francisco in rather less than seven days and nights, during which they have to feed themselves and pay extra for Pullman cars if they have any respect for their own comfort. The Pacific Steam Ship Company takes them in eight or nine days from New York to Colon, and thence across the isthmus to Panama, where another of their ships is ready to take them to San Francisco in seventeen or eighteen days more. The attraction to a passenger is that he is thus conveyed to his destination for about half what the railway journey would cost him; and, with the exception of drinking, he is fed for nearly a month into the bargain. It is therefore a favourite route for the impecunious: others also, to whom economy would be no consideration, sometimes allow themselves to fall into the trap, and groan helplessly over miserable food and intolerable crowding. By way of recouping themselves to some extent for 'alarming sacrifices,' the Company charged us for going only from Panama considerably more than the fare paid by the 'all-rounders' for the double voyage, and the railway over the isthmus!

When we went on board after breakfast, we found that nothing could be done until the arrival of the invading horde; and everything was so badly managed that, though it was known all day that the corresponding ship from New York had arrived at Colon, there was no message or telegram to say how many passengers might be expected. Consequently we could get no berths allotted to us, and no place to open a portmanteau in, till the evening. About sunset a steam-tug came off; and, when it approached, we saw to our horror that it was crowded like a beehive. Then came the 'ugly rush' to the purser's office, and in a short time every cabin was disposed of, and almost every possible berth provided with an occupant. On the upper deck the cabins or state-rooms, as the Americans are pleased to call them, were such little holes that it was barbarous to put two or three people into one of them for an imprisonment of about three weeks in a hot climate, without even the chance of choosing their own companions. The awning was peppered all over with holes, and the furniture was shabby beyond description. The crowding at meals, though there were other tables to spare, and the badness of the food, were things never to be forgotten. I have had a fair share of travelling, and have been looked upon as a sort of Mark Tapley for not complaining much about trifles, but I was fairly beaten by the salted salmon and miserable scraps, with cakes and treacle as substitutes for wholesome food. A very fat old lady sat next to me on the first day of confusion, and made signs for the treacle-pot. Not remembering that *molasses* is the American name for it, I handed it to her, saying, 'Would you like the treacle, ma'am?' She looked at me fondly, almost with tears in her eyes, and said, 'Oh my, now! Oh law! and you call it treacle, do you? We call it molasses, but my mother she came from the old country, she did; and she always called it treacle. Oh my, now!' I saw that I had touched a tender chord, and did not carry the subject further.

The difficulty of getting anything done was partly

owing to the fact of all the Chinese servants having struck work when the ship was on the point of leaving San Francisco, and the Company's agent being therefore obliged to go into the highways and byways to catch such heathens as he could. Dirt and disorder were in the ascendant: there were constant altercations with the stewards, and the captain had to adopt strong measures to preserve discipline.

Among the crowd of passengers there were a few pleasant and even delightful people, but there was a large majority on the other side. I hope never to forget two friends made there, an Englishman and an American; the first link of sympathy with the latter being a communion of admiration for the quatrains of Omar-Khayyám. On the other hand, close to us at dinner sate a man who every day contrived to get a large raw onion from the cook, which he cut up and spread about obtrusively, in spite of his neighbours' remonstrances. There was a positively filthy couple from one of the Southern States, with a young girl whom they were going to bring out at some Californian music-hall: the mother would sit for the hour together hunting like a monkey in the greasy head of her child, whom she kept between her knees. It was pointed out to me moreover that this lady spent a good deal of her time in a practice which I believe is, in the Southern States, called 'dipping.' All the world has heard of smoking, chewing, and taking snuff; but 'dipping' is not so generally known to the civilized world as perhaps it may deserve to be. It consists of taking a pinch from a snuff-box with a small stick, a toothpick, a bit of twisted paper, or even a delicate finger-tip, and applying it to the gums and teeth, where it is kneaded into a small pellet and rolled about till the time comes for consigning it to the spittoon which stands by the side of the fair operator. I need hardly say that this 'Rose of the South' was not popular as a first-class passenger. The doctor of the ship was always a charming companion, and was one of those honest gentlemen of the South who, born to independent fortune, felt it their duty to fight for the right of Secession, lost everything, and took good-humouredly to learning various trades or occupations, sustained by the possession of a good conscience. I have seen several men of this stamp and of similar antecedents who, however humble their present path in life may be, would not change places with Ulysses Grant. We had an interesting character in the mulatto stewardess, who had been a slave before the war. Her master was, I think, killed, or at all events he was completely ruined; and this excellent woman was bringing up and educating his penniless boy out of her own savings as a ship's stewardess. The negro barber was also a great institution on board; and, as usual in American ships, he had turned his large cabin into a shop, where he was equally ready to shave beards, or to sell oranges, cigars, hats, boots, paper collars, and all kinds of small goods. Altogether we had a motley party on board, when, after several days' roasting at Panama and acquiring wonderful complexions, we at last sailed once more for the North and West, at the same time as the 'Oroya' started on her return with the mails for the South.

For the first few days the heat steadily increased to about 95° in the shade by day, remaining at 86° in the cabins at night, when unluckily the dews were so exceedingly heavy that it was not particularly safe or pleasant to remain on deck. During this time we were needlessly crammed together at our meals as close as we could possibly be squeezed, and had to struggle with untrained Chinese waiters for our very unsatisfactory food. There was a great deal of natural grumbling and growling on all sides till the sight of land at San José de Guatemala gave us something else to talk of. From the sea there is very little to be seen of this place, with the exception of an iron pier long enough to get clear of the surf and breaking water, with warehouses at the shore end and a large shed at the other. The heat was intense, as the ship lay through all the middle hours of the day taking in 700 bags of coffee, which were brought off lazily in lazy barges. The sea was unruffled by breezes, but the long silent swell from the ocean broke in muffled thunder on the beach, dashing its torrents of foam almost up to the roots of the forest belt which clothes the land to the very edge of the coast. A few pelicans basked tranquilly at the furthest edge attained by the upward-rushing spray, apparently animated by the hope that a fish might thus be brought to them without their having the trouble of going to look for it; and a few coffee-coloured boys were bathing as near as they could venture to the rollers. Behind them rose the forest gently sloping inland, inconceivably lovely to the eye, gorgeous with every exquisite shade of green fringed with gold, and all bathed in a soft divine haze of mysterious light. Such is the Guatemala forest, rivalling in splendour the plumage of the long-tailed Trogons which inhabit its recesses, and whose colours of gold-tinged emerald make them brilliant even amongst the most glorious of birds. Here then was a place which immediately recalled the 'Lotos-eaters' of Tennyson. He must have had some spiritual vision of the coast of Guatemala when he wrote :

> In the afternoon they came unto a land
> In which it seemed always afternoon.
> All round the coast the languid air did swoon,
> Breathing like one that hath a weary dream.

And in the stillness of the glowing scene he might have thought:

> There is sweet music here that softer falls
> Than petals from blown roses on the grass :
> Music that gentlier on the spirit lies
> Than tired eyelids upon tired eyes;
> Music that brings sweet sleep down from the blissful skies.

Little did we dream as we gazed upon this sleep-inducing tranquillity that a very different scene would be presented to the 'Arizona' when a few weeks later she would call at San José on her return voyage. Then her passengers learned amidst the most profound excitement that a native commandant had caused a British Vice-Consul to be nearly flogged to death; and that, to avoid the wrath of his own Government, he was endeavouring to escape on board the American packet-ship. As his boat, however, neared the 'Arizona,' some of the free and independent travellers on board her showed their disapprobation of his conduct by firing revolvers at him and wounding him, mortally it was said, in place of allowing him the hospitalities of the ship. The population were in a state of wild excitement, and it cost the Government of Guatemala 10,000*l*. to pay for the outrage upon Consul Magee. Now I certainly am not disposed to be cruel; but if it was fated that this outrage and subsequent shooting were to take place at all, I should like to have been in the 'Arizona' at the right time instead of the wrong. If that man was to be shot, I hope I may be forgiven for wishing to have seen the shooting, and to have heard the remarks of those who did it, as well as those of the spectators. It must have been a lively scene.

Next day we ought to have called at a small port called Champorico, but we were buried in thick fog before arriving in the neighbourhood late at night. The captain took the ship very slowly and carefully towards the land till he found her in only five fathoms water, and we thought we could hear through the deep silence the distant booming of the swell ashore. Then he put her head to sea again, and waited for daylight; but when morning came the fog was as thick as ever, and to our great delight he made up his mind to give up looking for the port. Those merchants who were anxiously waiting to put 6,000 bags of coffee on board were no doubt proportionably disgusted.

After crossing the great bay of Tehuantepec, we came in sight of the coast of Mexico, which provided us with a long-continued succession of bold hills, backed by higher and higher ranges of mountains, presenting charming varieties of form and colour till they lost themselves in the blue haze of distance. At intervals were fine sandy beaches and snugly retired coves, probably beloved of pirates and buccaneers in the good times of old, and consecrated by many a deed of ancient violence. The great treat, however, was the beautiful approach to the renowned Acapulco. This was formerly the chief Spanish port upon the coast, whence every year a well-armed galleon loaded with treasure crossed the Pacific to Manilla, bringing back the silks and treasures of the East, to be sent across the country to Mexico and Vera Cruz for transhipment to Europe. Here it was that Anson, in 1743, in charge of a squadron for the suppression of Spanish interests in those seas, cruised about in the 'Centurion' under unheard of difficulties before he crossed the Pacific, and with the last fragments of his scurvy-smitten crew contrived after a battle within pistol-shot distance to capture a famous galleon with a cargo worth even in those days a million and a half of dollars, which he ultimately succeeded in bringing home to Spithead. Here too had been projected and essayed marvellous expeditions of buccaneers without even the pretence of war. And now what is Acapulco, after all the historic interest which surrounds it? Nature is the same, and the situation is lovely as ever; but the shrunken town and ruined fort tell of commerce diverted into other channels, and of countless disasters brought upon the country by the lawless people and contemptible institutions which have usurped the power of old Spain in Central America. Some people will probably conclude that all this is the Nemesis of what was done in days gone by, and that the present wretched state of Peru, Panama, Guatemala, Honduras, and Mexico is the legitimate reward of the barbarous cruelties that were perpetrated by the Spanish conquerors of the New World.

The approach from the sea was completely hidden till we turned a corner between rocky points crowned with rich vegetation, and saw a white, sandy, semicircular beach, fringed with white-stemmed cocoa-nut palms, varied with noble specimens of the *Cycas circinalis*, or sago-palm. The rambling town is clean but poor-looking, and the eye follows its stragglings upward to ranges of beautiful hills which easily lead the imagination towards Popocatapetl and the city of Mexico, only 180 miles away. A pleasant walk to the old Spanish fort passes under the shade of large and splendid magnolias; and, though many of the deciduous trees were bare of leaves at the time of our visit, yet few things could exceed the beauty of the foliage of live oaks in every direction. Close to the shore on the left was the perfection of a snug cemetery shaded by a grove of cocoa-nut palms, and bounded by a pure white beach where a boat's crew were sent to collect sand for scrubbing decks with. Within a few hundred feet of our anchorage, lofty rocks rose out of deep water, crowned with various sorts of cactus and prickly pears scattered among evergreen oaks and trees just bursting into the life of Spring. The calmness of this secluded retreat from the ocean was perfectly delicious; the water seemed swarming with fish, as it does everywhere on the coast of the Pacific, and the pelicans passing leisurely to and fro had an easy life of it: they seemed only to have to dip their great beaks into the water and bring them up again, shaking their heads right and left to help a victim down their capacious gullets. The fish jumped out of the sea close to the ship as if they had no hesitation about showing themselves, and I saw one of at least seven or eight pounds weight leap two or three feet out of the water, clearing a distance of three or four yards. Here too we luckily refreshed our larder with a stock of turtle, which comforted us much for a few days.

Jelly-fish abounded in the bay, and I was told a story concerning them in connection with an eccentric Englishman, who was tempted by the beauty of the beach to walk into the sea and bathe at Acapulco. He had little notion of the effect produced by a Mexican sun upon a white skin and a somewhat bald head, till he felt a sensation of roasting all over the upper part of his body. At this moment a jelly-fish floated by him. It looked so deliciously cool and soft that he immediately seized it and rubbed himself all over with it as with a sponge. The effect upon his blistered form was never to be forgotten, and he was nearly driven mad by the poisonous irritation which is produced by contact with these creatures, and which in his unhappy case must have caused double martyrdom.

A small fleet of boats and canoes came off to the ship loaded with shells, including the large 'Danish helmets,' as they are popularly called in England, corals of many colours, baskets of shells, baskets of shell-flowers beautifully made, bunches of green cocoa-nuts by the dozen together on the stalk, with piles of oranges, bananas, and limes. There was something very attractive about the people who offered them for sale; many of the women seemed to have a natural grace and smiling brightness which was not in the least affected by a refusal to buy any of the treasures offered; and as they laughed and joked, the mirth came from between rows of exquisite teeth, and illuminated the most brilliant of eyes. As a good type of them, I remember a handsome girl who came to the ship's side in a canoe paddled by two of her friends. She wore a loose white dress and a bright blue shawl, which she sometimes allowed to droop behind her shoulders, and sometimes gathered up like a hood over her magnificent head of black hair with as much grace and dignity as a '*grande dame*' with her opera-cloak. The plain blue and white of her dress contrasted charmingly with the golden heap of oranges and bananas by her side; and, as she held up her pretty corals and shell-baskets with a peculiarly graceful action of the hand and arm, accompanied by a beaming smile, I wished for an artist-friend to do justice to the portrait of such an attractive market-woman.

At Acapulco we were joined by three gentlemen who had made the overland journey from Mexico to that port amid much danger and difficulty. They gave a wretched account of the condition of the interior of the country. No one was safe; bands of brigands were in all directions, with dissatisfied store-clerks in prominent positions among them to facilitate plunder by their knowledge of business-men and business-doings. Murder and robbery were rampant in the land. In their journey across the country from the capital they had spent about ten days, during which they had to keep watch and ward by day and night. Several times they saw in the distance parties coming towards them, and prepared for action to the best of their ability, only to find, on coming nearer, that the supposed enemies were quiet people even more frightened than themselves. One of these gentlemen was already well acquainted with Mexico, and had been there for some time in the days of the Emperor Maximilian. Of late it appears that some of the leading robbers have taken a leaf out of the book of Greece and Sicily, and carry off rich gentlemen to enjoy the mountain air till they can find a ransom of about twenty thousand dollars. Some years ago, the most fashionable gang called themselves *Defendedores de la Iglesia*, or Defenders of the Church. 'Call it by any other name, 'twill smell as' badly.

In the afternoon of the 19th we sailed from Acapulco for Manzanilla, distant about 300 miles; and in the following morning we saw a whale making an amazing disturbance about a mile away on the port quarter. He lashed his tail, leaping and plunging in a furious manner, while another fish seemed to be attacking him savagely. The captain said that this was one of the celebrated battles between the whale and the 'thrasher,' in which the latter has the valuable assistance of a sword-fish under water. The thrasher leaps into the air and throws himself on the whale with all his weight and power, while the sword-fish assiduously bayonets him from below till the monster succumbs to this combination of forces. The battle royal was going on till we lost sight of the combatants; and it was remarked that it was lucky for Jonah that nothing of that sort took place when he was travelling inside his friend! Soon after this we passed through a vast shoal of porpoises, blackfish, and other finny companions, holding something like what theatrical acrobats would call 'Olympian revels.' On every side of the ship they were racing, jumping out of the water, playing leap-frog in the air, and apparently tumbling over one another like clowns in a circus. I only hope they enjoyed themselves as completely as they seemed to, for I certainly have to thank them for one of the most amusing entertainments that I ever beheld. There was an expression of business also with the fun; and no athletes of Lillie Bridge, even in the last rush, can show a greater appearance of eagerness and exertion than is displayed by half a dozen porpoises in a neck-and-neck race by the side of a ship.

After a lovely day, with heat slightly moderating, and aided by a young moon, we got through the intricate entrance to Manzanilla, and about 10 P.M. anchored and fired a gun to arouse the natives. Presently a swarm of boats came off and we were boarded by a motley crowd, some of whom came to trade and some from merely motives of curiosity. The stores of the black barber were in great request among a little crowd of men with hats as big as targets, ponchos of many colours, and the conventional *calzoncillos*, or white trowsers like pillow-cases, fringed round the ankle. Some of the women offered bunches of cocoa-nuts and bananas, but everything seemed to be done in the gentle sleepy fashion of those of whom it was said—

> Branches they bore of that enchanted stem.

Little groups of dark-eyed damsels in white garments were slowly promenading the deck with the silence of bare feet, and others were chatting in low tones over their cigarettes in a quiet corner; the young moon threw a gentle light upon the scene, and a red lamp, suspended above the stern of the ship, completed the Tennysonian vision:

> And round about the keel with faces pale,
> Dark faces pale against that rosy flame,
> The mild-eyed, melancholy Lotos-eaters came.

About midnight our visitors had all slipped off as quietly as they came, and I found myself sitting up for a pleasant chat with the doctor, till about three hours later the old

'Arizona' herself slipped off in a quiet fashion, which is peculiar to American steamers that have the slow pulsation of 'walking-beam' machinery.

Two days later we reached Mazatlan without any adventures beyond that of horribly frightening a huge whale who rose about eighty yards from the ship, and, finding himself so close, turned up his flukes incontinently and went down head foremost to where he came from. Mazatlan appeared by far the most important and flourishing place that we had seen since leaving Callao. Large clean-looking houses and buildings of various kinds stretched all along a curving beach of pure white sand; and the rising ground behind the main part of the town was scattered over with pretty residences and gardens. Splendid palms waved their green crests among the streets; and, behind all, the land rose in range above range of hills ending in the blue distance with lofty mountains, comprising several well-marked and precipitous points. Everybody longed to go on shore and see this bright-looking town at closer quarters; but there were such grave reports of virulent small-pox that, to our grief, the captain refused to have any communication with the land, except receiving specie and mails. Here we parted with one of the best and most pleasant of our fellow-passengers, who was bound for his mines in the interior. He described that part of Mexico as perfectly delightful in so far as nature is concerned. He lived among wild mountains abounding with bears, of which I think he had shot more than forty in the last autumn, with intervening valleys full of flowers and innumerable humming-birds. The drawback to all these charms was the presence of brigands, whom a miserable

Government allowed to exist. It had become so difficult to convey the precious metals in safety to the coast that he had been reduced to paying black-mail to some of the chiefs and entrusting them with the convoy of treasure, a duty which they fulfilled without stealing a dollar. On one occasion when a leading member of the fraternity was in trouble, as Obadiah hid the prophets in a cave, so my informant sheltered this man for several months by giving him an appointment of some trust in the bowels of the earth; and, when interrogated by the Government about his dealings with the brotherhood, he closed their mouths by saying, 'Señores, it has long been proved that you cannot defend me, and I must defend myself.' He told me that the influence of a degraded and ignorant priesthood was all-powerful for mischief, and the power of giving or withholding absolution was unscrupulously used for the furtherance of any nefarious designs they might entertain. He knew of one case where a priest, who was annoyed by the existence of a Protestant teacher in his neighbourhood, said in the presence of others, 'There goes a tree that produces no fruit.' The hint was sufficient, and the unlucky heretic was next day attacked, killed, and almost cut to pieces. Since this we have had news from Mexico that at Acapulco a small Protestant community of fifty or sixty persons were attacked during their service by a band of armed men, some of whom walked into the chapel and stabbed the congregation right and left, while others waited outside to murder those who might escape from the interior.

The only amusing story, however, that I ever heard about Mexican brigands was told to me by an American commercial traveller whom I met in Brazil about a dozen years ago. He wanted to go from Vera Cruz to the city of Mexico, and took his place in the *diligencia*, after having been warned not to take more than a few doubloons in cash, as the coach was pretty sure to be robbed on the way. In the course of the day they were stopped by a party of armed men who requisitioned the watches and purses of the passengers. My friend produced his eight doubloons, about 26*l*., and said that he had no more. 'I really hope, Señor, that you are not attempting to cheat me, *engañarme*,' replied the chief of the robbers. On receiving an assurance that there was no more, the rascal politely handed him back two dollars, with the remark that he might want some refreshments by the road. They went on their way, but before very long they were stopped by another gang, who were greatly troubled at finding they had been anticipated. His two dollars now disappeared: the thieves rummaged his trunks, took all the best of his clothes, and left the *diligencia* to pursue its journey once more. Their troubles were not over yet, however. A third gang appeared later in the day, in a very unpleasant temper: they took all that remained in the passengers' trunks and stripped them of most of the clothes on their backs. My unhappy friend was left with nothing but his straw hat and a marvellous pair of drawers with sundry steel-springs which had been made for him in Paris to compress the rotundity of his waist. Under these circumstances he asked the driver if he meant to go any further; and, getting an answer in the affirmative, he turned back and walked in this light costume till he found a decent house, where a worthy man who saw what had happened lent him a poncho and a horse, with which he rode back to Vera Cruz, arriving there in a most pitiable plight. 'Sir,' he said to me, 'I guess the first lot were the commissioned officers, and the second lot were the non-commissioned ones; but I'm darned if the last of them weren't the full privates, and no mistake!'

The authorities on shore were very dilatory in their proceedings, all the more so probably because the captain had refused on the strength of the small-pox panic to have more to do with them than was absolutely necessary; and it was not till late in the evening that we got away. The entrance to this land-locked bay is so narrow that the great ship had to be slowly backed out before her head could be put towards the open sea. Next morning we found that we had crossed the greater part of the entrance to the long Gulf of California, and that a sudden and astonishing change of climate had taken place. For several weeks we had been able to wear nothing but white trowsers, thin jackets without waistcoats, and the most shadowy of neckties: anything more than a sheet in bed was intolerable, and even that was often too much. Those even who wore large rings might have wished to change them for lighter ones, like the luxurious dandy of Juvenal, who

Ventilat æstivum digitis sudantibus aurum.

But, as we left Mazatlan, counterpanes were in request; and on the next day, when we came into the cool current of wind and water from the North, pilot-jackets and blankets were hailed with acclamation. The violent change was very trying, and even the doctor added himself to those who suffered from catarrh. As we drew near to Cape St. Lucas, at the foot of the peninsula of

Lower California, we could see the town of San José nestling at the base of an exquisite outline of mountains, varying in colour from Indian red to almost pure cobalt in the distance, rising above the white sandy beaches of the coast. About noon we rounded Cape St. Lucas itself, and lay-to near a grand collection of yellowish white rocky points rising out of the sea, in form like the Needles, though on a much larger scale, one of which was completely hollowed through as if by a splendid Gothic archway.

The sea here is so deep and so pure that for the first time in my life I saw real blue water of the violet type that ordinarily belongs to mid-ocean, reaching up to within a few ship's lengths from the land, where a belt of emerald green broke in gentle surf upon a shelving beach. The object of our stopping here was to land some despatches at one of the queerest little stations in the world. It is a settlement of a very few families which began with an eccentric runaway American, and would be a dull residence indeed if it were not in communication with San José on the other side of the cape. We sent a boat on shore with some letters; and, just as it landed on the open beach, we saw a solitary horseman ride down to receive them. Whilst waiting for the return of the boat, we had time enough to enjoy a thorough contemplation of the sea by the ship's side. Undisturbed by the reposing paddle-wheels, it spread around us, smooth as glass, clear as crystal, and purple like the violet. It was so transparent that a small silver coin thrown overboard seemed as if it would never get out of sight: strange creatures could be clearly seen far down below the surface; and now and then a huge circular ray-fish was seen rising slowly to the top, and clumsily rolling away upon his sluggish course. They seemed huge to us, at all events, but the doctor declared that he had seen them as large as twenty feet across on the coast of Florida. To those who were not afflicted with colds the change of temperature was deliciously refreshing, and, with the aid of exquisite colours to charm the eye by land and sea, the short halt off Cape St. Lucas will long fill a corner in my grateful memory.

Early next morning a great excitement was caused by picking up at sea a boat with six men and an officer, who proved to have been sent in search of us from another of the Company's ships which had broken her propeller and was lying helpless at Cedros Island, about 300 miles to the northward. There was nothing left for us but to go and look for her, especially as she was said to be short of provisions; the boat's crew had been four days at sea, luckily with fine weather, and immensely enjoyed a 'square meal' and a good sleep on board the 'Arizona.' In due time we came up with the cripple lying in a snug place near the island, where she had been detained for ten days; and, as we ranged up near her, we received volleys of cheers with much handkerchief-waving from her delighted passengers and crew. They were very short of food, and had lately subsisted chiefly on the quantities of fish that were caught by the passengers. Some hours were occupied in paying out two enormous hawsers and fastening them firmly to our stern; and then we settled down to the dreary task of towing for some 800 miles a ship nearly as large as our own. We had sent them a boat full of meat and other supplies, and the two ships communicated by means of writing with chalk on a large black board. Things did not go altogether smoothly in the few days following, and some of the messages were not altogether polite; there was a good deal of altercation about the whole affair at the end of the voyage, and something of a squabble among the Company's officers.

In spite of fresh breezes ahead we managed to tow the cripple at seven and a half knots an hour, but we were not so fond of our quarters or our provisions as to by any means enjoy the delay. Things got worse instead of better; quarrels between the stewards and Chinese were far from improving the comfort of the passengers; and I fancy everybody was as glad as myself when on the 30th we had our last horrible salt salmon on board, passed by the Cliff House, and entered the Golden Gate of San Francisco.

The city, which the inhabitants call 'Frisco' as a term of endearment, is admirably situated for the purpose of affording a great surprise to those who are lucky enough to approach it from the sea instead of by the railway. The Golden Gate is only a narrow opening between the low hills of the coast; and, after passing through it, a long bend round to the south has to be made before anything comes into view which could convey a hint of the close proximity of a vast city. We crossed a wonderfully well-defined boundary line between the clear water of the Pacific Ocean and the thick yellow flood which is poured into the bay by the mud-compelling power of the Sacramento river; we steamed between the mainland and a small fortified island; cast off our incubus, the 'Colima,' to take care of herself; and, curving round to the southward, we presently found ourselves in view of the great city. There was some trouble in bringing the huge form of the 'Arizona' alongside of the quay as the tide was very low; but we got there at last, and then began an entirely new phase in our wandering career. The first of many symptoms of the good practical way in which they do things in America made itself evident in the excellent system of the hotel-porters who instantly boarded the ship. Here were the badge-bearing representatives of the 'Lick House,' the Grand Hotel, the Occidental, the Cosmopolitan, &c., all of course anxious for customers, but without a particle of that detestable clamouring, jostling, quarrelling, and howling which in so many of our European cities drive a newly-arrived traveller to distraction, and make him tremble for his baggage if not for the safety of his coat. A word was enough, and a sign to a very jolly emissary from the 'Grand,' who looked more like a Kentish farmer than anything else I had seen since leaving England, brought him and his aide-de-camp to our cabins, where they marked every article of our luggage with the mark of the 'Grand,' and said we might go ashore without any further trouble. In a very short time everything was deposited upon a well-roofed quay; the Custom-house people gave us no trouble; we and our goods were stowed in the hotel coach, and in about a quarter of an hour we were beginning to compare the attractions of a delightful American hotel with the dirt and discomfort of the 'Arizona.'

CHAPTER IX.

Good living at San Francisco—'Oldest Inhabitants'—Living by Bears—Progress of Good Taste—Splendid Lupines—Cliff House and the Sea-lions—The Redwood Tree— Wild Flowers—Berkely University — Buildings in Earthquakia—The 'Heathen Chinee'—A Chinese Theatre—The Chinese Immigration—The Mission Church of Dolores—Detestable Tramways—Californian Hospitality.

AH! WHAT A BLISSFUL CHANGE it was for the wanderers in the ' Arizona'! Cleanliness, comfort, order, civility, and good living were all supreme in the Grand Hotel. The whole of these valuable articles were supplied for the very moderate charge of three dollars, or 12s. 6d., a day, which includes everything except wine. Large as the house is, a new one of nearly double the size was already springing up on the opposite side of the street, of which all I have to say is, that bigger than the Grand it may be, better it can hardly be. The bread was as good as that of Vienna, which is generally considered the finest in the world; milk and butter abundant and delicious; pork, which would have soothed the soul of Charles Lamb; salmon, which converted me from my home opinion that two or three appearances of it in a season are quite sufficient; vegetables in perfection, and oysters at a shilling a score, were among the daily delicacies of San Francisco. We were too soon for any fruit except strawberries, but we heard wondrous tales on all sides about the peaches, pears, grapes, &c. &c., which would come in due season. One apparently trustworthy man told me that he had seen a single bunch of grapes weighing fifty pounds exposed in the scales of a shop, and kept there as a curiosity till it rotted! I have seen a great many of the finest fruit-shows in England, but this old gentleman's account made me think of nothing less than the pictures of Caleb and Joshua coming back from the Promised Land. Of course we have all heard the stock jokes about Californian turnips and beetroots growing so deep that it takes two horses to pull one up; and that, if they are left a day too long in the ground, nothing can stop them from growing out at the antipodes; but, without travelling into the realms of romance, it is certainly true that the fertility of California is altogether surprising to Europeans.

The wonder of wonders, however, is San Francisco itself. Twenty-five years ago there was hardly anything in the settlement but a small mission church of Saint Francis, with its school and the few small houses necessarily connected with it. Now here is a city with a population drawing towards 250,000, sweeping round the edge of the bay and covering the high lands which look down upon it; here are magnificent streets with hotels like palaces, and miles of suburbs ever stretching farther from the sea; here is everything that wealth and prosperity can bring together; and yet San Francisco was only two years old at the time of the Great Exhibition! Everything there dates from 1849, and if you talk to one of the 'oldest inhabitants' you will see he is as sure to tell you that he came out with the first party in that year as every old pensioner in Greenwich Park was certain to declare that he carried Nelson in his own arms into the cockpit of the 'Victory.' These oldest inhabitants must be pretty tough, and very fortunate to have survived at all; many of them must in a few years have had more opportunities and chances of shuffling off their mortal coil than would fall to the lot of ordinary mortals in a century. The bullet and the scalping-knife must have often been far too near to be pleasant; they have faced the ' Grizzly,' knowing that they will have no dinner if they do not kill him, even though the odds were probably in favour of the bear; they have toiled all day with the deadly hunger of gold upon them, doubtful even if success would not attract the murderous hand of a comrade ; they have figured in scenes where shooting a man was thought no more of than treading on a caterpillar ; they have passed through a 'hell upon earth,' and they have lived to see it purified. To such a one we can only say with Virgil, '*Fortunate senex !*'

As I wandered about the streets of the huge city full of handsome banks and shops and stores, swarming with a dense population of active, industrious, and orderly people, and contemplated the comforts of the Grand Hotel, I often thought of the adventures of one of my friends, since dead, who about twenty years ago went to California in search of sport. He was a good rifle-shot, and having killed lions in Africa, he was anxious to try his hand at the grizzly bears of the Rocky Mountains or the Sierra Nevada. Starting from New Orleans for San Francisco by way of Cape Horn, he was one of the first to catch the yellow fever which broke out on board soon after leaving port. There was a mob of miners and intending emigrants on board, discipline was very bad, and as he lay sick of the fever he could not get any attendance except by bribes of a few dollars for even a glass of water. Some of the people on board, thinking probably that he was sure to die, began to help themselves prematurely to his dollars; and when he recovered by something like a miracle, he found that he had no cash left. Under these circumstances he complained to the captain that he had been robbed. The captain, apparently a man of the times, answered in a manner which in these days would be called at all events rude, 'What the devil do I care? Do you mean to say I robbed you? I only wish I had chucked you overboard as soon as you got the fever; and I'd have done it too if it warn't against the law.' After this rebuff he was obliged to take comfort in the reflection that he had still preserved his letters of credit to two houses of business in San Francisco. On going ashore, however, they found things in a dismal state: a big fire had destroyed a great part of the rude town and caused general ruin; and, when he came to inquire about the people whom he expected to supply him with money, he found that one had been 'burnt out' and the other 'bust up,' and nobody knew anything more about them. He had nothing but his weapons and ammunition and a box of clothes: he was in a new country without a dollar or the prospect of one, unless he got it for himself. However, he proved equal to the occasion; he went up the country and held his own among the rowdies and miners by shooting bears, and supplying them with the meat at a dollar the pound. Some of his bears weighed 600 and 800 lbs., and in the course of about six months he had realized enough to retire honourably from the profession of butcher to a somewhat turbulent mining population.

The early years of anarchy and reckless dissipation must indeed have been awful ; and the intervals of cruel work and privation were too often devoted to drinking, quarrelling, and various forms of vice. But when things get to their worst they begin to mend; the sounder men saw that something must be done, and Vigilance Committees undertook to sweep out the Augean stables. Many rogues perished abruptly, and a better class of men came to fill their places. Gold-digging was found to be in many cases a delusive toil, or at all events not such a profitable occupation as many others; and comparatively steady habits of business came to the front. Speculations in land were wonderfully successful ; building followed, with commerce from all parts of the world to supply the increasing community; and, lastly, agriculture has come to employ a solid steady class of country farmers, who are bringing more gold out of the soil of California than was ever brought by the gold-diggers. Moreover, a very important change has taken place in the manner of mining; and a great benefit has accrued to society in the gradual extinction of the reckless, dissipated, individual digger. In passing through various parts of the gold districts we saw no diggers, except here and there a wretched old Chinaman, all skin and bones, scraping among the *débris* left long ago by his predecessors. The main work is now done by Companies, with of course very various and uncertain results; but with this advantage over the solitary digger with no capital, that they are not driven to the desperation of hunger by a short period of bad luck, and with the further benefit of encouraging more orderly life among the men by the payment of regular wages. We saw several establishments of the kind which appeared to be going on prosperously, and the men that we saw there behaved extremely well.

With the return of order, churches of every denomination sprang into existence, and some of them are handsome. The inquiring traveller in San Francisco can, if it so pleases him, investigate the peculiarities of every form of service, from purest Catholic and High Church down to that of the Chinese joss-houses. The Jewish synagogue, with its two towers like pepper-pots, is more conspicuous than anything else in the city, but it is extremely ugly. The Hebrews everywhere have no notion of architecture; and, however rich the temple of Solomon may have been in gold and decorations, I can hardly believe that the external effect was successful. The Roman Catholic cathedral is a very handsome Gothic building, and several of the churches on Easter Sunday were as beautifully decorated with choice flowers as anything of the kind that could be seen in England. There are many indications that a few years have not only sufficed to bring order out of lawlessness, but to produce a considerable amount of sentiment among a people who are not generally credited with it, and who are too often supposed to care for nothing but the almighty dollar. There is a great taste for flowers in San Francisco, and the charming villas of the suburbs in every direction are ornamented with gay and well-kept gardens. The cemetery which we visited was another proof of this, and was to me quite unique in its arrangement. The situation has been chosen with perfect taste on the irregular hilly ground which rises behind the city, with a full view over the deep blue of the Pacific. Advantage was taken of the scattered old native ilex-trees, amongst which have been planted cypresses, Australian gum-trees, and mimosas. The ground is divided by broad paths winding up and down among the trees, and known by various names, such as 'Lily walk,' 'Rose path,' 'Acacia avenue,' &c., so as to avoid all trace of those horribly long and monotonous lines of tombstones which are to be seen in many of our English cemeteries. Between the trees the graves are arranged in irregular groups surrounded by flowers, and here I saw Gloire de Dijon roses in full blossom hanging over the tombstones, mixed with tall fuchsias and veronicas, pinks and double daisies. The inscriptions were for the most part excessively simple, such as 'Our dear Nelly,' or 'To our dear Parents:' there was little ornamentation, but in several places I observed that a sculptured lamb was a favourite headpiece to a child's grave. Reflecting upon the fact that most of us have to be buried somewhere, I came to the conclusion that the cemetery of San Francisco would be one of the pleasantest spots that could be chosen for the purpose.

A tramway leads thus far from the heart of the city, and a further ride or walk of a few miles over an admirable road brings us to the Cliff House on the edge of the sea. The greater part of the way is flanked by sandy hills, almost covered down to the edge of the road with innumerable plants of perennial lupines, in varieties of blue, white, pink, and yellow. In England these plants die down to the ground in winter, and are obliged to make a fresh start every spring; but the mildness of a Californian winter allows them to grow into great bushes, some of them as large as haycocks ready for carrying. These were all coming into bloom when we arrived in the country, but a few weeks later we saw them in perfection, when the dense thousands of brilliant flower-spikes in their various colours formed some of the most striking floral displays that can be imagined. A sharp bend of the road led us down in a few minutes to the verandah of the Cliff House, where the eye which had been dazzled with lupines for the last hour now had nothing to contemplate but the vast ocean which stretches over to Japan, five thousand miles away, without the smallest intervening land. The only exception is to be found in the Farallones and a few small island rocks which rise out of the sea about two hundred yards from the cliffs above which the hotel is built, and which in fact form the chief attraction towards that excellent establishment.

These islands of rock are the abode of a colony of several hundred sea-lions, *Otaria Stelleri*, whose behaviour and evolutions afford a fund of amusement to everybody, from the philosopher to the baby. We all know how popular a very similar animal has been of late years in the Zoological Gardens of London, but the islands opposite Cliff House are covered with others, and the blue rollers of the Pacific dash showers of spray over their lazy backs as they break against the well-worn rocks. Being a large family, of course they are of many sizes, amongst which our London friend would look very small. The larger ones must weigh, I should think, about as much as a cow; and there was one notable sovereign among them who went by the name of 'King Tom' or 'Ben Butler,' whose weight has been estimated at 2,000 lbs. Their abode is so near to the hotel that an accustomed visitor armed with a good binocular could soon learn to know many of their faces as a shepherd knows his sheep. Scores of them are enjoying themselves in the broken surf made by the long sleepy swell which is turned into white spray by contact with the rocks. When they have dined sufficiently on the innumerable fish, they clamber in their awkward fashion up the rough precipices; and the proceedings of the next few minutes depend upon their respective size and importance in the community.

The nature of the rocks prevents their seeing far ahead of them, but they take the best places they can find for drying themselves in the sun and digesting their meal. They come out of the water black and shiny; but if they are left to dry in peace they soon assume a dull brown appearance. It often, however, happens that 'King Tom,' or some other leading member of the family, comes out intent on the same purpose. Woe be to a youngster who has taken possession of a spot which the sovereign has set his heart on! A loud roar and violent shaking of the head gives quite sufficient notice to the intruder that he must turn out, and out he turns panic-stricken for a header into the sea. Meanwhile the great man establishes himself comfortably to dry in the sun, and by an occasional sleepy bellow warns all intruders not to disturb his repose.

Here again the American Government has shown its good taste and sentimental feeling. In the same way as they have converted the Yosemité Valley and the Big Trees into inalienable parks for the benefit of the nation, so have they protected these creatures by law from all sort of molestation by the public, well knowing that

SEA LIONS, NEAR SAN FRANCISCO.

some of their enterprising citizens would not leave King Tom and his family many days of life if they were permitted to get at them. No one is allowed to disturb them, or even to bring a boat near enough to frighten them ; and with this compact they live at peace and are content to amuse the visitors to Cliff House, who enjoy their luncheon and cigars in the verandah of the hotel while they watch the performances of the sea-lions on their sacred rocks. One day we heard an unusual bellowing amongst the monsters, and saw that it was caused by a sailing-boat which had come out from the Golden Gate and approached nearer than usual. Till then I never knew how many of the creatures there must be ; but, as the boat drew nearer to them, they seemed to emerge from every cranny of the rocks, and with terrific roarings cast themselves violently down steep places into the sea. The people on board, seeing what a tumult they had created, put helm up and went about, as if they were afraid of being boarded by phocal pirates, while we were naturally delighted by the strange scene. The Cliff House is deservedly a great attraction to the dwellers in San Francisco ; and, apparently, the correct thing is to drive a friend out to it in a very light-built carriage, with large wheels not much thicker than a finger, behind a pair of horses trotting about fifteen or sixteen miles an hour. There are always excellent eatables, pleasant rooms, and, down below, a charming walk or gallop over one of the purest sandy beaches in the world.

Almost our first expedition from San Francisco across the water was to San Rafael and the very pretty hill country on the north side of the Golden Gate. One of the small but very fast steamers which traverse the land-locked bay in all directions soon took us over to San Quentin, where we had an opportunity of looking at a Chinese establishment for catching and drying shrimps upon a large scale. Then a little railway took us quickly up to San Rafael, a delightful appendage to the great city. We had made friends with the captain of the steamboat, who went up with us in the train and very kindly showed us something of the place. All was new, very new, but evidently growing quickly; and the green valley, backed up by wooded hills, would be an immensely valuable property to hold now with an eye to a speedy future. We got some luncheon and walked westwards towards a range of hills studded with pines and other forest trees, which promised a view from the summit. The road wound up from the green meadows through a park-like region, shaded in many places by groups of 'Redwood,' or *Sequoia sempervirens*, a very elegant conifer peculiar to the coast range of California. A further interest attaches to it from the fact that this name was given to it before the discovery of the so-called *Wellingtonia*, which was properly named *Sequoia gigantea* by the botanists on account of its near resemblance to the *S. sempervirens*. The original name was given in honour of a peculiarly intelligent half-breed Cherokee Indian who was called Sequoyah; he had, among other things, devised something of an alphabet and written language for his tribe, and was therefore called by an American punster 'the best red- (-read) man out.' Such is the origin of the received scientific name of the 'Big Trees,' as they are universally called in their own country; and we can hardly complain if the Americans are unwilling to designate one of the greatest of their own national wonders by the name of a British hero.

Here and there oak-woods bordered the road, and the banks were full of flowers. For the first time I found the beautiful blue *Anchusa* in a wild state, together with a scarlet columbine, yellow *Enothera*, yellow borage, two species of blue iris, a kind of dwarf sunflower, and lovely beds of both the blue and white *Nemophylla*. Besides these, in the same neighbourhood we found abundance of *Dodecatheon*, very much like a cyclamen in appearance, and called 'shooting-stars' by the American ladies. A little farther on, I made a dash down a grassy slope among the thickets, to see what was the meaning of some brilliant orange patches on the hill-side, and to my delight I found the *Eschholzia* of our gardens in its native splendour, larger and fuller in colour than we find it in cultivation. Close by were large branches of 'Southernwood,' *Artemisia arborescens*, the perfume of which reminded me of many an old fashioned garden and cottage-door in England, where it is fondly cherished under the name of 'Old Man.' This was a very satisfactory batch of flowers for the first short country walk in California, and when we got to the top of the ridge we found a variety of new trees, including the *Madrona*, as it is called throughout the country. It is properly speaking a magnificent species of *Arbutus*, covered when we were there with dense clusters of white bell-like blossom, which with its dark foliage and smooth red stem makes a very handsome figure in almost every part of the coast ranges that we saw. I was in the humour to enjoy in all thankfulness and happiness a lovely view from the highest point of our ridge, whence we overlooked a broad wooded valley, out of which rose up in the next distance the graceful summit of Tamal Pais, about 3,000 feet above the ocean immediately behind it. We intended to take another long day to ascend Tamal Pais, and to look upon the Pacific from its crown, but time and fate were against us, and the project came to the same end as many other 'good intentions.'

Another line of steamers runs over to Oakland, on the opposite, or eastern, side of the bay, where is the terminus of the Great Pacific Railway, and where the train is ready to take you to New York, a distance of 3,300 miles, in a week, if you like travelling continuously day and night for that period. We, however, now only wanted to inspect Oakland itself and the neighbourhood, which is the favourite and most fashionable resort of those who like something of a country house not too far off to prevent their daily business in the city. Oakland is rightly named, and, even amidst the exigencies of building, the inhabitants have left enough oaks in and about the town and surroundings to form shady groves and break the monotony of the streets. We walked on about three miles to see the buildings of the new Berkely University, which are well placed on the lower slopes of a line of grassy hills facing the bay and commanding a good view across it. There were two large handsome blocks with excellent lecture-rooms, and all proper appliances; but all was perfectly new, and had scarcely escaped from the hands of the builders and carpenters. There appear to be two rival theories concerning building in countries subject, like California, to earthquakes. One is to make use of light materials, so that, if the structure falls, comparatively little harm may be done : the other is to build in such solid fashion that nothing short of a very extraordinary earthquake can knock the place down at all. On the coast of Peru, the earthquake-power has shown itself in such irresistible might that the former of the two methods is almost uniformly employed, and those who have learnt by experience build low wooden houses which might fall to pieces quietly like a house of cards ; but in San Francisco, where earthquakes, though frequent, are not severe, there appears to be a division of opinion. The Berkely University is built upon the solid principle, and long may it remain so ! There are also now many large stone houses in the city ; but the greater part of them, including the hotels, are chiefly built of wood, coated with paint and sand so as to look exactly like stone. The wood theory appears to me to have a great deal to say for itself as long as the houses are small, but I think that I would quite as soon be knocked on the head by a big stone as by a beam of wood, if it fell from a fourth-floor elevation. Moreover, for my own part I am much more afraid of fire than earthquakes, and the chances of being roasted alive, especially in a dry climate, are greatly increased by living in a wooden house. At the back and by the sides of the University large grounds were being laid out with roads and paths among the masses of wild lupines and *eschholzias*; and quantities of young *eucalyptus* and various trees and shrubs had been planted, so that, though the place is very bare at present, there will soon be Academic groves for the future philosophers of California. We followed up the grassy side of a small adjoining glen, watered by a rippling stream and

P

shaded by trees, among which I made my first acquaintance with the Californian laurel, or *Tetranthéra Californica.* This large and handsome tree is in appearance very like our bay-tree grown to a huge size, and the scent of the leaves is almost as good, though not so lasting : the wood is something like that of our walnut, but more varied both in colour and marking, and is deservedly taking a high place in the estimation of the cabinet-makers. We climbed the hill behind the University, over long slopes of grass and flowers, much to the alarm of many ' gophers,' a species of rodent about half-way between a rat and a rabbit, who bolted into their holes before we could get near enough for a close inspection. Down below us was spread a broad expanse of the rich alluvial soil, still rather damp from the effects of an unusually wet winter, but green with thick growing crops of young wheat ; and far away over the great bay and its islands we had a lovely view of the green and wooded hills which cluster around Tamal Pais. We soon began to find that we had come to California at the best season of the year for seeing it. In April and May it is like a vast garden, and the climate is equally enjoyable in either town or country. During the succeeding months of full summer, the country becomes very hot, dusty, and burnt up ; while, by a strange contrast, in the city of San Francisco midsummer is the season when people shiver with cold ! The cause of this anomaly is that in those months a cold north-westerly wind sets in through the Golden Gate, and folds the city in a continuously cold and raw fog, whilst everything is in the blaze of sunshine on the other side of the bay. Thus it comes to pass that in a place of about the same latitude as Sicily people wrap themselves up in the month of July.

The Chinese element is naturally one of the most striking features in San Francisco, and we felt obliged to pay some attention to the 'Heathen Chinee' before leaving for the interior of the country. One section of the city is specially designated the Chinese Quarter, where a sudden turn round a corner brings the astonished visitor into the presence of the Celestials. Their habitual conservatism induces them to make everything look as if they were at home. I was told by one of the chief police officials that there are about 25,000 of them in the city. Here they have streets entirely filled with Chinese houses, covered with the flaunting flags, lanterns, scrolls, and gay devices which give the towns of China the appearance of being decorated for a perennial fête-day or fair. Here they have their theatre, their joss-houses, their brilliant shops full of precious wares from the East, and their filthy stalls of garbage to dine upon. Here, too, they have their opium-shops and dens of debauchery which exercise the minds of the Californian police, and which are considered unsafe for curious visitors excepting under their protection. One evening we went to their theatre, and I vowed to myself that I would never go to a Chinese theatre again. Nor will I. For a quarter of an hour the extraordinary novelty of such a scene was great enough to overpower the general feeling of disgust, but the latter soon turned the tables, and in half an hour I was glad to beat a retreat. We were helped by the presence of a detective accustomed to the language and manners of John Chinaman, who explained to us something of the plot and action of the play, which appeared to be at a rather indecent stage of its protracted existence. The constant banging of gongs and strident noises from detestable instruments of music, accompanied with harsh and screaming voices; the grotesque masks, the vile painting, the ceaseless rushing about the stage, the terrific combats, the yells of the foes, the universal hubbub, all conspired to drive me out of this temple of Chinese dramatic art with the sensation of having suffered from a hideous nightmare. The only redeeming feature was a group of tumblers, who, for no apparent reason, came forwards during a serious part of the performances, and did their particular work right well. They turned summersaults over the tables, alighting on the very tops of their heads, and thence taking a fresh departure with such astounding coolness that I could not help wondering at the thickness of their skulls.

The chief part of the clothes-washing of San Francisco is done by Chinamen, and is done so admirably that I often wish for their aid in London when I contemplate the contents of my shirt-drawer. In every part of the suburbs are small houses with boards at the door announcing that Loo Sing and Ah Sam, or other gentlemen with similar names, devote themselves to taking in washing. They are masters of their craft, and send home the linen as white as snow and as smooth as glass. The ironing process struck me as peculiar. Each shirt when ready was placed on the table in front of an industrious little man, who had a hot iron on one side of him and a bowl of clean water on the other; he dipped his mouth into the water, and by some curious action of the lips squirted out the contents in a spreading shower of almost invisible dew; then down came the iron and the result was perfection. If these useful heathens were not there for 'washee washee' purposes, I do not know who would fill their places in a country where there is a great prejudice against domestic drudgery. In California it is very difficult to get your boots cleaned decently; and even in contemptible little inns a charge of twenty-five cents, or a shilling, is made for the luxury. Many gentlemen travellers take their own brush and blacking among their luggage, and do the work for themselves; but I fancy that many men who could clean their own boots respectably would collapse before the difficulties of washing and ironing a shirt. The Chinese in California have also done good service to the State in making its roads and railways by their cheap labour, and I have heard it said that the Great Pacific Railway could never have been made without them; but the individual working citizen is selfishly ungrateful for this; he simply vows vengeance against the Chinese for underselling him in the labour market, and no one need be surprised if he hears some day of a serious attack being made upon them by those who want to raise their own wages and are not very particular about having their shirts washed.

Meanwhile there has been a very large and continuous emigration from Canton and other parts of Southern China, which has been an important source of income to the Pacific Steam Ship Company, whose vessels sometimes bring over 1,000 or 1,200 at a time. The whole arrangements for this traffic are carried out on fixed principles, which would be very well worthy of imitation elsewhere.

The Chinese have often been laughed at for their worship of ancestors and other old-fashioned ways, but these things are in truth only illustrations of the intense love of family and country which pervades their nature. If they are induced by the hope of profit and future wealth to leave their country for awhile, their next care is to see that they go back to it, dead or alive. Firmly convinced of the superiority of China over the rest of the world, they refuse to take root in other lands where they may have a temporary abode; and they are by no means prepared to admire the American or any other Constitution. It is only on certain conditions that they condescend to make themselves useful and hoard up dollars among the Californians. Their coming over is a matter of solemn contract; and, dead or alive, they go back to China.

The Celestial emigrants in a foreign land are under the care and guardianship of the Hweis, or guilds, representing their native provinces; who look after their interests in this life and take care of their bodies after death. If they die on shore they are buried in a spot set apart for them for a period of two years, I think, by the end of which time the Californian Government is content to let their bones be dug up and properly prepared for sending home to their friends. If they die on board one of the Company's steamers, it becomes the duty of the surgeon to embalm or prepare their bodies by some similar process, and to have them put in coffins to be kept safe till they reach port. If one of them were thrown overboard there would be a mutiny at once, and a cessation of the Company's trade in carrying them for the future. There are many amusing stories of Chinese devices to combine economy with affection by carrying home their departed relations without paying for them. The purser of the 'China' told me that a quartermaster came to him one day and reported that some of the Chinese had got very queer-looking baggage down below in their berths. He insisted on overhauling it, and found sundry travelling-bags full of bones, which proved to be the remains of scraped friends surreptitiously concealed among their bed-clothes. This was considered a very mean trick, and resented accordingly. When properly sent home in coffins they are treated with the greatest possible respect, and the inviolability of a coffin is so piously maintained at the Chinese ports, that, as I have been told, it is sometimes made use of as a convenient means of smuggling goods in coffins through the Custom-houses instead of honestly carrying dead men.

The Chinese are as fond of saving money as the peasantry of France, and generally they seem to use it for very sensible and creditable purposes. Sometimes one of them, when he has hoarded together a comfortable sum, will take it over to China and buy a house for his father and mother, or do anything that may be considered most desirable for the benefit of his family; and he will then go back to California and make another fortune for himself. If he wants to invest his money in a wife, he commissions a friend in the old country to get him the best he can find for 300 or 400 dollars, or whatever sum may be specified as the highest price that he can afford to give. Her passage also has to be paid out of the money; and, as I do not suppose that Chinese peasants indulge in photographs, he must look with some doubt and anxiety for the appearance of his expected bride. There was a story that one of them was being laughed at for the unusual ugliness of her who came out to be his partner for life; but he answered, 'Never you mind, handsome wife cost too muchee money, and kick up dam bobbery all the time too.'

The only 'antiquity' of the neighbourhood is the mission church at Dolores, where the visitor is soon reminded of St. Francis in connection with San Francisco. The church was built in 1776, and its centenary will therefore be identical with that of the American Republic; but in the general rejoicings I fear that the Saint will be made to look very small in comparison with General Washington. The building is a very poor affair, surrounded by a neglected churchyard, robed in weeds and disorder, and making a painful contrast with the neatness and beauty of the cemetery on the other side of the city. Thence with the aid of a map we found our way to the Mission rock through a new suburban district, where houses were rising like mushrooms in every direction, while the untouched land was gay with flowers, conspicuous among which were beds of the Californian violet, golden yellow in colour with a very handsome brown eye. A beautiful blue iris was abundant in moist places. Hence a tramroad is carried over a wooden causeway back towards the city; and, as we happened to come in for a windy day, we had a good opportunity of testing the misery of these wooden roads. Pines of many descriptions supply the timber for all ordinary purposes in California, and wood of this kind when subjected to horses' feet breaks up into chips as thick as small straws, which when driven by a strong wind, and mixed with all kinds of small sand and dusty rubbish, makes a most irritating compound: it fills up eyes and ears, smothers one's clothes, and produces slow torture as it works its way down the back of the neck.

Altogether I found the tramcars by far the most disagreeable institution in California. They run through the city in many directions, it must be admitted, and they are generally neat and clean; but the cause of complaint is the way of managing them. At first starting all looks comfortable enough to the passengers who take their seats; but, as the car pulls up every minute or two, it soon becomes evident that the conductor's object is to put as many human beings into it as it can by any means be made to contain. The seats on both sides are soon crammed so that it is impossible to move an elbow, and the next lot have to stand between them till there is no more standing room. When the seats are entirely full, women do not hesitate to crowd in and stand, as a sort of challenge to the men to get up and make room for them; and if the hint is not soon taken they have various ways of pushing, squeezing, or parasol-poking which generally succeed in making one of the recalcitrants turn out. Even this is not all, for when every part of the inside is full, another batch of people crowd on the steps, cling to anything they can lay hold upon, and hang behind like a swarm of bees in such a way as to make escape difficult for those who want to get out. I often left the cars and walked rather than run the risk of suffocation. What would be said in England if conductors were allowed to fill an omnibus on the same principle as would be employed in stuffing a coal-sack? It is astonishing that the people submit to such treatment with equanimity; the only explanation I can think of is that they are all in such a habit of being in a hurry that they sympathize with fellow-creatures who absolutely refuse to wait a few minutes for the next car. I must, however, give them the additional credit of being apparently a very kind-hearted people; and, at all events, San Francisco is the only city in the world where on several occasions I have asked a question of a perfect stranger in the street, who, not being able to give an answer directly, has most goodnaturedly invited me to come with him to his own office where he could find what I wanted by referring to a directory, though he had to go considerably out of his way.

Another feature of national character which struck me very forcibly was the remarkable frankness and politeness manifested by the officials of San Francisco in many various departments. One day we merely presented our cards at the door of the Mint, and asked if we might be allowed to see the establishment. With scarcely a minute's delay, and without asking any sort of question, a very pleasant and intelligent officer led us through all the departments, remarking that we were lucky in the day, as they were engaged in coining gold twenty-dollar pieces. He called up men to show us each of the processes in action; from the rolling of long bars of gold and bringing them to the exact thickness by delicate machinery, to the punching out of the plain pieces of metal, and the final coining and stamping in machines, each of which turned out eighty to the minute. This coin, worth about four English guineas, is by far the handsomest I ever saw in circulation; the taste of the design and the beauty of the execution appeared simply perfect. Our *cicerone* took all possible pains to show and explain to us the details of everything. Nobody seemed to consider us thieves *in posse*, and we left the place with a feeling on my part of wonder as to whether in any other country a perfectly unknown foreigner, bent upon a similar errand, would have been so well received and so kindly entreated.

CHAPTER X.

A good pace over the Bay—Calistoga—The 'dare-devil' Coachman of California—Corn and Wine—Poison-oak—Pine Flat and a Tragedy—A long jolting to the Geysers—Close to Gehenna—Nothing to eat—White Sulphur Springs—A Happy Valley—Californian Quail—The Poison-oak again—Return to San Francisco.

LIFE IN SAN FRANCISCO was thoroughly enjoyable, and great was the temptation to linger in such good quarters; but we were thirsting to see the marvels of the inland country, which through the medium of photography invited us every day as we walked along Montgomery Street. The Geysers, the Sulphur Springs, the Yosemité Valley, the Big Trees, and the snows of the Sierra Nevada must all be seen before we should again tempt the perils of the ocean.

Accordingly, early in April, making up a party of four, we started by a steamer at 4 P.M. to cross the bay to Vallejo, which, though said to be twenty-six miles distant, was reached in one hour and a half. This is a very lively pace, and would appear impossible to anyone who saw for the first time one of these clumsy-looking vessels, which look about as incapable of speed as one of the old yellow hulks that may be seen near any of Her Majesty's dockyards. Their looks belie them; for underneath their huge upper works they have fine lines, and they go like the wind as soon as they are started. As far as comfort is concerned, they leave nothing to desire. There is an abundance of room, and seats of every description; every convenience for eating, drinking, and smoking; with the additional luxury of a barber's shop. I was compelled to assume that many of these busy people can find no time for such trumpery work as shaving except when *in transitu*, for I always observed that on board the local steamers a rush was made to the barber almost before we left the quay. The lower deck accommodates piles of cargo, mixed up with poultry, carts, horses, machinery, Chinamen, and other useful articles. In one of them I saw a huge tub of live fish, with several people employed in changing the water continually by baling out and pouring in fresh supplies.

On arriving at Vallejo we found a train ready to take us through the fertile Napa Valley to Calistoga, which we reached a little before 9 P.M. in a state of complete resignation to an excellent supper at the hotel. This establishment is rather peculiar. All feeding-operations are conducted in the principal structure; but after supper we were conducted to our sleeping quarters in one of several neat cottages, built along the edge of a very unfinished and imperfect sort of garden, ornamented with a few scattered palm-trees and flower-beds, conspicuous among which stands a tall trophy-like pile of huge blocks and stumps of various kinds of stony wood collected from the neighbouring petrified forest. We were getting into a region of natural curiosities and prodigies; and a petrified forest sounds very well in connection with hot sulphur springs, boiling geysers, and other indications of the arch enemy of mankind.

The cottage was clean and comfortable, and contained four or five neat little bedrooms, which we were left to divide among ourselves as we pleased. There were no symptoms of anybody to answer the bell, if a bell had been there; we were left entirely to our own devices and our own company; and after the evening pipe and gossip we had an undisturbed sleep in what seemed at that season of the year the quietest place that could well be imagined. Next morning we got up early and went to the hotel for breakfast at half-past six o'clock, as we were informed that the coach would start for the Geysers at seven, under the personal guidance of a celebrated man named Foss, known familiarly as the 'famous dare-devil coachman' of California; and, as we were almost the first pioneer party of the season when the roads were sure to be bad, we expected some excitement under such auspices. Presently we saw a large *char-à-banc* approaching us with the great man on the box driving six horses, two abreast; and, as there was a round flower-bed in front of the hotel, he gave us a first touch of his quality by driving round this at full speed, so that for a moment the wheelers were seen going in exactly the opposite direction to that of the coach. He pulled up at the door, flung down his reins, and descended to receive a morning greeting from a little circle of admiring friends. And really it was a pleasure to an Englishman to look at his big burly frame and honest rosy face, reminding me of a jovial English farmer rather than of anything that we are usually accustomed to associate with the United States. He was a cheery companion and good fellow, and I trust I need not describe him in the past tense;

but soon after our return to England I saw in a Californian paper the account of an accident on the same road that we travelled over with him, which was of such a nature as to make me tremble for the fate of the jolly 'dare-devil.' He in some way or other lost command of his team, and they dashed down a hill-side, upsetting the coach, smashing the harness, and scattering the passengers in all directions. They were picked up by degrees, grievously wounded, if not dead; poor Foss was very seriously injured, and four of his six horses cleared out into the surrounding space.

On the present occasion, however, no thought of danger entered into our heads; and we started off merrily in company with about half a dozen other people. Soon after leaving Calistoga we began to see that a road in that part of the world has no connection with Macadam and stonebreakers. It is merely a broad line fenced off by wooden rails from the cultivated lands on each side of it; and in the spring, when the rich alluvial soil is still saturated with the winter snow and rain, the depth to which the wheels may sink is a matter of complete uncertainty. Through what is called Knight's Valley the country was very pretty, in spite of the many inroads which cultivators of the soil were making upon what was very lately the unsophisticated home of lovely Nature. Here were occasional flourishing farms, with clean happy-looking homes, surrounded by gardens and orchards of pears, apples, plums, peaches, and apricots, now all in sheets and masses of brilliant pink and white, and glorying in the warmth of the April sun. The greater part of the land is of course cleared and planted with corn and grape-vines;

but in many places the farmers have had the good sense as well as the good taste to leave some of the magnificent oaks and other forest-trees which formerly covered the country.

A great breadth of land is covered with vines, the newly-planted ones looking like thin walking-sticks, and the old ones cut back nearly to the ground in thick black stumps. The wine manufactures of California are becoming of very high importance, and I can testify to the excellence of several of them which we used to consume in the Grand Hotel. I took the opportunity of asking Foss and a fellow-passenger about the matter, and I was informed that wine costing the grower only thirty to fifty cents (from 1s. 3d. to 2s. English) per gallon is the same that is sold in the hotels for a dollar a bottle, which would give about 1,000 per cent. profit on the transaction. Not a bad trade, it would seem. Wheat-growing too ought to be tolerably profitable if, as I was told, a fairly good crop gives a yield of sixty bushels, or $7\frac{1}{2}$ quarters, per acre without the aid of manure. In course of time no doubt the natural soil must be greatly weakened, but the difficulty of manure will probably then be met by a great increase in the stock of animals. I have previously alluded to the enormous bunches of grapes exhibited occasionally in California; but before leaving the subject of its vines, I should like to quote a passage from a recent letter of the *Times* correspondent in those parts. 'Among other things to be sent to the Centennial Exhibition at Philadelphia is,' he says, ' the Montecito big grape-vine, from the Santa Barbara county, perhaps the largest vine in the world. It has been taken up and cut into sections and otherwise prepared for exhibition. The dimensions of this vine are fourteen inches in diameter at three feet from the ground, and nearer to the ground it has a diameter of eighteen inches, while its foliage has long covered a space equal to 10,000 square feet. Its produce has often reached the immense number of 7,500 clusters of an average weight of $1\frac{1}{2}$ lbs., or nearly 12,000 lbs. in the whole. Its age is between fifty and sixty years, and it has for several years shown symptoms of decaying vigour.' It appears, however, to have thrown up an offshoot sixteen years ago which has already nearly equalled its parent, by producing last year between 8,000 and 10,000 lbs. of grapes. California, like Chile, began with mining; but, like her, is finding her truest wealth in the resources of the vegetable kingdom.

There was, however, one product of the vegetable world against which the 'dare-devil' warned us with an earnestness which surprised me. The road had been getting worse and worse, until at a part where it was carried along the sloping side of a hill covered with grass and bushes mixed with occasional trees, he found his leaders sinking so deeply in the mud that he doubted the propriety of trying to take the loaded carriage through it. At his request we all got out to walk along the grassy slope, and rejoin him after a few hundred yards, while his team floundered through the mire. But we had hardly set foot upon the bank when, pointing to some small bushes, he implored us for Heaven's sake not to touch them. He said they were 'poison-oaks,' and were never so dangerous as at that time of year. They were mean-looking bushes, just opening their young leaves, in appear-

Q

ance much like those of our blackberry; but I soon found that no fabled upas-tree ever inspired more fear than the 'poison-oak' produced in the minds of the natives. We were assured by our fellow-passengers that a touch from it would produce boils and blains, and poison all the blood in the system; and one of them declared that for two years he had suffered nearly all the ills that human flesh is heir to in consequence of unluckily coming in contact with one of them. Their stories were so circumstantial that we kept at a respectful distance from the dreaded bushes; but, as on subsequent occasions we found ourselves inadvertently among whole thickets of them, where both hands and face must have been in contact with them at every step, without any evil consequences happening to either of us, I am compelled to suppose either that the effects were exaggerated, or that some constitutions are much more sensitive to the poison than others are. The plant is no more like an oak than a currant-bush : it is one of the *Rhus*, or Sumach, family, the *Rhus toxicodendron*; and its name clearly implies its poisonous nature; but I cannot understand why it did not poison us. It is rather an interesting, though by no means handsome, plant. It is naturally a creeper, and attaches itself like ivy to a tree or rock when it finds one at hand, and in this way it grows freely to a considerable height: but it sows itself everywhere; and, when it grows upon an open hill-side or similar situation, it accommodates itself to circumstances and does the best it can, though the result is only a scraggy bush of five or six feet high. I have since talked about it to a physician in London, who says that the poisonous qualities of *Rhus toxicodendron* are well known in the Materia Medica; and that its dangerous qualities are undoubted if it comes in contact with a skin in any way damaged. We must therefore have been in a satisfactorily undamaged and unwounded state. A practical use of this detestable bush is the composition of a powder eminently destructive to fleas and other vermin. The Californians seemed to have a very genuine dread of it.

One of the best and prettiest of the isolated houses and gardens in the valley belonged to our distinguished coachman; and, when we stopped there to change horses, we were not a little disgusted to find that horses were not the only things to be changed. There was to be an end of the commodious glories of the big *char-à-banc*, the great man considering it too heavy for the rascally state of the road. We were to be jammed into two smaller traps in company with several other people; and we were deprived of half the very small amount of baggage which we had brought for the excursion, and which was to be left at the house till our return next day. We were packed three on each seat where there was only room for two, and I was pinioned against the most atrocious little wretch of the 'Jefferson Brick' type that I have ever encountered. Almost a beardless boy, he displayed a noisy bumptiousness and vulgarity that were simply astounding, and I believe I was only restrained from throwing him out of the carriage by my doubts as to the legality of the action, and the strong probability of his putting a bullet into me the moment he recovered his legs. The Americans, as I have already remarked in the matter of tramcars, seem to have no objection to overcrowding in their vehicles; and the squeezing in of extra passengers is submitted to with a calmness which would be inconceivable in England. As we advanced over a road which was getting continually worse and worse, the fact of our being pressed like herrings in a barrel to both sides of the carriage had a very disagreeable effect. The wheels on one side were often up to the axles in mud of seemingly bottomless depth, while those on the other side were on firm ground; and on these occasions the luckless people on the lower side felt that they must inevitably be capsized; the driver would look over his shoulder and shout to us to throw ourselves as much as we could to the other side, and we did so to the utmost of our ability; but again and again it seemed that nothing could prevent the wheels from breaking and the carriage from turning over, often on the side of a hill where an upset would have been fatal to somebody; but at the last moment an encouraging yell to the horses, accompanied by an exciting larrup from the whip, always contrived to pull us through the difficulty in a manner which would astonish an ordinary coachman. Without any worse result than constant alarms we emerged from the worst part of the country, and found ourselves about noon on the good turf of Pine Flat, where we halted for about half an hour. Providence was merciful enough even to preserve the objectionable youth, and leave him free for further mischief, a doubtful blessing to the American community.

Pine Flat is the top of a kind of grassy pass over the hills, and was, when we saw it, clothed in the sweet fresh verdure of early spring. Scattered clumps of fir-trees among the grassy openings formed a kind of advanced guard to the forests on each side, and there were manifest signs of their becoming still more scattered, and dispersed in the form of planks. A few, very few, new wooden huts adorned the place, of which one, I think, was devoted to stabling purposes; two were inscribed with the names of land-agents, who did not, however, appear to be ready in their offices for the purpose of selling the surrounding land; and two, at all events, were devoted to the sale and consumption of liquors. We had been bumped about for a good many hours since a light and early breakfast; we had had every muscle in our bodies strained in hanging out of the vehicle, first on one side and then on the other, to prevent a wholesale smash; our boots were wetted by going on foot in places where even the 'dare-devil' thought it safer for us to alight; and I need hardly say that we stepped with triumphant joy across the elastic turf into a hut where we were soon supplied with light refreshments by an amiable old man who professed, as became his years, to have been one of the original pioneers of California. We were greatly comforted by the time when fresh horses were ready for the forward march.

It seemed, moreover, that the worst of our troubles had come to an end. Clearing the region of fir-trees and turf, we soon began a long gradual ascent over a more rocky line of country, where the comparative hardness and cleanness of the road made walking pleasant for several miles, while horses and carriages wound their way slowly upwards over a sinuous route among the hills. Trees here became rather scarce, but the hills were for the most part covered with what is universally known in California as 'chaparal,' a dense undergrowth of shrubs and bushes, conspicuous among which is the *Manzanita*, a kind of arbutus (*Arctostaphylos glauca*), so named from the Spanish diminutive of *manzana*, an apple, in reference to the small berries with which it is supplied. There are also immense quantities of disagreeably thorny bushes, which, in company with the poison-oak, have hitherto prevented the full exploration of vast regions of the Californian coast range. A great excitement had lately arisen about discoveries of quicksilver in this region, and we saw many indications of the peculiar red rock (cinnabar) from which it is extracted. We passed near a house occupied, I believe, by some of the people connected with these mines, and stopped to deliver letters to a man who came out for them; but we had no idea at the time that this place would soon become famous for a remarkable tragedy.

A few months after our departure from California one of the best, most successful, and most popular of the photographers in San Francisco was furnished by a discontented nurse with letters which left him no room to doubt the infidelity of his wife with a young Englishman, whose adventures and escapades numbered more than the hairs on his head. The photographer heard that he had gone up country to the quicksilver mines beyond Pine Flat. He went by steamboat and railway to Calistoga; ordered a trap, and tried his revolver by the way. He arrived by night at the place which I have spoken of, and asked to see the man he wanted, with whom he wished to speak for a minute on matters of business. The latter came to the entrance, and the photographer, simply saying 'I have brought you a message from—my wife,' shot him dead as he pronounced the last words. The photographer was tried for murder, and the Californian papers, afterwards sent to me by a friend, described a curious state of things connected with the trial. Every one of the jurymen empannelled was challenged as to whether he had any decided opinions for or against capital punishment. Every one who expressed an opinion decidedly on either side was rejected: a jury of neutrals was chosen to hear the case, and they found a verdict of 'Not guilty.'

Uphill and downhill, sometimes riding and sometimes walking, we followed many a turn of the twisting road between the hills amongst rather dreary and uninteresting scenery, till at last a long and continuous descent brought us down again to the region of fine trees; and a sudden stench of sulphurous fumes proclaimed that we were near our destination. Presently we stopped at the door of a queer-shaped country hotel, and thankfully descended from the detestable vehicle. The distance was said to be only twenty-eight miles, and we had spent eight hours and a half in struggling over the road. Moreover, we had had nothing to eat since our very early breakfast, and looked for substantial refreshment in addition to the luxury of stretching our limbs, which were cramped with oversqueezing. However, it was not to be. The barbarous people of the house said that the dinner would be at six o'clock, and positively refused to give us any food whatever till that time. We were naturally irritated by such a heartless proceeding, and by the utter indifference to the comfort of visitors which evidently reigned in the whole establishment. Remonstrance was useless, and there was no rival house to appeal to. The owners knew that everybody who came there was in a *cul-de-sac*, from which there was no possibility of escape till the next day, and chuckled over their victims in the same spirit as that which must animate a spider when a fly tumbles into his web. It was four o'clock, and we had to spend the time till dinner in a visit to the Geysers, under the guidance of a young showman with a thick stick, whose sickly and miserable appearance testified strongly against spending a life amongst the intolerable fumes and stenches of the under world.

Crossing a small stream ornamented with some handsome ferns, we were in a few minutes at the entrance of a steeply inclined and irregular rocky ravine, extending upwards for about a quarter of a mile. In following up a slight path through this place it was quite impossible to avoid the consciousness of being unpleasantly near to the infernal regions. The ravine is bursting with jets of steam; its rocks bristle with sulphur, alum, magnesia, and pure Epsom salts: in some places the earth seems bubbling like a saucepan, and in others it groans and grunts like the Devil at home, as he ought to be in a place where every spot is peculiarly dedicated to his comfort and convenience. The sickly showman pointed out the Devil's kitchen, and the Devil's armchair, his office, his laboratory, and his pulpit! Then there is the Witches' Cauldron, a darksome hole which looks as if some one were perpetually boiling tons of walnut-pickle in it. A little higher up are the Steamboat Geyser and Whistling Geyser, giving forth volumes of steam and dismal roarings; and in one of them some ingenious person has placed an iron pipe over the orifice in such a way as to improve the tune.

Throughout the whole ravine the heat was very oppressive, and the odours were sickening. Moreover, the very soil seemed rotten, and the whole place suggested the notion of a plague-spot of foul disease on the fair body of our Mother Earth. To the foot it felt rather like hot suet-dumpling, with an admixture of stones; to the eye it presented many tints of dirty ochre, and in some places which we walked over rather gingerly, the firm pressure of a stick or umbrella-point went right through and tapped a stream of hot black ooze, which flowed sluggishly as if it were the blood of some fabled dragon. It is certainly a very wonderful place, and, as such, is well worth seeing for once in a way; but I would not recommend a very fat man to try it, as he might possibly break through into the Tartarian pie. For my own part I was not very sorry to emerge at the head of the valley, and preferred turning to the right over a fresh grassy hill and finding a new way home with one of my companions, instead of traversing Avernus again with its by no means interesting or agreeable *cicerone*.

I do not know if the fumes of sulphur and other abominations promote appetite, or whether our hunger was naturally due to the fact that we had had nothing to eat since early morning; but I do know that we were remarkably ready to enjoy the expected dinner, and that we were most lamentably disappointed. When at last we sat down to table in a shabby room we found the repast to consist of nothing but indifferent eggs and ham, as hard as iron, with bread *ad libitum* by way of an *entrée*. We fell back upon smoking in the evening; but, need I say that we were rather sulky after such treatment till we were consigned to miscroscopically small rooms where the only comfort was that the beds were clean ? Early next morning we had some ham and eggs, the only change from eggs and ham, for breakfast, and started to return to Calistoga by the way that we came. We observed a conspicuous notice to the effect that boots might be cleaned on payment of twenty-five cents : mine were very dirty, but I would rather have carried off all the mud in a Suffolk turnip-field than let the inhospitable natives of this Californian Inferno glory in the acquisition of a shilling more by cleaning them. It is true that we were rather early in the season ; but there were several other visitors besides ourselves, and there seemed to be no wish to oblige and no idea of apologising for deficiencies. It was a strange contrast to the pleasant and delightful ways of the hotels at San Francisco. We left the land of smells in the distance behind us; crawled up the long slopes to the land of hills ; had some more of the veteran's beer at Pine Flat ; struggled once more through ruts in unfathomable mud, girt about with divers flowers; recovered our baggage at Foss's house ; and rattled gaily along through the vineyards and peach-groves of Knight's Valley to the hotel at Calistoga, which we reached about two o'clock, in time for the starting of the train southwards.

We retraced our steps in that direction only as far as the St. Helena station, from which a very pretty drive of about two miles brought us to the establishment of the White Sulphur Springs, which are frequented for sanitary purposes as well as for the picturesqueness of the situation. Here we found everything in delightful contrast to the disagreeables of the Geysers hotel. The place is kept by Mr. Alstrom, a Swede, and is a very delightful retreat from the bustle of the world. The main building stands a little back from a road which follows the course of a pretty river winding between hills not unlike those of Matlock on a large scale. Near this are the baths and taps of the hot sulphur springs, said to be as wholesome to the body as they are disgusting to the taste. On the other side of an open space are the public dining-room, bar, and reading-room; and a little farther are several small detached cottages, with a few peach-trees in front. We were consigned to one of these called the 'Laurel,' where we spent several very pleasant days. There was a neatly furnished sitting-room with three or four bed-rooms opening out of it, and we had the house to ourselves; so that, after being out all day and then disposing of dinner in the public *salle à manger*, we retreated to our own cottage for a rubber of whist by the side of a comfortable wood fire.

We were not long in finding a delightful rivulet babbling down behind the establishment, like a bright trout-stream in Hampshire; and, crossing this by a plank bridge, we followed up its course till the faint path lost itself among the woods of a peaceful valley terminated by a waterfall among a wild scene of fallen rocks, huge trees lifting their heads to Heaven, and ruined trunks that had crashed down towards the stream with the downfall of the banks whereon they had lived for ages. There was a peculiar charm about the silence and solitude of this wildly beautiful spot; untouched by man, it recalled stories of Indians who have long been driven from their old haunts, and it seemed a fitting place for the wildest adventures of our old friends 'Hawk-eye' and the 'Last of the Mohicans.' There was not a sound but that of falling water, as we wandered beneath the dark shade of oaks, or stopped to measure the stem of some gigantic conifer. Here were magnificent specimens of the Red-wood (*Sequoia sempervirens*), apparently of very great age, and of another kind of fir with immense cones, the name of which I am not acquainted with. In openings among the bushy undergrowth and rocky places of the sloping sides of the valley, and on cool shady banks of the stream, we found a great variety of choice ferns and flowers. Among the ferns that were perfectly new to me were two exquisite species of the *Platyloma* family, one of them almost as finely divided as if it were made of dark green lace. I have never seen these in any part of the world except in some of the Californian valleys. Among flowers I saw for the first time a large quantity of the *Trillium album*, whose three-petaled blossoms of snowy whiteness were frequently more than six inches in diameter. Another beauty of the valley was a tall Saxifrage with very delicate stalk, and a profusion of white flowers with a fringed edge. There were two forms of *Convillaria*, one of them with white star-shaped flowers instead of the usual bells; but among other beautiful novelties, that which I think most surprised me was a magnificent *Fritillaria*, with a tall spike of flower two or three feet high; the individual blossoms were almost the same in appearance and colour as our English fritillary, but instead of being single on each stalk they hung gracefully one above the other, to the number to about eight or ten.

We frequently explored the recesses of this delightful valley, diving among the bushes to look for flowers, or scrambling on the rocks for the chance of a new fern; and I am the more anxious to record its quiet charm because there were manifest signs that its solitudes would soon be more invaded. Already, at the lower end of it, preparation was being made for a road, and though this in itself may not much damage the beauty of the surrounding scenery, yet it will go a long way towards dissipating such dreams as I indulged in about the presence of Mohicans upon the scene. Who shall say how soon this enchanted spot may be turned into a Cockney garden with Ethiopian serenaders, instead of Uncas and Chingachgook, with the waterfall flaring in the light of many-coloured lamps like the unfortunate Giessbach, or illuminated like the Great Pyramid of Egypt for the Prince of Wales? *Absit omen!*

Two of our party took guns one day, and went to seek for adventures among the dense woods and thickets which clothe the hills forming the southern barrier of this favourite valley, with the hope of being able to descend into it on the other side. They found nothing to shoot, though they thought they saw the traces of a bear, whom it is probably fortunate that they did not come in collision with. *En revanche*, they lost their way, and had to make a heroic struggle down hill through a horribly thorny and dilapidating thicket, from which, after some hours, they emerged by dint of hard labour, and arrived at Laurel Cottage in such a condition that one pair of trousers at all events had to be thrown away at once, past all hope of redemption by any arts of the tailor. We all saw at different times among these hills sundry specimens of the Californian quail, which, however, it would have been as illegal to shoot then as it would be to kill a partridge in England at the same season of the year. These very pretty birds are entirely unlike the quail of Europe, and are ornamented with a black feathery crest which, widening towards the end, hangs over in a graceful curve above the beak.

While the sportsmen were trying their pluck and the endurance of their garments, I with our other friend followed up a narrow footpath behind the sulphur springs, which promised to lead us to the top of some very tempting hills rising above that side of the valley. Nor did the fair promise in any way delude us. Up and up we walked, among groves of trees and among sheets of many-coloured blossoms, as if we were in a continually ascending Richmond Park with the combined attractions of an endless flower-show. As Tennyson says in the 'Two Voices,'

> You scarce could see the grass for flowers.

Here, amongst other beauties, were three species of blue and white lupines in immense abundance, together with *Gilia tricolor*, *Collinsia bicolor*, and brilliant clumps of the golden *Eschscholtzia*; a lovely species of yellow tulip, purple larkspurs, Indian pinks, and scarlet columbines. Grand oak-trees were rejoicing in the first tender green of spring, and formed a beautiful contrast with masses of ilex and other evergreen shrubs and trees, conspicuous among which were some grand specimens of the 'madrona,' whose large shining leaves and countless clusters of white bell-like flowers covered them with beauty to the very summit. We wandered for some hours about the tops of these undulating hills, every point adding something fresh to the charming views around us, and introducing us to something new in the world of trees and flowers. It was with no small reluctance that we began our descent towards the valley, the general direction of which we knew, though we had lost all traces of a path. We left the region of park-like openings alternating with forest-trees, and presently found ourselves obliged to push our way down through thickets, much as if we were 'going with the beaters' in an English copse. Suddenly it occurred to me to look more closely at a leaf, and I was at once conscious of the fact that we were up to our necks in a mass of the much-dreaded 'poison-oak.' There was the enemy round to the right of us, round to the left of us, above us, and beneath us; pressing against our hands and tickling our noses as with outstretched arms we laboured to make our way. Unconsciously we had run into the jaws of *Rhus toxicodendron*, and were in the middle of the trap before we had a suspicion of it. We were philosophical enough to know that under these circumstances the fatal mischief was done already, if it were to be done at all; and we had no doubt in deciding to push ahead and take our chance of some of the awful consequences which had been predicted by our American friends. In due time we got home after a delightful ramble, only tempered by the reflection that after taking such a powerful dose of 'poison-oak' we were bound to be covered with boils and blains and other horrors in a day or two. Nothing, however, happened to either of us;

and we might say with Tom Ingoldsby in the 'Jackdaw of Rheims:'—

> But what gave rise
> To no little surprise,
> Was that nobody seemed one penny the worse.

So I will take my leave of this alarming vegetable in a spirit of gratitude for its gentle treatment of us, and with the hope of hearing more of its real properties from those who have had more experience of it.

We found another charming walk along a broad path cut on the side of deeply wooded hills, and leading for a few miles over the high land and among the forest looking down upon the valley of the waterfall, before reaching which it lost itself in dark and shady wilds. Some of the conifers here were magnificent, and the open spaces were as usual full of flowers. The lilac bunches of *Dodecatheon* raised their heads higher and more densely than usual, and several species of ferns were flourishing better than in the valleys beneath. Among these was a peculiarly handsome one, with waving fronds about five feet long, and in appearance very like the *Woodwardia radicans*: but in this excursion we had very little baggage and no materials for preserving plants. The more I saw of this delightful neighbourhood, the more I enjoyed it. The park-like hills, the noble trees, the countless flowers, the shady walks, and rippling streams, must make it a paradise in the hot Californian summer. When we saw it, it was waking into the lovely resurrection of a genial spring, and there were abundant signs of endless hunting-grounds for a botanist or a general lover of Nature in some of her sweetest forms. I was very loath to part from 'Laurel Cottage' and the many attractions and peaceful retreats round the White Sulphur Springs of Calistoga; but the inexorable hand of Time was pressing us upon the shoulder, forcing us into the railway, and driving us back to the crowded life of San Francisco. We had enjoyed some delightful glimpses of the pretty scenery of the coast ranges: we were now to make a fresh start towards the sublimer wonders of the Sierra Nevada.

CHAPTER XI.

Geographical comparison of Chile with California—Start for the Yosemité—Judging distances—Deserted Diggings—Lonely Chinamen near Mariposa—Skelton's—A lively Mule in the Forest—The 'Devil's Gulch' and the 'Bishop's Creek'—Hite's Cove and the Miners—The Demi-john defunct—A Miner's Inn—The Mule beaten—Fallen Rocks—Arrival in Yosemité Valley.

THERE IS A REMARKABLE SIMILARITY between the geographical position of Central California and that of Chile. The fertile plains of Chile extend for a distance of nearly 500 miles from north to south, and are enclosed between the vast wall of the Andes on the east and the comparatively insignificant coast range on the west. The great central valley of California, traversed by the Sacramento and San Joaquin rivers, is about 400 miles in length, and is also enclosed throughout that distance by a coast range on the west and the snowy range of the Sierra Nevada on the east. These two ranges gradually converge at each end, meeting on the north near Mount Shasta, in about the latitude of 41° N., and meeting at the other extremity near the Tejon Pass in about 35° S. The great plains of Chile extend through the almost exactly corresponding latitudes of the southern hemisphere, namely, from about 33° to 41° south latitude. The coast range of California is lowest in the middle, near the neighbourhood of San Francisco, where the Monte Diablo, with its 3,856 feet, and Mount Hamilton, with 4,400 feet, are the highest points. Northwards and southwards the elevation of this range rises considerably as it converges towards the main Sierra Nevada. Mount Shasta at the northern extremity is 14,400 feet above the sea; many peaks of the Sierra Nevada are from 12,000 to 14,000 feet; and the highest of them in the south, which is named Mount Whitney in honour of the head of the geological survey, rises to 15,000 feet.

The Sierra Nevada itself is only the western limit of the lofty mountainous plateaux which terminate on the east in the Rocky Mountains, properly so called, and which combine to form part of that marvellous mountain backbone of America which extends from Alaska to Patagonia, through more than a hundred degrees of latitude and sixty degrees of longitude, with a probable total length of about eight thousand miles! In the greater part of this distance it divides the vast continent so as to cut off a comparatively narrow belt of more or less arid climate from the boundless regions of luxuriance towards the Atlantic; and though California does not suffer from the amazing drought of Western Peru, Bolivia, and a great part of Chile, nevertheless a large part of the State is apt to endure a very parching heat for a considerable portion of the year, and, like its South American sisters, it is finding the value of irrigation. Like Chile, its first fortunes were derived from mines and minerals; and, like it also, it has become alive to the fact that a rich soil properly managed produces results better than gold in the manifold forms of the vegetable world.

For the present, we are concerned mainly with the

most central districts of Central California, that large region of the State which is enclosed between the coast range on the west side and the Sierra Nevada on the east. 'This portion of California,' says Professor Whitney, 'is by far the most important, both from an agricultural and mining point of view. It does not embrace more than one-third of the State ; but it holds at least 95 per cent. of its population.' The upper half of the central valley is watered by the Sacramento river, and the lower half by the San Joaquin, both which rivers, aided by many branches, find their way from opposite directions into the Bay of San Francisco. The famous Yosemité Valley, for which we were first bound, is the cradle of the head waters of the Merced river, which, running nearly east and west, forms one of the chief feeders of the San Joaquin. The chief groups of 'Big Trees' are at no great distance from it, and can generally be combined in an excursion of about ten days from San Francisco.

There were plenty of agents in the city ready and eager to open the tourist season by selling us tickets for the 'round trip ;' but it appeared evident from the few reports as yet received from the mountains that the extraordinary amount of winter snow had made the season a month later than usual. The best and most attractive route is to go first to the Mariposa group of trees by way of White and Hatch's to Clark's Ranch, and down into the valley by a place called Inspiration Point, so named from the grandeur of the view afforded by it. Everyone, however, agreed that the depth of snow would make it quite impossible to go by the Mariposa 'trail,' as it is customary to call a mountain road in

California. We were advised to go to the Yosemité by a new route passing a place called Hite's Cove, and thence joining the trail from Coulterville. We were to be taken to the Yosemité and back for 58 dollars apiece, or nearly 12*l.*; and, judging from the style and the amount of accommodation afforded for that sum of money, I imagine that somebody must have made an uncommonly good thing out of us.

One afternoon in the middle of April we left at four o'clock by train to Lathrop and Merced, arriving about eleven at night in clean and comfortable quarters at a hotel called 'El Capitan.' Next morning, after a very early breakfast, we went to inspect the vehicle which was announced to take us on to the town of Mariposa. It was a small and seedy-looking *char-à-banc* with three seats very close together, each intended apparently for two people. Still we thought we might do pretty well, until to our horror we saw by degrees six more people emerge from the hotel with their bags, evidently intending to share the wretched trap with us. Remonstrance was useless; the jobber who was making the arrangements declared that only one trap had been ordered: there it was, and we could have no more. It had a low roof supported on stanchions, with side-curtains, and it required an acrobatic feat with singular powers of bodily contortion to get in or out of it. The whole party was jammed in somehow or other, nine inside and one on the box by the side of the driver, who rejoiced in the name of 'Buffalo Jim,' and signed himself accordingly in the book of visitors when we got to Mariposa. We were full of wrath, but three of our fellow-passengers were

American ladies who took it all so quietly that we had nothing to do but submit also, and devote ourselves to making friends with our new companions for the next few days. We got on very well together, and amused one another to the best of our ability, whenever the jolting of the vehicle did not make speaking dangerous, for fear of biting off the tip of the tongue before coming to the end of a sentence.

Our new friends were from Michigan and Wisconsin, and had crossed the continent in the Great Railway; and I was amused to find that on coming from the more Eastern States to California, they talked as if they were travelling in some foreign country. They could not understand our being in California without having gone to see 'the *States*,' and I felt obliged to apologise on the ground that New York and Liverpool are so near that Englishmen think they can make a journey of that sort at any time. Certainly it seems strange to reflect that the continuous railway journey from New York to San Francisco is about 500 miles longer than the voyage to Liverpool! The idea of vastness in this journey had, I fancy, powerfully impressed the mind of one of the party, a very pleasant elderly man, and he told me an illustrative story which ought not to be lost. He said that a solitary Englishman once on a time arrived at some wild station in the Far West, where he found the landlord of the lonely inn with nothing to do, in default of travellers. The Englishman saw across the open expanse of country what he imagined was a small hill at no great distance, and asked his host to walk there with him. The American consented without a word, and they walked on together for some hours, but the hill looked no nearer than before. The Englishman walked faster, followed by his host, who was determined not to give in, if he could help it. Presently he saw the Englishman stop and deliberately take off his shoes and stockings. As he was next turning up his trousers to the knee, the American came up and found him standing by the side of some sort of narrow ditch. 'Hulloa!' said he, 'what on airth are you about?' The Englishman said quietly, 'Well, I am going to ford this river.' 'River!' said his host, 'why it's only two foot wide! why don't you jump over it, as I do?' 'Oh!' said the other, savagely, 'it's all very fine for *you* to talk like that, but how the devil *am I to judge of distances* in a confounded big country like this?'

For some time we followed an excessively bad road near the side of a small river on our left hand, and a boundless extent of unfenced corn-land on the right. The immediate sides of the road were lined with brilliant flowers, and I observed that the countless lupines were all white on one bank of the river, and all blue on the other. Here, in addition to the masses of blue and white nemophila, poppies, borages, escholtzias, and others of our beautiful old friends, were two magnificent species of larkspurs, one of them with flowers of the most intense purple that can be imagined. There was also a great quantity of a liliaceous plant, closely resembling the blue *Agapanthus* of our greenhouses; and in open places farther on there were acres of a dark-yellow composite plant, whose starry flowers were tipped with a delicate primrose tint. Now and then, as the road turned close to the river, we put up a few ducks and other startled water-birds from under the steep bank. The road was as bad as bad could be; full of deep ruts and quagmires, which on more than one occasion made Buffalo Jim prefer taking his team across country for awhile, and then rejoining it. Once we met a loaded waggon with a team of twelve horses coming towards us: there was no room to pass, so we, being the weakest, went to the wall, and were nearly capsized in charging up into a cornfield. What we endured in the way of bumping and jolting can hardly be described. Suffice it to say that we frequently were thrown upwards till our heads struck the roof, and the seats were so narrow and so abominably contrived that those on the outside, after a jump of this kind, came down again violently upon an iron rail in a manner which fills my bones with aches as even now I think of it. In my agonies I hit upon the device of keeping my hand upon the hateful bar, and found it was decidedly a more comfortable substance to alight upon. After all, however, I believe, from what I have since heard, that we were suffering the joys of Paradise compared with those who travel in California in summer; when in place of mud and jolting tempered with sweet air and myriads of flowers, they are too often choked and blinded with intolerable dust as they rattle over a brown and thirsty land.

We stopped to water the horses at a small farmhouse, by the side of some trees which were crowded with birds' nests of very curious construction, each of them made fast to a single twig. The scenery improved vastly as we gradually rose above the damp and level corn-lands, and wound along among the rolling hills and scattered groves of trees which make a large part of California like one gigantic park. No landscape gardener could place the groups of various trees in better position than they have been left in here by the hand of Nature; and the open spaces as far as we could see presented all the colours of the paint-box, according to the nature of the predominant flowers with which each hill-side was covered as with a glorious carpet. Here and there we saw very singular-looking groups and irregular rows of slaty rocks, projecting almost vertically out of the ground, and coloured gaily with red and yellow lichens. At first sight, they suggested the idea of a vast deserted cemetery, full of ancient tombstones, and ornamented by scattered groups of oak and fir trees.

As we drew nearer to the famous mining town of Mariposa, there were abundant signs of deserted diggings by the road-side. Heaps of broken stones testified to the patience and labour of those who had worked hard and gone away with very different results. All was quiet and peaceful now; but as I looked at those piles of stony fragments, I could not but think of the scenes that must have been enacted here a few years ago. What wild joy, what dull despair, must have passed through the minds of those whose very soul was devoted to tearing gold out of the earth! What savage quarrels, what wild orgies, were entered into by some of those who washed, and pounded, and piled up those heaps of now deserted stones! Nearer the town we came upon an occasional ghastly Chinaman, a mere bag of bones, trying to extract a treasure from the leavings of departed diggers, poking laboriously among the *débris*, and looking just like a very old woman investigating the contents of a dust-heap. Poor wretches! It was hard to believe that a Celestial could look so profoundly miserable.

The distance to Mariposa was said to be only thirty-five miles, but the state of the road was such that we spent eight hours over it; and the amount of bumping and cramping that we had endured made us all uncommonly glad to wriggle out of the vehicle at the door of the little hotel of Mariposa about four o'clock in the afternoon. The house was kept by a very pleasant German from the neighbourhood of Baden-Baden; a store opposite to him, where we went to get some first-rate tobacco, belonged to another German family from Wurtemburg; and I soon found that in both cases the way to the German heart was to talk to them a little in their native tongue about their native country. A very amusing inhabitant of the hotel was a large brindled dog, who, at the word of command, went into the back garden, where he popped into the interior of a vertical wheel about ten feet in diameter, and drew the water for the house by trying to run up the inside of the wheel and turning it after the fashion of a squirrel in his cage. He worked with a steady energy which was delightful to behold.

Mariposa is a scattered little place permeated by the Mariposa Creek, and it seemed to have been shorn of some of the dignity it might have formerly possessed by the diminution of the gold-digging interest, added to the effects of one of those disastrous fires which are constantly devouring the wooden habitations of America. Pretty wooded hills rise on both sides of the valley; I rambled up one of them while waiting for dinner, and found a floral novelty in a delicate yellow *Erythronium* (*E. lanceolatum*, I believe): a family which is represented in Europe by the well-known 'dog-tooth violet' of our gardens in early Spring. Everything in the house was, as might be expected, of a very simple description; but we were tolerably supplied with materials for food and sleep, and went off early next morning with light hearts as soon as Buffalo Jim and his four horses were ready for us.

Turning to the left at a place called Mormon Bar, we began steadily rising into higher regions with occasional glimpses of the snowy mountains towards which we were travelling; and passing gradually from the park-like country of oaks and grass-slopes and wide belts of flowers, we entered into the true forest-land of giant pines and firs of every description. We were at the height of about 5,000 feet above the sea, in the finest zone of the grandest conifers in the world. Here were the pitch pine, or *Pinus ponderosa*, the sugar pine (*P. Lambertiana*), the white cedar (*Libocedrus decurrens*), and the *Abies Douglassii*, the famous Douglas fir. The sugar pine is remarkable for the size of its cones, which I have picked up more than sixteen inches in length, and which may be well described as hanging like ornamental tassels from the ends of the branches. The timber of this tree is said upon very good authority to be the best in California, and its size gigantic, being not unfrequently 300 feet high, and from seven to ten feet in diameter. Passing through the dark shades of these magnificent forests we arrived, after about fifteen miles of atrocious road, at a lonely farmhouse in a clearing of the forest. This place is known as Skelton's, and here we were fairly on the new trail to the Yosemité.

Buffalo Jim put up his horses in a rough shed which did duty for a stable, and we soon made the acquaintance of Mr. and Mrs. Skelton. If it had not been for the surrounding scenery and the astonishing trees, the idea of being in the Far West of America would have been dispelled as an illusion. Our host and hostess looked as if they had just stepped out of a cozy farm in Kent. Yet they had been for many years in this utterly lonely spot, had cleared the forest immediately round them, were growing corn, and had made for themselves a happy and prosperous home. Mrs. Skelton, if ever she sees these pages, will, I hope, forgive me for saying that her ruddy and healthy countenance reminded me of the old country; her skill as a cook, with very simple elements to work upon, was admirable; and the excellence of her eggs, milk, and butter could not be surpassed. The route being new, and the season very early, they were not expecting company, but they exerted themselves to the utmost in a kindly way not to be forgotten. A gigantic pine-tree had been lately felled, and lay so as to make a bridge over a ravine leading to the road, and this led me to ask Skelton about the height of the trees, which I could hardly believe to be so great as I had heard they were. 'Ah! nobody understands that at first,' he said; 'one of my relations came to see us out here some time ago, and offered to bet me that I had nothing over 150 feet; so we set to work and cut down one which turned out to be 270!'

After a midday dinner, we were jammed once more

into our wheeled prison, and were carried about five miles farther through the forest over a road which grew worse and worse, till we pulled up at a very small and lonely house, and here to our great joy we found that we were at the end of all things on wheels. Two guides, Joe Ridgway and Harry M'Cready, had been sent forward, and were waiting for us with a dozen rough horses roughly saddled, and a never-to-be-forgotten grey mule for carrying the baggage. The party had been increased by a small trap carrying a married couple with two young children, one of them a baby. The gentleman turned out to be a minister of one of the many sects prevalent in America, though there was not any kind of external symptom in dress or appearance to make a stranger think so. However, he and his wife were very agreeable, intelligent people, who had travelled in Europe and made a pilgrimage to the Holy Land. The baggage was reduced to a minimum by leaving sundry articles at this place, and the guides began to load the mule with everything else. At the first attempt to touch him, he jumped into the air and kicked in all directions; but he was in the hands of strong men who only laughed at him as we did; and we soon saw that we were going to be favoured with a very entertaining companion.

It was certainly a rather difficult load to pack on account of the number of small bags, and the guides seemed to think that we probably had no right to any baggage at all; but there was one thing with which we insisted on crowning the edifice, namely, a wicker-covered demi-john of the best whisky in San Francisco, as we had been told we should probably get something more like petroleum than the genuine article in the Sierra Nevada. It was put on at last, but not without sundry gibes from the men which made me greatly doubt if it would arrive at its lawful destination. Then the ropes were hauled fast, and at the finishing knot the mule rose once more into the air, kicking out in ludicrous attitudes as if it were trying the weight of the burden imposed upon its back, and estimating the chances of being able to get rid of it prematurely. By degrees each of the party picked out the horse which he or she preferred, and I waited quietly to take the last when the rest were all suited. When it did come to the last I found myself with a little bushy-maned animal, such as an old gentleman is supposed to give to his favourite grandchild; and remembering that I was probably the heaviest of the party I had some doubts as to the result. But, as I jumped into the saddle, the old man of the house said with a cunning laugh, 'You've waited till the last, and you've got the best of them, *you* bet.' I found the old fellow was about right; I had got a genuine mustang of the native breed, sturdy and sure-footed, and the most comfortable beast that was ever invented for riding-purposes in the mountains. I had brought with me a South American *revenque* which I picked up some years ago when riding in the Pampas, but my pony had no need of it. This is the most punishing style of whip that I am acquainted with, consisting of a thick leather strap about two feet long and cut to a point; the handle is about a foot long, heavily loaded with iron inside, terminating in a strong ring of silver, through which is passed a circular leather strap large enough to pass over the right hand and wrist. The Gauchos thus armed can ride with the hand free for throwing the lazo or anything else; when wanted, it is caught up rapidly by the handle. Sometimes they use the heavy handle like a truncheon, and they have been known, when in a rage with a horse, to rise in their stirrups and kill him by a blow between the ears.

The party filed away under the shadow of forest giants, and the mule soon began to give us trouble by breaking out of line and rudely charging past some of those in front, who got heavy thumps on the legs from his projecting burden; it was no use bringing him back, he did it again and again, till at last he was allowed to 'gang his ain gate,' and then we found out what he wanted all the time. My friend, Mr. Rawson, was mounted on a white horse in front, and for some reason of his own, the mule insisted on walking behind this particular animal, and when he got in that position he was perfectly happy. After several miles we reached a high point on a ridge, from which a very fine view opened before us. A deep valley with many ramifications descended from our feet, and a steep hill-side rose up beyond it, above which, still far away, rose mountain over mountain, clad with pine forests looming darkly out of the still deep snow.

Hence a narrow road lately cut in the mountain-side led us slowly and with many a steep zigzag down about two or three thousand feet to a valley which, according to the map before me, appears to be known as the 'Devil's Gulch.' The name is ominous, but I am happy to see that the same map gives a 'Bishop's Creek' close by, which sends down a stream to meet that which flows from the valley with the evil name. Much of the way down was cut through oak-scrub and thickets, with a considerable undergrowth of ferns and flowers, which induced me to dismount and dawdle behind the rest of the party; however, as I found at the bottom of the valley nothing but a narrow sandy path close to the river on one side and bounded by rugged rocks on the other, I encouraged my gallant steed into a gallop to rejoin my companions. We went on merrily enough for some time, till my attention was arrested by something on the side of the path, and I found to my horror the carcass of our demi-john! I dismounted to look after the state of our poor friend, but he was past curing and totally empty. In spite of strong wicker-work the bottle was broken inside, and the contents were gone. The rascally mule had caused a violent scene at this point, and smashed the bottle against a neighbouring rock. Soon afterwards the path turned round a corner and revealed the existence of a small collection of buildings on the other side of the river; a very frail bridge was crossed, and we dismounted at the mining station of Hite's Cove, where we were destined to pass the night.

The *raison d'être* of the establishment at Hite's Cove is the existence of a valuable gold mine in the barren hill above, and a crushing-mill is worked by water from the river which we crossed at its base. A managing man very civilly showed us the working of the mill, where powerful crushers in perpetual motion pound the ore to powder, which with the admixture of water forms a substance like blue mud. We were told that they were turning out gold to the value of 15,000 dollars a month. Probably the fact of its being on a new route to the Yosemité will do something towards civilising the place, but at present it is decidedly in the rough. The hotel, as I suppose I must call it, was a remarkably small one, and was apparently presided over by a sturdy elderly German whose general post was at the bar on the left hand of the principal room, and opposite to him was a stove and chimney, round which there was generally a party of rough-looking miners playing at cards with little heaps of dollars and cents by their sides. Now and then a couple of them would get up to play a game of billiards on a filthy table which occupied the upper half of the room. Both here, and at many similar places which we afterwards saw, I was particularly struck with the quiet way in which everything was done by this class of men. They would just give a passing stare to a stranger, as we all had to enter the same room; and then resumed their games in a silent fashion, each getting up and moving off without saying a word, as soon as he had had enough of it. Whether the presence of strangers acted as a *gêne* upon them, or whether the progress of civilisation had anything to do with it, I do not know, but I was frequently surprised at the total absence of incivility, bad language, and riotous conduct among them in public.

Food and feeding-accommodation were remarkably capable of improvement, but the people did their best for us in such a wild place, and apologised for not being 'fixed up' just yet. Some very limited sleeping-quarters were found for the ladies, either in the house or in the few small adjoining cottages. What became of some of the men I have no idea. Two of my companions with myself were at night escorted by a man with a lantern to a little wooden hut on the side of a bare steep hill, and left there to make the best of the situation. Our abode was in shape like a bathing-machine without the wheels, and was certainly not larger than ten feet by eight: it had some large holes in it, and was so loosely constructed that it was penetrated through and through by a howling gale that had set in for the night. If there had been no holes in it, it would perhaps have been blown down into the river. It contained two small truckle-beds, and no other furniture of any sort or kind, so we had the excitement of tossing up to decide who was to have a bed to himself. the other two having to 'double up.' Undressing was useless, as we had nowhere to put our clothes, so we blew the candle out; and, by a happy tendency of human nature to be merry sometimes in the most disagreeable circumstances, we babbled about the Babes in the Wood, and laughed ourselves into a comfortable sleep. In an establishment of this kind the only washing arrangements, for the male sex at all events, are out of doors. We had to take turns at a couple of tin bowls and a piece of soap in a small open balcony, at the end of which was suspended what is called in English kitchens a round-towel, but is known in America as a towel-bag.

A very tolerable notion of one of the rougher places may be derived from the document which I am now going to copy, and which was sent in print from a friend in the Far West; and, though the last words are sufficient to show that it is not meant to be taken *au grand sérieux*, yet, after what I have said of Hite's Cove where people were on their best behaviour, it may easily be imagined that the following is scarcely a caricature of a still wilder place in which ordinary tourists are not expected. It professes to hail from Reese river, and to contain the rules of an hotel there. It runs as follows:—

RULES AND REGULATIONS.

Board must be paid in advance; with beans fifteen dollars; without, twelve dollars; salt free. Boarders not permitted to speak to the cook; no extras allowed; 'pocketing' at meals strictly forbidden; no whistling while eating; gentlemen are requested to wash out of doors and to find their own water; no charges for ice; towel-bags at the end of the house; extra charges for seats round the stove; lodgers must find their own straw; beds on the bar-room floor reserved for regular customers; persons sleeping in the bar are requested not to take off their boots; lodgers inside arise at 5 A.M.; in the barn at 7; each man sweeps up his own bed; no quartz taken at the bar; no fighting allowed at table. Specimens must invariably be left outside the door. Anyone violating the above rules will be shot.

With regard to this remarkable notice it should be explained that 'specimens' are understood to refer to revolvers; and it must be remembered that these useful articles are always 'there,' even if not much displayed. If a Californian tailor makes you a pair of trousers, they are sure to contain a pocket which is unknown in Bond Street; and if a man finds himself in a 'difficulty' without wishing to be too quick in showing that he is prepared for it, he does not hesitate to spoil his 'pants' by firing surreptitiously through his own pocket. At the same time let it be observed that the knowledge of this fact is no secret, and the result is contained in the old saying that 'to be forewarned is to be fore-armed.' I was forcibly reminded of this one evening when I chanced to be standing at the door of the Grand Hotel in San Francisco, chatting with some English and American friends. A very tipsy citizen of the lower classes passed close by us in a somewhat noisy, singing, and ridiculous condition. One of the Englishmen made some joking remark to him of a very harmless character, but a Californian of the party whispered, 'Never you say anything to one of those fellows, it's just as likely as not that he would have turned round and fired into us right and left.' Nevertheless, I am bound to say that during the time we were in California I heard of no murderous catastrophe except one which occurred between a couple of photographic clerks who had crossed one another in love. One was said to have shot the other when his head was in the camera!

After our rough toilette, followed by a still rougher breakfast, we were all mounted early in the morning, and crawled slowly up a barren hill-side to a point which I supposed to be nearly 2,000 feet above Hite's Cove. On the road we crossed a tramway which is employed for bringing down from the mouth of the mine the ore which is sent to be crushed in the mill at the bottom of the valley. As far as I have seen, from Cornwall to Chile and California, the most valuable mining regions are indissolubly connected with an otherwise unfruitful soil; the grand pine-forests we had lately passed had nothing to say to the gold-hunters; and the gold-mountain we were crossing had nothing to offer to the lover of the woods. On the top of it, however, we had new views of natural beauty. Far, far below us ran the Merced river, which we knew to be the aggregation of the wondrous waterfalls of the Yosemité; and beyond it rose the dark woods and summits of the Sierra Nevada.

We all halted some time to admire the wild scene

around us, and then began a very long and winding road cut partly through woods and thickets down to the bottom of the valley of the Merced. Again we reached the land of ferns and flowers, amidst scattered groups of oak and fir and undulating slopes of soft grass. In damp places by the wayside I found our old European friend, the *Cystopteris fragilis*, which appears to be one of the most cosmopolitan and self-accommodating of all the mountain ferns in the world. It is found all round the northern hemisphere, at all events outside the tropics; and while not objecting to Italian heat, it yet flourishes at the base of the Riffelhorn in Switzerland at the elevation of 9,000 feet above the sea. Here, too, was a profusion of a white *Ranunculus*, which appeared to me to be identical with the *Ranunculus aconitifolius* of the Alps: the two species of *Platyloma* ferns, which I have already mentioned, were in great beauty; and a little farther on I met, for the first time, the *Cheilanthes gracillima*, one of the most lovely of that elegant family. As we descended to the neighbourhood of the bright and dashing Merced river we met a man on horseback, who told us that the furious wind of the past night had blown down several trees across our path, but that he had sent men to cut them across and open the way, which, as we afterwards found, was a very necessary proceeding.

Meanwhile I found myself again with the rear-guard of the party. The minister and his wife were pretty well mounted, but something went wrong with her saddle, and as Joe Ridgway was carrying their little girl on his knee I waited to take care of the child while he dismounted. The father was carrying the baby on a pillow in front of his saddle, and had already been shot off once, with baby and pillow and all, by his horse shying at the stump of a tree; so he was obliged to be careful, and I devoted myself to helping them as much as I could, whilst the rest of the party got far ahead of us. Presently we met M'Cready coming back to look for the mule, who, as it appeared, had been greatly disgusted at being cut off from his favourite companion by Mr. Rawson's superior pace on the white horse. The beast had taken the opportunity when nobody was looking at him to leave the path and charge down a steep hill into the thickets. M'Cready, with the sagacity of an Indian, was looking for his tracks, and soon found him down below trying to get rid of his burden by rolling on it; he was kicked up and brought back in triumph, but it required a great deal of pulling and hauling to make things straight again. After a charming ride of several miles among the scattered woods on the margin of the river, we came up with the rest of the party, who had tethered their horses, and were preparing for lunch under the shade of an oak-tree. It was a delightful place for a picnic as far as nature was concerned. We were on clean dry grass among small rocks which were eminently adapted for chairs and sofas; we had the fair Merced river, clear as purest crystal, running close by our side; we had comfortable shadows from the oaks and other trees about our camp; 'all save the spirit of man was divine,' but man proved himself unequal to the occasion by having provided us with a luncheon beneath contempt. This was owing to the very limited resources of poor little Hite's Cove, from which we certainly had no reason to expect great things. We found a few respectable scraps for the ladies, but most of us had to be thankful for a mere mouthful of bread and cheese. As this magnificent repast at the end of a six hours' ride came to an end, the party gradually mounted and rode ahead. As I felt it was my destiny for the day to take charge of the rearguard and look after the baggage, I saw them all off, and then found myself alone with M'Cready looking for the dreadful mule. The rogue had contrived to slip away from the bush to which he had been tied, and we found him in the position which he had long desired. He had completely got rid of his load, and was happily rolling amongst our bags with nothing to trouble him but a network of loose ropes about his back. One man by himself could never have restored order from this chaos; but stout M'Cready and myself managed the brute. We got everything on his back again, thrashed him, and tied up his load so efficiently that, whatever his wishes may have been, he was apparently incapable of further mischief for the day.

The rest of the party were making good running entirely out of sight, except the minister with his wife and babes, and Joe Ridgway who still had the charge of one of them. We picked them up, going on in a very tired fashion, and as I had helped to take care of them all day, I thought it was a point of honour not to desert them. We left M'Cready to urge the mule along as best he could, and followed in the rear at a funeral pace. The path became as narrow as a footway across a ploughed field, winding along the course of the river, which was often separated from us only by a steep and precipitous slope with an equally steep mountain side on the other side of us. In the middle of one of the worst places we met a man running towards us, and almost breathlessly crying out that he had three loaded mules coming in the opposite direction, and that it was impossible to pass. We had to dismount, and back our horses till a more convenient slope allowed us to drag them up a little way, and let the mules with their excited owner pass beneath us.

A few miles farther we were astonished a little by the sound of a gun; and on turning a sharp corner we found a small boy holding the weapon just discharged. He smiled affably, and we, being delivered from any idea of immediate assassination, asked him what he was about. It appeared that an attempt was being made to improve the road, which I must say was capable of improvement: John Chinaman and others were employed in the task of blasting rocks, and it was the duty of this youth on seeing or hearing any symptoms of travellers to fire his gun as a signal for these people not to destroy life by blasting at the moment when peaceful citizens were on the point of passing. The Celestials and their commander stared at us sleepily as we went by them, and I could not help thinking of the strange destiny that had brought them there. A few minutes later a tremendous bang behind us announced that they had resumed business. Not far from this we found that the wretched path led us through a labyrinth of the most amazing fallen rocks that I have ever seen. The rushing river on one side, and the rocky, pine-clad slopes on the other, reminded me rather of the upper part of the way to Saas in Switzerland, where vast blocks are sometimes precipitated crashing through the pine-woods till they make a final leap across the river into the meadows beyond. But the blocks of granite among which we were winding surpassed anything in my experience. Some of them were many times larger than the Bowder Stone of Derwentwater, or even the renowned Pierre-à-Bot of the Jura not far from Neufchatel. In comparison with these huge rocks, men and horses filing between them, with scarcely elbow room, looked like dolls, or monkeys riding dogs in a circus.

By one of the most sudden changes of scene that could be imagined we emerged presently from this chaotic confusion on perfectly smooth and level ground. The horses trod silently upon a soft carpet made by the spines from the fir-trees, the thick masses of which threw a sombre gloom upon all around us; and the river, no longer a torrent bounding down among masses of granite rocks, appeared like a sheet of smoothest glass, in which every leaf was reflected as from the surface of a mirror. The utter tranquillity and stillness of the scene were in strange contrast with the turmoil and savageness which we had just left behind us, and marked the fact that we were close to the portals of the mysterious Yosemité Valley. From this point the land was as nearly level as is compatible with allowing a glassy stream to glide along the bottom of a valley, and it would have been easy to gallop quickly over the remaining miles, but I could not bear deserting the tired worn-out family with the children: they could only move at a foot-pace, and so we went very slowly and wearily, close to the bank of the smooth and silent river, darkened by the shade of mighty overhanging trees, and opening out frequently into broad shining pools where it was almost impossible to distinguish between the reflections and the reality.

We were cheered by a lovely view of the 'Bridal Veil' waterfall on our right, and that of the 'Virgin's Tears' on the left; and we passed through what is probably the grandest gateway in the world, where the portals are 'El Capitan' on one side and the Cathedral Rock on the other, each being a mass of nearly perpendicular granite rising about 3,000 feet above the valley, and scarcely half a mile apart. The evening was cold and late when we reached a house which is dignified by the name of Leidig's Hotel, three hours later than most of the party; and we had spent eleven hours in getting over less than thirty miles, which I could have easily walked in two-thirds of the time.

CHAPTER XII.

The Yosemité Valley—Its discovery—Indians—Size of the Valley—Inspiration Point and the Domes—Theories of formation—Erosion or Subsidence—The 'Bridal Veil'—El Capitan—Leidig's Hotel—The great Yosemité Fall—The Sentinel Rock—The work of ancient Ice—The Mirror Lake—Avalanche Snow—Comparative Scenery—Return to Mariposa and Merced.

THE YOSEMITÉ VALLEY is undoubtedly one of the most remarkable wonders of the world. It is not only grand and surprising, but it is also entirely unique in situation and appearance; and the air of romance and mystery which accompanied its first discovery still produces a charming influence on the imagination of the visitor.

It is situated in the heart of the western slopes of the Sierra Nevada, a few points to the south of east from San Francisco, and at a distance from it of 150 miles in what the Americans call a 'bee-line,' though nearly 250 miles by the ordinary routes. The general appearance is that of a complete *cul-de-sac* among the surrounding mountains; and in that capacity it served as the last refuge and hiding-place of the neighbouring Indians. In their earlier fights with these savages the white men, who were first brought into these regions by the gold fever in 1849, used to lose all trace of their red enemies in some mysterious manner, till at last in 1851 a friendly Indian, named Tenaya, treacherously betrayed the secret and guided a party under the command of Captain Boling into the recesses of the Yosemité, which had never before been trodden by a white man's foot. The Indians were horribly frightened at being surprised in a retreat which they had imagined to be impregnable; some of them were of course killed, and the rest 'made peace.' In 1852, however, they again ventured to attack a party of miners and killed two of them. This filled up the cup of their iniquities. A second expedition killed many of them, and drove the survivors entirely out of the valley, and over to the eastern side of the mountains, where they joined the Monos Indians. The hospitality of the Monos was badly requited. One day the Yosemité Indians stole the horses of their friends and escaped into the depths of their old valley. Thither the Monos followed them, and fought a battle which ended in the almost entire extermination of the Yosemité tribe. The name Yosemité means 'Great Grizzly Bear,' but it appears to have fallen out of use among the Indians, perhaps in consequence of the recent destruction of the tribe to whom it was familiar. The present Indian name is Ahwahnee.

The grand oak-trees of the Yosemité still tempt the Indians to the harmless pursuit of picking and storing up acorns, their staple article of food; a fact which will perhaps give some notion of what manner of men they are likely to be. There are, however, very few of them; and, like the rest of the so-called 'digger' Indians, 'they are a miserable, degraded, and fast-disappearing set of beings, who must die out before the progress of the white man's civilisation, and for whom there is neither hope nor chance.' These are the words of Mr. Whitney, the State Geologist of California, to whose excellent work, called 'The Yosemité Guide-book,' I am indebted for many facts beyond the scope of my own eyes and ears in a single visit to this astonishing region. The few Indians we saw in our Yosemité rambles were the most wretched representatives of humanity that I ever chanced to see. They were little wild-looking creatures, and their general appearance reminded me immediately of a queer little image often to be seen in the window of a shop where electrical toys and instruments are for sale. It has an ugly head with coarse features, with a reddish-brown complexion, and a thick shock-head of long black hair, which is intended to illustrate one of the powers of nature by standing up like a broom when put under the influence of an electrical machine. It is exactly like a 'digger' Indian. The contrast afforded by these little wretches when compared with the amazing grandeur of their native country would almost induce one to think that Nature had in those regions so exhausted herself in making marvellous precipices and gigantic trees that she had not enough time or energy remaining for the creation of a respectable race of men. The last fragments of these aborigines show no signs of any capacity beyond that of picking up acorns and sleeping on the store. If they have any idea of a future state, it is probably something relating to one in which they will wake up under a magnificent oak-tree which drops golden acorns into their mouths without necessitating the trouble of even looking for them.

Such being the history and condition of the original

proprietors of the Yosemité Valley, let us consider its position under its present owners. The fame of the valley soon went abroad, and assumed a national importance. In 1864, an Act of Congress granted to the State of California the valley of the Yosemité and the neighbouring Mariposa grove of Big Trees upon trust to hold them for the public use and recreation, inalienable for all time ; they were, however, to be permitted to grant short leases, subject to the condition of spending all accruing profits upon the maintenance and improvement of the premises. This grant was formally accepted by the Californian Legislature ; but in spite of the best intentions they have been hampered with the claims of previous squatters, and, be the reason what it may, it is certain that very little has hitherto been done in the way of making the promised roads, bridges, and improvements. So much the better, many people will say ; but the fear is that if the valley gets into the hands of private individuals, vexatious restraints and annoying charges will be multiplied, till, as Mr. Whitney says, 'the Yosemité Valley, instead of being "a joy for ever," will become, like Niagara, a gigantic institution for "fleecing the public."'

The base of the valley is 4,000 feet above the sea: it is about six miles long, and from half a mile to a mile in breadth; and is so nearly level that the Merced river flowing through it only descends thirty-five feet in the course of the whole six miles. It is barred in on all sides by granite precipices of stupendous proportions; and the valley may be compared to a gigantic trough of irregular form, hollowed out to the depth of nearly a mile below the general level of the surrounding region, and nearly at right angles to the main Sierra. To compare great things with small, if any of my Alpine friends will imagine themselves at the bottom of a *crevasse* six miles long and nearly a mile wide, with a perfectly smooth floor, and surrounded by vertical or nearly vertical walls of 3,000 feet above their heads, they will have a good notion of the proportions of the great Yosemité Valley. The only visible outlet is the way by which we entered, where the Merced river, throwing off its placid and mirror-like character, suddenly plunges roaring through the rocks and boulders of the cañon, whose steep and rugged sides had been considered till lately as a very sufficient bar to any approach in that direction.

The only known routes to the valley were the Coulterville or Big Oak Flat trail on the north side of the river, and the Mariposa trail on the south side; and, so extraordinary is the natural formation of the surrounding country, that by each of these routes it was necessary to climb to a height of nearly 7,500 feet before getting a chance of descending to the Yosemité, 3,500 feet below. This has, however, one very great advantage in the fact that an astonishing prospect is suddenly presented to the view. The best and favourite way to this valley of wonders is by the Mariposa trail, which, before descending, leads to a spot called Inspiration Point, whence the accompanying illustration was photographed. The Coulterville route descends towards the valley in a very similar manner from an almost equal elevation, where some of its adherents, not to be outdone in sentimentality by such a name as Inspiration Point, have boldly taken a still higher flight and christened their favourite point of view the Stand-Point of Silence! The Americans, however are not the first in adopting sentimental names for various places in this region, for the Indians had fanciful and poetical names for every mountain and waterfall in the neighbourhood. In the illustration, the wonderful peak on the right, about 5,000 feet above the valley, and known as the Half Dome, is the Matterhorn of the Yosemité. The Indians appear to have called it Tis-sa-ack, or the Goddess of the Valley. On the left is the North Dome, which the natives called To-coy-a, or Shade of Indian Baby-Basket.

This mountain, rising 3,725 feet above the river at its feet, is a singularly perfect specimen of the dome-like form which characterises granite peaks; and the curved lines of natural fracture which may be seen upon its flank in the illustration, and which are known as the Royal Arches, give a sort of notion as to the structure of these wonderful domes, by showing the lines in which the curved concentric plates tend towards exfoliation. Throughout the whole of the Yosemité the features which distinguish it from all other known valleys are the immense height of its nearly perpendicular walls, and the very small amount of *débris* which is to be found at their feet. The first thought that must occur to any reflecting mind upon entering this unique and marvellous valley of giants is, how could it possibly have been formed? And before speaking further of its separate and individual charms, it will be worth while to consider this general question for a little.

Most valleys may be supposed to have been dug out,

THE DOME AND HALF DOME, YOSEMITE VALLEY

or at all events greatly deepened by water or ice. Mr. Whitney says (p. 81) : 'Most of the great cañons and valleys of the Sierra Nevada have resulted from aqueous denudation, and in no part of the world has this work been done on a larger scale. The long-continued action of tremendous torrents of water, rushing with impetuous velocity down the slopes of the mountains, has excavated those immense gorges by which the Sierra Nevada is furrowed on its western slope, to the depth of several thousands of feet. This erosion, great as it is, has been done within a comparatively recent geological period, as is conclusively demonstrated in numerous localities. At the Abbey's Ferry crossing of the Stanislaus, for instance, a portion of the mass of Table Mountain is seen on each side of the river, in such a position as to prove that the current of lava which forms the summit of this mountain once flowed continuously across what is now a cañon over 2,000 feet deep; showing that the erosion of that immense gorge has all been effected since the lava flowed down from the higher portion of the Sierra. This event took place, as we know from the fossil bones and plants imbedded under the volcanic mass, at a very recent geological period, or in the latter part of the Tertiary epoch.

'The eroded cañons of the Sierra, however, whose formation is due to the action of water, never have vertical walls, nor do their sides present the peculiar angular forms which are seen in the Yosemité, as, for instance, in El Capitan, where two perpendicular surfaces of smooth granite, more than 3,000 feet high, meet each other at a right angle. It is sufficient to look for a moment at the vertical faces of El Capitan and the Bridal Veil rock, *turned down*

T

the valley, or away from the direction in which the eroding force must have acted, to be able to say that aqueous erosion could not have been the agent employed to do any such work. The squarely-cut re-entering angles, like those below El Capitan and others, were never produced by ordinary erosion. Much less could any such cause be called in to account for the formation of the Half Dome, the vertical portion of which is all above the ordinary level of the walls of the valley, rising 2,000 feet, in sublime isolation, above any point which could have been reached by denuding agencies, even if we suppose the current to have filled the whole of the valley!'

The water-theory failing to account for such a remarkable depression, the next theory liable to be jumped at is that the work was done by ice. Now, though I do not profess to be a geologist, yet I have served my apprenticeship for a sufficient number of years among the Alps of Europe to know something of glaciers and of what they have contributed towards modifying the surface of the globe; and I can have no hesitation in confirming Mr. Whitney's statement that nothing can seem to be more improbable than that the Yosemité Valley has been scooped out by this agency. The re-entering angles, the deep bays, with their sharp corners, and the precipices with double faces at right angles to each other, are conclusive proofs against such idea. It is nothing like the true work of a glacier. The ice theory of the Yosemité may be pretty safely dismissed: and, though in the higher regions of the Sierra Nevada there are abundant signs of moraines and smoothed rocks to testify to the work of ancient glaciers, there is nothing to induce the belief of moving ice having ever penetrated into the bottom of this valley.

The Yosemité is too wide to have been formed by a fissure like the Via Mala of the Splugen; it is about as wide as it is deep; moreover there is no sort of correspondence between the two sides of it. A hollow bay on one side is faced by a flat precipice, or even an oppositely concave hollow on the other side; and the fissure theory may be said to fail in accounting for the phenomena as completely as those of water and of ice. The direction of the valley being transverse to the main chain of the Sierra prevents us from attributing its formation to any folding or upheaval of the range. After this almost exhaustive process, what remains? The State Geologist, who has spent many a long month in surveying this district and the whole of the surrounding mountain-land, has come to the conclusion that the Yosemité Valley can owe its origin to nothing but the subsidence of the rocky surface of the earth between faults or fissures. That is to say, he thinks that a portion of the earth's surface, during the upheaval of the Sierra, gave way, and dropped, perhaps slowly and perhaps suddenly, for about 3,000 feet below the level of the adjoining region.

After having compared the real scene with the maps of the Government survey, I am perfectly unable to suggest any other solution of the problem; and, having tried to glance at the general features of the country, we will return to the bottom of the gigantic crevasse which I have suggested, only remembering that the mighty walls are of shining granite instead of ice, while a smooth stream flowing gently through the midst of the valley reflects with mirror-like accuracy the vast precipices and glorious trees that look down upon it.

I have explained how the two established routes are carried over steep mountain-paths to a height of nearly 3,500 feet above the level of the valley, which is itself 4,000 feet above the sea. As we had only just passed the middle of April, the snow still lay very deep over these high places, and both routes were considered impracticable for the present, though I have no doubt that a little Swiss energy would soon have cleared them. Thus it was that we were compelled to be thankful for the new route by Hite's Cove which follows the cañon of the Merced in a gradual ascent to the valley instead of a long and steep descent into it. This is the natural and direct line, and the Chinamen were at work in making a decent road when we passed, but the natural difficulties of the position may be imagined from the fact that people had so long been content with much longer and more out-of-the-way routes. Though, however, we were thus debarred from entering by Inspiration Point or the Stand-Point of Silence, I am not at all sure that we were not rather gainers by entering the valley as we did. There would, of course, have been a more extensive view at first from the high ground, but I feel sure that the appearance of such rocks as El Capitan and the Cathedral is far more sublime and astonishing when first seen from below.

The excessive flatness of the base of the valley and the narrowness of the neck through which we entered it, leave little room for doubt that it has been occupied by a lake whose waters gradually increased the passage through the steep sides of the entrance, exactly as a former lake in the well-known Oberhaslithal of Switzerland forced a way for itself into the valley below. An open space of about a mile in every direction lay before us decked with several kinds of oak and alder, mixed with clumps and groves of magnificent firs of many kinds. The river flowed glassily by our side: through the gaps of the trees on our left we could see the thin but lofty cascade of the 'Virgin's Tears;' and on our right came dashing down the 'Bridal Veil,' which I consider on the whole to be the loveliest waterfall I have ever seen. It breaks out from among noble pine-trees, and makes a clean leap of 900 feet before losing itself again in the depths of the forest below. The height is the same as that of the Staubbach, but its breadth and volume are many times greater, and its immediate surroundings are incomparably more beautiful. Moreover it leaps so cleanly from its perpendicular rocks, and, in spite of its breadth, it is so delicately broken up, that when seen, as we saw it, with a wind slightly swaying it from side to side, and the bright evening sun shining upon it, the shadows of the moving water gave the semblance of another waterfall behind it, cast upon the glistening rock. Crowned by overhanging pine-trees, and with its base hidden by still grander forest, it is as perfect a waterfall as can be imagined.

Immediately in front, the plateau, which is a kind of ante-chamber to the valley, draws in towards the narrow entrance to the main valley. The awful precipice of the massive El Capitan rises perpendicularly for 3,400 feet on the left, while the almost equally steep, and perhaps more picturesque, Cathedral rock stands at a nearly equal height on the right hand. These amazing precipices seem to rise straight up from the ground, and look as if it were easy to walk only 200 or 300 yards across the level sward and rub shoulders with their wall-like sides; the accumulation of *débris* at their base being so insignificantly small that it is entirely hidden by the adjoining trees. Some of the most conspicuous among these are the beautifully formed pitch pines (*Pinus ponderosa*), with *Picea grandis* and *Abies Douglassii* rising to the height of 150 feet, and scattered about in graceful negligence among the oaks, maples, and alders on both sides of the river. Weird-looking roots and trunks of fallen trees, stranded in shallow water and bleached by the hand of Time, mingle with the lower boughs of the noble firs which wave above them: the bones of the dead lie quietly at the feet of their glorious and heaven-seeking successors.

The fast-falling shadows were deepening the silent, sombre gloom of the woods as we rode over the last few miles at a very slow foot-pace, and it was rather weary work; but I resisted the temptation to whip up my mustang and gallop ahead. Happily, however, οὐδὲν ἄμικτον κακόν: there are 'sermons in stones, and good in everything;' and, as I dawdled along over soft sands left by former overflowings of the river, amidst a stillness in which the falling of a fir-cone was startling, trying every now and then to comfort the little girl and her weary mother with hopes based upon ignorance as to our distance from the hotel, I felt that this was after all perhaps a more fitting way to approach the solemn grandeur of the Yosemité than if I had been galloping joyously forward, without time to drink in, as it were, the whole marvel and sublimity of the scene.

At last, we came to a wider opening, where the spread-

THE YOSEMITE VALLEY AND SENTINEL ROCK.

ing oaks and towering firs were more scattered, and the hand of man had evidently been busy in the neighbourhood; the Great Yosemité Fall was casting down its 2,650 feet of foam and water-rockets on our left; the Sentinel Rock, with a form resembling the invincible obelisk of the Aiguille Dru at Chamonix, was towering over our right; and nestling among the trees at its very base was the little hotel which we were seeking. A huge barricade of still unmelted snow extended along the front of the house, at the end of which we dismounted, and I don't think anybody in this world ever felt so stiff as I did after having been cramped for eleven hours in an unaccustomed saddle.

Leidig and Davanay's house is rather a humble apology for a hotel, but I believe it is generally considered the best of the three little establishments which are dignified by the title. It is exactly in front of the Great Fall, and has the further advantage of being the first that offers food and shelter to the approaching traveller. The provisions, cooking, and furniture were all of very primitive simplicity; but, instead of complaining of such matters, I prefer to think of Dr. Johnson and the dancing dogs, and wonder that they 'do it at all.' The house is of course built of wood, with two floors, each having a roofed passage round it, into which the rooms open outside. The wood is so thin and the joints so imperfect that every sound goes right through the whole edifice, and the droll little rooms into which they contrive to stuff two people made me think of a row of large deal bonnet-boxes insecurely fastened together and arranged in a row. One of the party made a pretended snore directly he got into bed: it was taken up by another, and in the next moment from every room issued a round of laughter and jokes in which every voice, including those of the ladies, was recognised by everyone else. So we all ended a long day by going to sleep in a happy humour.

There was a sufficiently sharp frost at night to give a white coating of ice to the rocks for a considerable distance on each side of the Great Fall, wherever the spray could reach; and as the day grew and the sun came into play, it was a beautiful sight to see great sheets of this ice come slithering down from the vast height as if they were racing headlong against the water-rockets. We soon found our way to the foot of the Lower Fall amongst a wild chaos of fallen rocks shaded by dense clusters of pines; and then, keeping to the left we searched for some trace of the path which we knew led somehow or other from the valley up to the front of the Upper Fall. The intervening precipices seemed from below quite as unsuitable for a path as the rocks of the Gemmi; and the soil, which consisted of sand covered with the dead spines of conifers, made it exceedingly difficult to follow up a track. At last we hit upon one which led us among a mass of trees and bushes to the regular mountain-path, which, though very narrow and very steep, is clear for the rest of the way. The thickets among these stony places are famous for dangerous snakes, and we saw a few wriggling away. I have an indescribable hatred of snakes, but after all it would be a pity to be seriously afraid of going near them. They generally run away if they can, and in the many snake-countries where I have rambled on foot, I have always contented myself with driving a stick or umbrella into suspicious places as a warning to them to get out of the way before I put my hand into a tuft to pick a fern or a flower.

A long zigzag led us steeply upwards through stony slopes and among scattered firs and oaks till we reached a point whence begins a long succession of magnificent views over the valley below, and away to the snowy summits which surround it at a much greater elevation than its immediate walls of rock. The path is here carried for a long way without much ascent by means of a natural ledge in the precipitous granite, and here, among the snug clefts, I found a great quantity of one of the *Platyloma* ferns already mentioned, and also of the lovely *Cheilanthes gracillima*, with bunches of young fronds of velvety whiteness like those of *C. elegans* in our hothouses. Presently the path rises very steeply again, twisting upwards to a higher range of ledges, where we began to find considerable patches of snow, and a few men were working to open the way for the season. Then turning to the left round a corner where stunted trees were growing among rocks in the wildest and most picturesque of positions, we suddenly found ourselves face to face with the amazing rush of the great waterfall. In the middle of a horseshoe or *cirque*, as it would be called in the Pyrenees, it comes down with a single leap of 1,650 feet; and when, as we saw it, it is full from the melting of the snow above, it expands in the middle to a width of several hundred feet. A few weeks later it would have been still fuller. The foot of it was hidden from our point by a huge pyramidal mound of ice and snow, looking like a small Silberhorn, which was piled up in front of it, and gave it the appearance of falling into a snowy tomb. To the right of this it emerges among a mass of battered fallen rocks, through which it rushes down in a series of cascades for a depth of about 600 feet, and then it takes its final leap of another 400 feet into the bottom of the valley.

Later in the season it is easy to follow the path we were upon to the base of the Upper Fall, or as near to it as the traveller's power of enduring a good ducking may admit of. We were cut off by an immense slope of snow on our left, which lay at so steep an angle that I knew it to be highly dangerous to attempt a crossing. It was in a soft and rotten condition; and, if the feet had started an avalanche, it would soon have rushed down the slope and then thrown the intruders over a thousand feet of nearly perpendicular rocks. One or two of the party went a little way across it in spite of my warnings, but soon came back, finding that the farther they went the worse they fared. We halted for some time and smoked the calumet on the top of a commanding rocky point, with dwarf oaks and bushes growing out of the clefts, where we enjoyed a full view of the waterfall in front, the river winding silently among the trees at the bottom of the valley a thousand feet below, and the white peaks and snow-fields on the other side of it. Conspicuously beautiful among these is the Sentinel Rock, rising like an obelisk to more than 3,000 feet above the valley, with a broken waterfall of nearly the same height on one side, and a steep ravine on the other, then covered with masses of snow and remains of avalanches.

There we long time sat in broad sunshine upon our rocky perch, close to the edge of the snow-slope, taking in what we could of the wondrous view in front of us, beneath us, and above us all around; watching and trying to count the water-rockets in their headlong flight through nearly five times the height of St. Paul's, some of them traversing the whole distance in unbroken beauty, and some shattered into dust in mid-career by a wind that from time to time swayed the whole cataract from right to left, and played with it like a downward plume of snow-white feathers. Then, dreaming over the weird history of this mysterious land through the ages that had passed before its yesterday's discovery by civilised man, I was thinking of it as the last *penetralia* of Indians who jabbered over the tidings of an incursion by an unheard-of race of men, and who swore to bury their tomahawks in the accursed heads of the foreigners; thinking of the Indians who had perished in the unequal encounter with the white man, and had left nothing behind them but a few miserable descendants to pick up acorns and beg for the crumbs which fall from the rich man's table; thinking of the 'Grizzly Bears' which had given their name to the valley, and had met with the same destruction as the tribes who had fought with them and lived upon them for ages; I was thinking, I say, of all these things, when my reverie was cut short by the merry laughter of the American ladies, who had walked after us from a point beyond which their horses could no longer be safely taken, and who by their presence turned the current of my thoughts, bringing to my fond remembrance Tennyson and his 'Morte d'Arthur' with the words :

> The old order changeth, yielding place to new,
> And God fulfils himself in many ways.

Next morning we mounted horses soon after breakfast and rode for a few miles up the Tenaya cañon to see the Mirror Lake. Soon after leaving the few houses in the valley, none of which except Leidig's were as yet open for the season, the valley divides into three cañons, the Tenaya on the left and the Illilouette on the right, with the main cañon of the Merced river in the middle, into which last the Nevada and Vernal Falls precipitate the only permanent waters of the central stream. The Bridal Veil, the Virgin's Tears, the Sentinel Fall, the Illilouette, and even the Great Yosemité Fall, only depend upon the melting of comparatively low-lying snow; and all of them disappear before the conclusion of the hot Californian summer. The main stream of the central cañon which dashes down through the Nevada and Vernal Falls, comes from the far higher level of some of the main peaks of the Sierra, where the snow never entirely disappears, though there are now no true glaciers. Among these, Mount Lyell rises to 13,227 feet above the sea, and Mount Dana and several others are about the same height; and from these it seems certain that a vast glacier must formerly have filled the Upper Tuolumne Valley at about 8,000 or 9,000 feet above the sea. Mr. Whitney reports having found an immense area of beautifully polished rocks, and all the manifest phenomena of lateral, medial, and terminal moraines which characterise a true glacier; and he calculates from the markings which he observed that the moving ice must have been a thousand feet in thickness. These marks, however, are not found in the Yosemité Valley.

Among other attractions to this elevated region are the traces of widely-extended volcanic action by the side of the ancient glacial phenomena, and Mr. Whitney mentions that in the neighbourhood of most fantastic mountains he found the edges of lava-beds 700 feet thick which had flowed over granite rocks 3,000 feet above the adjacent valley. Everything he says will more than confirm an idea which must suggest itself to anyone who gets even a few distant glimpses from the intermediate heights of the Yosemité precipices. There must be a very interesting and enjoyable region for a tour of some weeks among the snowy mountains and lofty passes which head in the Yosemité Valley and its branches. The full summer would be the proper season for it, and he shows how a party might live for weeks and months in these beautiful highlands, climbing, wandering, observing or collecting, all day, with almost a certainty of unbroken fine weather, and camping where they please in a delicious climate, with an abundance of wood and water to help them with the stores which baggage-mules carry from each camp to the next.

To return, however, to the Mirror Lake. This beautiful little lake is formed by the stream which flows through the Tenaya cañon, at a point where the valley is less than half a mile in width. Groups of noble firs fringe the greater part of its banks, and its marvellously glassy surface reflects the surrounding scenery with such vivid brightness that we sometimes thought the reflection looked more real than the reality. It is looked down upon by the precipices of the North Dome on one side and by the still more awful summit of the Half Dome on the other. This latter rises from almost close to the lake to a height of 4,737 feet above the valley. The upper 2,000 feet present an absolutely vertical surface towards the lake; the rest falls off with a very steep slope of about sixty or seventy degrees to the bottom of the cañon. Strange to say, this slope is 'not a *talus* of fragments fallen from above; it is a mass of granite rock, part and parcel of the solid structure of the Dome: the real pile of *débris* at the bottom is absolutely insignificant in dimensions, as compared with the Dome itself.' This may well be when we consider that the valley is scarcely half a mile in width, that the lake occupies about a quarter of this width, and the Half Dome rises nearly a mile in height directly above it. The form and appearance of this wonderful mountain certainly suggest a strong confirmation of the subsidence theory; it looks as if the original dome had been split vertically from the summit by some cause which dragged half the mountain 2,000 feet nearer down to a subterranean gulf. It is difficult to imagine any other solution of the problem. Considering the close proximity of a district in which volcanic action once operated upon a stupendous scale, it does not require a very strong flight of fancy to suppose that the lower foundations of the fallen mountain may have been vomited up with the vast lava-streams which formerly swept over the upper range.

Such are the giants which keep guard over the lonely little Mirror Lake. We wandered at our leisure about its banks watching the effects of every reflected rock and tree from different positions till about an hour before noon, when the sun peered suddenly over a shoulder of the Half Dome and produced a very singular appearance among the reflections on the water, as it seemed to creep downwards into the bosom of the lake. In some very shallow water at the edge I observed curiously rounded pieces of wood and bark, and after a short search I found some much more perfect specimens. I put the best I could find into my pocket, and I have it still. It is a piece of pine about eight inches long and three inches wide, perfectly worked and smoothly rounded into a flatly oval form by the action of water in its long and rough voyage from somewhere in the farthest forests of the Tenaya. One would suppose it must have been stopped on the way and pounded for many years among the rocks at the base of a waterfall until some extra flood floated it away into a harbour of rest.

In the gallop back to join the route to the Vernal Fall and the Nevada I contrived to lose myself in the forest which spreads over the wide part of the valley where the three cañons unite. A reckless young guide who led the way thought very little of how many there might be behind him; and while I waited a few minutes to speak to a friend coming in the opposite direction, the rest went on at full speed, and left the track by which we had come at some point without anything to mark it. I had gone a long way beyond it before I found my mistake. Then I rode back and found the marks of their horses' hoofs, but lost them again among thickets and grass. I made my way to the river, which I knew must be forded somewhere, and tried it in several places, but nothing could induce the animal to cross. Persuasion and force were equally useless: whenever we got at all near the middle he made it perfectly clear that he was prepared to throw me into the river, or roll with me, or do anything else except taking me over to the other side. At last I was obliged to give it up in despair and content myself with a distant view of the Vernal Fall instead of climbing up its curious ladders and hunting for *Adiantum pedatum* amongst its damp rocks. After riding about some time by myself I went back to the hotel, and in the afternoon had an interesting walk by a steep path which winds upwards from the base of the Sentinel Rock to the summit of the Glacier Point. My companion and I found that this path had not been touched since last season, and we crossed a very wide and steeply inclined *couloir* of avalanche snow piled up in strange confusion with fragments of trees and rubbish brought down in its descent; and we had some very fine views over the valley beneath us, with the Half Dome and Cap of Liberty in front. The Nevada Fall takes its leap of about 600 feet from close to the foot of this so-called Cap of Liberty, whence the river passes through a line of rapids to the Vernal Fall, where it descends another 400 feet, just as if it came down a perpendicular step. This is the main stream of the Merced river, and all the other waterfalls dry up in the summer.

On the whole I am disposed to think that we were a little too early in the season; but that is far better than being too late. Probably May is the most perfect month for seeing the Yosemité. We found the waterfalls in grand order, but so they would have been for another month or two, and we should have found more ferns and flowers; among the most conspicuous of which would be the fragrant blossoms of the white *Azalea occidentalis* and *Penstemons* of various species, blue and scarlet. On the other hand, we had the full glory of the countless flowers which carpeted the lower-lying lands which we travelled over in going and returning, and which only enjoy a very short season before drying up in the sun. The abundance of the snow still remaining on the mountains and among the forest added a great deal of variety and beauty to the appearance of a region to which the adjective 'beautiful' can hardly be said to apply. The Yosemité scenery is grand and even sublime, but it is not beautiful in the picturesque style of Switzerland. Many people ask what the valley and its mountains look like as compared with the Alps. I can only say that it is almost impossible to compare them at all. The precipices of the Yosemité are stupendous; and the solemn seclusion of the valley enclosed by them, its silent mirror-like river, its unequalled waterfalls, are impressive to a degree bordering on a sensation of awful grandeur; the deficiency is in colour and form. The colouring is cold, and the inherent faults of granite as an element in scenery are seen to the utmost on a gigantic scale.

It loves to appear in huge dome-like forms, with a complete absence of all the salient pinnacles, narrow ridges, and wild ravines which distinguish the greater part of our Alps. In tropical countries under the influence of constant heat and frequent moisture it disintegrates easily, and assumes such fantastic forms as those of the Organ Mountains in Brazil; but in California it looks hard as steel, and gives off scarcely a particle of its massive forms. The only outline in the Yosemité which at all approaches the exquisite form of the European Alps is the Sentinel Rock, which, as I have said, somewhat recalls the Aiguille Dru at Chamonix. The want of the green slopes which give their name to the Alps is another serious defect in this Yosemité scenery, and nothing can atone for the absence of glaciers in a mountain-land. It may properly be called solemn, sublime, grand, and marvellous ; but with regard to beauty, in the strict sense of the word, it is not to be compared with the charms of Switzerland. The form of many of these wonderful rocks is anything but beautiful, and El Capitan himself might be profanely compared to a steeper but decapitated Wetterhorn.

After two days spent in rambling and scrambling about among the woods and rocks and waterfalls of this extraordinary region, we turned our steps back by the way that we had come. The family with the babes had been so thoroughly knocked up that they stayed behind to rest for another day or two, and our pace was something very different from that to which I had been reduced while in attendance upon them. One of our American lady friends appeared to be an accomplished rider, and led off in a style which would have carried her well with many a hunting-field, so we were not long in galloping over the first half-dozen miles among the dark woods by the side of the glassy river, and saying good-bye to El Capitan on one side and the downward plume of the Bridal Veil on the other. Then the narrow and precipitous path reduced us to crawling again at a foot-pace for a good many miles, after which came another lively spin over a very pretty piece of grassy country with groups of handsome trees and bushes, among which there was a quantity of plants that at a distance looked like lilacs in full bloom, but proved to be papilionaceous shrubs. We managed rather better this time in the matter of lunch by the side of the river, and pushed on to Hite's Cove in time to go on the same day over the next range of hills and sleep at Skelton's.

This second pull up of about 2,000 feet was very hard work for horses at the end of a long day, and there were still many miles of bad road before we got to our sleeping quarters; and I imagine that neither man nor beast was sorry to come to the end of it. Buffalo Jim kept his appointment, and brought up his coach and team to be ready for the early morning. Cheery Mrs. Skelton bustled about to get something for supper in a small back room; but, knowing the bedroom resources of the house to be very limited, I rather wondered what they would do for us in that way. They were equal to the occasion, and led four or five of us into what appeared to be a large barn. Strange to say, however, it was meant for a ball-room, decorated with evergreens and simple ornaments. As the house is one of those lonely places in the forest clearings which are scattered at distances of miles apart, I wondered very much where the guests came from and how they got home again. However, it had been done in some way or other. We now found low truckle-beds scattered about this apartment, and slept well; but there was a sharp frost at night, and the strong currents of cold air which blew through the interstices of the planks close to my head were anything but agreeable.

In the morning we had, according to custom in such places, to turn out and wash under the open verandah, though there was a sharp frost and fresh ice. Then came a very early breakfast, and at seven o'clock Buffalo Jim had stowed and crammed us into the car, which, after about three hours of bumping over picturesque roads among hills and forests and sheets of flowers, once more landed us at Mariposa. We halted for food and a fresh team of horses, with which we went on to Merced the same evening, and, across the level plain, had a race against the setting sun to see which of the two would first reach its resting-place. The sun beat us by a couple of minutes.

CHAPTER XIII

Stockton and Milton—Fine drive to Murphy's—'Trap-door' Spiders—'Shakes' —The Big Trees of Calaveras—Cutting down a Giant—The 'Mother of the Forest'—The Prairie Owl—The Rising Generation—Sacramento City—Farewell to California—The Farallon Islands—Sea-li onsand countless Birds— A Flying Escort across the Pacific—John Chinaman on board—'Perdidi Diem'—Our Escort departs—Arrival at Yokohama.

HAVING BEEN DEBARRED by the state of the snow from combining the Yosemité with the Mariposa grove of 'Big Trees,' we now had to take a fresh departure on our way to see those of Calaveras. This involved going by the railway from Merced to Stockton and Milton, before taking to the road for an expedition of three or four days. Stockton is one of the most painfully uninteresting cities that can well be imagined, and seemed to me to be scarcely more suggestive of dollars than of a school of landscape-painters. Situated on the dead level of a fertile alluvial plain, it was just recovering from the effects of the winter season, which had apparently converted it into a sea of mud, which we were told would be speedily reconverted into dust that would endure through the summer. At Milton station we were uncarted from the train, and found that, as usual in that part of the world, there was nobody to tell us anything, or in any way assist a wanderer. The railway-porter of Europe seems to be almost unknown in the Far West; at all events his representatives, if they exist, are too proud to indicate their calling by wearing a distinctive costume. The theory appears to be that everybody should be able to take care of himself, and that nobody has a right to have more luggage than that which he can carry in a hand-bag. I daresay this primitive simplicity is delightful when people get accustomed to it; but to a stranger it is rather a nuisance. He generally has to stand by his bag upon the platform, and take his chance of finding some one to answer a question.

Some of these lonely stations at the half-built centres of future prosperity call up the story of an unusual number of passengers having been seen to alight at one of them, and attracting the attention of a looker-on who could not resist indulging his curiosity. He began to ask what they were about, and it appeared they had come to start a new settlement in the neighbourhood. He found young men and maidens, healthy carpenters and builders, farmers and shoemakers, all in due proportion. Then his eye fell upon a crumpled up and very ancient man with one foot apparently in the grave. 'Well, what are you going to do with *him*?' he asked. 'Well, you see,' said the other man, 'we are going to open a church, a theaytre, a hotel, and a cemetery; and we shall open the cemetery with *him*! I reckon he'll do his part.'

Milton looked quite the place for such a scene. Our pleasant American friends, who were still going on with us, looked as much puzzled as ourselves about things in general; but by degrees we straggled with our bags across an open space surrounded with irregular buildings, and found that the coach that would take us to Murphy's was another of the detestable narrow-seated *char-à-bancs* from which we had suffered so many days of torture. The Americans were again good-humouredly resigning themselves to a squeeze, and indeed there seemed no alternative till I fortunately looked into an adjoining stable and found a very neat car that would just hold four people, including the driver. I knew that my friend, Mr. Rawson, was an admirable coachman, and it was arranged that our party of four should take this machine to ourselves instead of joining in the general cram. A capital pair of horses were found, and away we went, following the coach as closely as we could, the road being often uncertain.

This was an altogether delightful expedition. We were immediately once more among the rolling hills and park-like slopes, the scattered groups of trees and countless sheets of flowers, which characterise the charming region of California that separates the lower plains from the high mountain-land. Here we found, in addition to the blue and white species of *Nemophila*, another with purple spots at the edge of the white petals, a very lovely flower which I believe is *N. atomaria* of the gardeners. Damp places produced an abundance of a large handsome yellow *Mimulus*; the openings in the thickets were now and then occupied by enormous purple mounds, which proved to be masses of blooming lupines; a scarlet *Lychnis* made brilliant patches among the bushes; and the bright green foliage of the 'buck eye,' *Æsculus Californica*, or Californian horse-chestnut, shone out in fine contrast to the darker foliage of the black oak. There was a great deal of hard work up-hill as we drew towards the higher belts of conifers, and this gave many a welcome opportunity of taking to our feet and looking more closely into the treasures of the road-side; but it was always necessary to keep an eye on the coach, for in the wet season things on wheels have to pick out the best way they can in default of a regularly made road; and sometimes that which looks only like a couple of stray wheel-marks leading into the forest may be the only practicable way to take. The land was only beginning to dry up, though the weather was already delicious, and we had many places on the road which required a coachman like Mr. Rawson, who drove as if he had been 'in a manner born to' the exigencies of coaching in California.

About sunset we passed a very rough part of the ascent, and were rather surprised to find ourselves for the last hour of our thirty miles on a piece of tolerably good road parallel to a lively river which, thanks partly to a good moon, led us for supper to the famous mining-station which rejoices in the name of 'Murphy's.' The present proprietors of the 'hotel' are very intelligent and agreeable men; and here again, as at other similar places, we were much struck with the apparent quietness and peaceableness of the rough-looking miners who frequented the house and amused themselves with cards and billiards in the public bar-room, which we all used in common. One or two lads showed a desire to trade in some of the natural curiosities of the place, especially in the clay nests of the wonderful 'trap-door spiders,' of which they had a good collection of better specimens than I can remember having seen in Brazil. The spiders are very large, and the beautiful construction of their clay-door and hinge, which enables them either to shut themselves up invisibly, or to put out their limbs in search of prey, has long been a matter of interest to naturalists. Sets of studs and buttons made of the pretty wood of the *madrona* and *manzanita* were in considerable request.

Next morning we were off early with the same horses to drive fifteen or sixteen miles to the 'Big Trees.' The greater part of the way was through forests of magnificent pines and firs, getting larger and larger as we advanced, and many of them were eight or ten feet in diameter with a height of about 250 feet. It was a cruel sight to see with what recklessness these noble trees are sacrificed in the manufacture of 'shakes,' or short split pieces of wood like our 'shingles,' only much larger, and used in a similar way. The tree is cut down, and sawn across at about a yard from the stump; if it splits up easily into good straight 'shakes,' it is worked through in similar lengths, but if it proves knotty or twisted so as to split badly, it is abandoned at once, and left to rot upon the ground, as we saw them very frequently by the side of the road.

By degrees we got into larger and thicker patches of snow, and the air was exceedingly keen; presently we found ourselves between walls of snow five or six feet high, between which the road had been lately cut through a drift by the people of the Calaveras Hotel. The forest, which for a long time past had prevented us from seeing anything except the trees in our immediate neighbourhood, now opened out a little to the left, and turning slightly in that direction we found ourselves face to face with the Calaveras Grove of Giants. Through snow about a foot deep on an average the road led us between two of the outlying monsters, whose clean reddish stems, rising to the height of about 275 feet, formed royal portals nearly half as high again as the Monument of London. Two minutes later we drove up to the door of a comfortable-looking hotel which would be a charming residence in summer, but was now almost surrounded by vast piles of snow shovelled together in trying to clear the approaches; and a drift of twenty or thirty feet deep still lay undisturbed at the back of the house, darkening the lofty dining-room and filling it with an atmosphere of piercing cold. The little garden in front was literally buried in snow which had drifted up over the fence; but above us was a cloudless blue sky, and a brilliant sun to sparkle on the snow and gild the trees with glory.

Everybody has of course heard and read abundantly about the 'Big Trees' of California; but so many vague and incorrect statements have been made about their size, their age, and their distribution, that I need not apologise for giving a few general remarks concerning them, and a few facts mainly derived from the Report of the State Geologist who surveyed the whole district with the utmost care. It appears that this Calaveras Grove was the first to be discovered by white men, in the person of a hunter who in the year 1852 brought down the news, and was of course disbelieved. However, the reputation of the trees spread about, and the first scientific description of the tree was given by Dr. Lindley in the 'Gardeners' Chronicle' of December 24, 1853, from specimens sent to him through Messrs. Veitch. Overlooking its close affinity to the already described 'Redwood,' which had been named *Sequoia sempervirens* by Endlicher in 1847, he treated it as a new genus, and called it *Wellingtonia gigantea*. In the following year, however, at a meeting of the 'Société Botanique de France,' the eminent botanist Decaisne exhibited specimens of both species. together; and, giving his reasons for considering them to belong to the same genus, he gave the name of *Sequoia gigantea* to the latest discovered and the largest of the two. I fancy that nobody who could compare them together would hesitate to confirm this decision, though it is very probable that the English public, having been accustomed to the name of Wellingtonia, will stick to it to the end of the chapter.

A very remarkable point about this tree is its very limited locality. Mr. Whitney only knows of eight groves in which it has been found, and he estimates that the whole of them together do not cover more than fifty square miles. They are limited to the western slopes of the Sierra Nevada between about 36° and 38° of North latitude; and their elevation above the sea-level is nowhere much less than 5,000 feet, or more than 7,000 feet; the most northerly being at the lower, and the most southerly at the higher elevation. They are always in connection with various other conifers, almost as high as themselves; and the pictures of a gigantic tree spreading out by itself in an open space are completely fictitious. The *S. sempervirens*, or 'Redwood,' is, on the contrary, entirely confined to the coast ranges, and flourishes nowhere unless it is frequently enveloped in the ocean fogs. Moreover, though it rarely attains anything like the dimensions of its gigantic congener, it seems that it does so occasionally. Near Santa Cruz is a grove of

'Redwoods' in which one tree measures 50 feet in circumference and 275 feet in height. Near Crescent City one was measured 58 feet round at four feet from the base; and there is a story of a hollow stump of one seven miles from Eureka, 38 feet in diameter, in which thirty-three pack-mules were corraled at the same time. Though at present only known to exist in California, there are several *fossil* species of Sequoia, one of which is found in the Miocene Tertiary of Greenland at 70° N. latitude: it is called *Sequoia Langsdorffii*, and is so difficult to be distinguished from the 'Redwood' of California that it may, perhaps, be identical with it.

The Calaveras Grove where we now were occupies a belt about 3,200 feet long and 700 feet wide: it contains about ninety or a hundred Sequoias of large size, but very few young ones, except on the outskirts. In the deep gloom of the main part of the grove I saw none, though the ground was covered with thousands and thousands of cones in all stages of ripeness and decay. The upper soil, wherever it was clear from snow, seemed to me to consist of scarcely anything but an agglomeration of the cones and spines of various species of firs, and this barrenness of soil, combined with the darkness caused by the vast canopy of tree-tops, must naturally be extremely unfavourable to new growth. One of the freaks of Nature is that the cones of these gigantic trees are much smaller than those of any other conifers that I know, while some of the pines growing amongst them, and comparatively insignificant in size, sprinkled the ground with cones sixteen inches in length.

When our teeth had chattered over a hasty meal in

the ice-cold dining-room, we sallied out to explore the grove. Snow-shoes were ready for those who liked to use them; but the snow was so soft and wet with melting that, dreadful as may be the word 'legs' to an American ear, it is nevertheless true that the ladies submitted to having those limbs encased and tied up in sacking to do duty as gaiters. Then we wandered into the vast 'contiguity of shade.' We had lately passed through so many leagues of forests which had gradually accustomed the eye to trees of more than 250 feet in height, that I felt at first a certain sense of disappointment at finding that the biggest of the 'Big Trees' were only seventy or eighty feet higher than many of the other pines around and amongst them. When, however, we came close up to them this feeling was soon lost in an ever-increasing wonder at the sublimity of their proportions and their marvellous superiority to anything near them.

There is something positively stupendous about their magnitude. You stand upon the polished stump of one that was twenty-seven feet in diameter at six feet from the ground: you hear that five strong men spent twenty-five days in cutting it down, and almost broke through the crust of the earth in felling it: you enter a wooden kiosque which has been built upon the stump, and you know that forty or fifty people have danced in it without any more sacrifice of fans and jewels than is customary in a London drawing-room: you crick your neck in trying to look up to the top of its nearest living neighbour, and compare yourself to the London cocks and hens which Darwinically develop long necks and legs by trying to reach over the area-railings: against the deep blue sky you see the last crest of glorious green, waving at a height which you know to be not much less than the top of St. Paul's: you steady your eye by turning to your feet and counting thirty long strides round the base of a giant; and then— and then—you begin to comprehend the marvel of the 'Big Trees.'

The *modus operandi* of bringing the monster down was very ingenious, and the marks of it are plainly visible upon the end of the trunk. Axes and saws would have had no effect upon a tree nearly thirty feet thick; so it was resolved to sever it by boring with gigantic augers, each hole working in the same horizontal plane towards the centre from every inch of the circumference. This occupied twenty-five days; and it required three days' work with wedges to upset it after the severance was complete. The trunk was afterwards cut again at thirty feet above the former place, and this section was carefully examined by the Survey party. They counted the rings of growth, and found 1,255; they separated them into periods of a hundred years, and have given a table of the result; from which it appears that, beginning from the outside, they found the first hundred rings occupying three inches; the gradation was nearly uniform up to the twelfth or inmost hundred, which extended over thirteen inches. Inside this were fifty-five more rings, occupying 9·4 inches, and a slight hollow, allowing for which and for the time taken for the first forty years of growth, it may be considered that this tree was about 1,300 years old. It was one of the finest in the grove, and there is no reason for supposing any of them to be much older.

The principal trees are all named and marked with

The Foot of a Fir Tree.

white labels, and there is something very amusing in the incongruity of some of the titles. The 'Keystone State,' with its 325 feet, is the highest of the Calaveras trees; and amongst them we find ' Abraham Lincoln ' and the ' Three Graces;' 'Florence Nightingale' and 'William Cullen Bryant;' 'U. S. Grant' and 'George Washington;' 'Uncle Sam' and 'Lady Franklin;' *cum multis aliis quæ nunc perscribere longum est.* The ' Mother of the Forest ' still remains a ghastly monument of human cruelty. She was flayed alive some years ago, and an extent of 116 feet of her skin was set up in England for the gratification of visitors to the Crystal Palace, where it was ultimately burned. Many of the posts and bars which were driven into her sides to support the scaffoldings are still there, sticking out like spears in the flanks of an elephant.

Pieces of the tree which was cut down are every now and then made into cups, candlesticks, and other souvenirs. There is plenty of it yet, however, and it is likely to be almost as prolific in relics as the wreck of the ' Royal George,' the True Cross, or Noah's Ark upon the top of Ararat. We supplied ourselves with a few of them, and had our last look at the Big Trees while the horses were being brought out. Then we put on all steam, and drove back over the sixteen miles to Murphy's with as much speed as was compatible with the nature of the road. Next morning we were off again very early, and long before noon had said farewell to the hills and forests of California. We gradually came down again to the region of cornfields and flowers; the blue and white *Nemophilas* seemed, if possible, more countless than they were a few days before; and when the necessities of the road made us turn a little aside, and I saw the wheels crushing through solid beds of blossoms, I felt what Tennyson makes his dear old 'Talking Oak' express:

> I felt a pang within
> As when I see the woodman lift
> His axe to slay my kin.

It reminded me too of my sensations a dozen years ago when, in company with a 'Gaucho,' I first found myself riding at a hand-gallop through sheets of our scarlet verbena upon the rolling plains of the Argentine Republic; '*Que lastima!*' 'What a pity!' I said to my companion, pointing to the brilliant flowers which we were trampling under foot as if they were mere heathens in the way of the car of Juggernaut. '*Quiere flores?*' 'Do you want flowers?' he replied; and, without checking speed, he threw himself out of the saddle in Indian fashion low enough to sweep the ground with his fingers, and came up again with a handful of them.

As we drew near Milton among the flat country, everything in the scene changed rapidly. Huge grey squirrels, nearly as large as rabbits, were playing about the trunks of the oak-trees, and we passed a good many of the placid little owls that sit about upon the grass of the North American prairies in company with the so-called prairie-dogs, in exactly the same fashion as they do on the Pampas of South America in company with the biscacha, a somewhat similar rodent, but of far larger size. In the last few miles of the journey we had a taste of what Californian dust would be in the coming dry season. It nearly smothered us in a very short time, and on arriving at a humble hostelry dignified with the name of 'Tornado Hotel,' we had to take half our clothes off and souse curselves with water before we could do anything else.

Here, in front of the railway station, was the end of our delightful cruise upon wheels in combination with horses. The proprietor of the latter, who also drove the coach, was a very intelligent man and capital companion, with whom I had many opportunities of a pleasant chat. I was talking to him once about the rising generation in the many lonely places we had seen where isolated families were growing up without much chance of schooling except what little their parents, and very busy parents too, could find time to give them.

'Well,' he said, 'I'm sure I don't know; in most countries I should say that a considerable lot of them would come to be hanged; many of them don't care for man or God either; boys and girls, when they grow up a bit, do just what they like, and go pretty much where they like; and if they get into trouble they clear out where they please. I know of a man, not so far from where we've been passing, who has got two boys, Sam and Joe. In the work of the house it was Joe's business to set out the knives and forks and plates for their meals. He didn't seem quite to get on with Sam, and one evening he laid out nothing for him. Sam said, "If you do that to-morrow, Joe, I'll shoot you." The same thing did happen next day, and Sam went to his father and asked for his revolver. "What do you want that for, you young cuss?" said his parent. "Why I mean to shoot Joe, as I said I would." The father reflected, went to his room, quietly took the charges out of his pistol and gave it to the boy with only the caps on. Sam was as good as his word, and "commenced shooting" at his brother the moment he saw him, but of course under the circumstances no harm was done.'

My friend said he thought everybody was satisfied. Sam was very proud of not having hesitated in his intention to shoot his brother; Joe was very glad to get off so easily; and the father was doubly gratified by the pluck of his first-born and the safety of the younger brother! Such was the story gravely told me by our coachman, as characteristic of the rising generation in the backwoods.

Knowing that Sacramento City is the official capital of the State of California, we made a point of going to see it before returning to San Francisco. If anyone asked me whether I should advise him to follow our example, I should emphatically say, 'Don't.' We had no means of going there that day except by a luggage train, or 'freight train,' as it is called in America, and we spent five hours and a half in getting over forty-eight miles. On arriving at Sacramento we found ourselves four desolate individuals at 9.40 P.M.; and, as usual, saw no responsible person to tell us anything. However, with some difficulty we succeeded in getting our traps to the nearest hotel, where, though desperately hungry after a very long day, we found we could get nothing whatever to eat at that not very late hour. We sallied into the streets and looked into all the shop-windows that were open, till we found shelter in a dirty little place where, however, we were truly thankful to get a tolerable chop with oysters and beer. *En passant*, we saw the half-open door of a fire-engine station, in which the horses stood ready harnessed, and the men 'at attention' with lights and everything ready to rush into the streets at the first word of alarm. The inhabitants of these American cities have abundant reason to be afraid of fire.

The water in the bedrooms was about the colour and consistency of thin pea-soup, and the proprietors would not or could not give us anything better, so I postponed washing till the return next day to the luxuries of 'Frisco.' In the morning, daylight revealed the fact that we were in a perfectly flat city, scarcely raised above the level of a river which appeared to combine the attributes of the yellow Tiber and the dirty Thames. We visited the Capitol, a really handsome building something in the style of that at Washington, and climbed to the top of the dome for a view over a fertile but uninteresting plain. Mr. Rawson and Mr. Wheatley went down the river by an early steamer at a fare of one dollar for the 138 miles, and had a race with an opposition boat which did the same work for two 'bits,' or a shilling, so I was happy to find that they had not been 'bust up.' I waited to see our other friend, Mr. Hedges, off by the train to a place in the middle of the vast continent, and took an afternoon train to San Francisco by Vallejo. In crossing the Bay we were very coolly bumped by a rival steamer, which evidently tried to disable us and run in first. Going on a nearly parallel course she deliberately steered down upon our quarter, and 'collided.' There was a considerable amount of smashed bulwarks and cracking planks, accompanied by much shrieking and execration, all of which I fear I took very phlegmatically, perhaps because I felt sure that the affair would not be very serious.

I ought not to leave Sacramento without saying how I gave a small lesson upon 'inflation' to one of its citizens. After seeing my friend on his way, I had nothing to do till my train started, and there appeared to be nothing on earth to see, so I strolled along the street till I happened to find a pleasant-looking man at the door of a money-changer's office. The window was full of various coins and notes, as such windows are all the world over; and, as I felt rather desolate, I thought this gentleman would do very well for a chat. I made the excuse of having a few English sovereigns in my purse, which I asked him to turn into dollars. As I opened my purse I found a Buenos Ayres paper dollar, which I had kept as a curiosity. 'There,' said I, 'did you ever see such a thing as that? That's a paper dollar, and it is only worth 2d. sterling.' He was very much surprised, and called up a friend who was as much surprised as himself. 'That,' said I, 'is the result of issuing paper money at discretion till it is hardly worth the cost of the paper and print.' He thanked me very much for making him a present of this curiosity for his collection; and then, going to a drawer, he said, 'Well, you have been kind enough to give me a dollar worth 2d. sterling: allow me in return to make you a present of this twenty-dollar Confederate note; but I'm afraid I'm hardly square with you then, for the note I give you is not worth two cents.'

The time had now come to wind up affairs in the New World and prepare for the great leap of 5,000 miles across the Pacific. We paid a farewell visit to Cliff House and the sea-lions, who showed themselves to great advantage as the surf was running rather higher than usual, and plunged grandly among their island-homes. We saw a few more city sights, and in company with our charming Boston friend, Mr. Clarke, saw a May-day fête of some thousands of children at Woodward's Gardens. It was a very pretty sight, and everything was admirably managed. Next morning, May 2, we left our comfortable quarters and kind friends of the Grand Hotel, and went on board the good ship 'China,' of 4,000 tons, and one of the finest vessels of the American Pacific Mail. She was a marvellous contrast in matters of order, comfort, and cleanliness to what we had found on board the 'Arizona' of the same Company; but the route to Japan and China is considered altogether a superior service to that of the line to Panama.

The quay was crowded with people who came to see the great ship start, and conspicuous amongst them was a group of Chinese women in their best dresses of plum-coloured silk, with their black hair combed out to its utmost distension. It seemed to me like leaving home as we moved in stately fashion out of the Golden Gate between the familiar hills, now really golden with escholtzias and lupines; and I thought of all the happy days we had spent among the trees and flowers, the beauties and the grandeurs of California in the freshness of early Spring. The great beam of the engine beat solemnly up and down, and the paddles pounded away with the jerky motion caused by the 'walking-beam' engines of America; and we knew that if all went right, they would never be checked till we anchored in Japan, unless we happened to fall in with the returning ship of the same Company.

With the prospect of a voyage of twenty-five days before us, during which we ought not to go within about a thousand miles of any sort of land, we started with the enormous quantity of 1,600 tons of coal, the result of which was that we travelled faster in the second half of the voyage than in the first, but only made up an average of about 200 miles a day.

There is, however, one remarkable little group of islands close to which we passed only four hours after leaving San Francisco. These are the Farallones, mere wild masses of fantastic rocks, against which the ocean-swell is perpetually breaking, and dashing up towers of foam. There is a good lighthouse, and the men in charge of it are the only regular human inhabitants, though at a certain season of the year there is an incursion of seekers after the eggs of the countless sea-birds that live upon the islands. As we approached, we found ourselves in the midst of an extraordinary scene. The air all round the ship was absolutely alive with gulls of various descriptions, as thick as snow-flakes, jostling one another in their flight, hovering over the deck, screaming, clamouring, and dashing down in dozens to fight for each scrap which was pitched overboard from the remnants of the first meal at sea. Innumerable cormorants were passing to and fro, in their very intent and businesslike fashion ; and at every moment the progress of the ship startled huge flocks of their young flappers, scarcely yet able to fly, who scuttled across the smooth surface of the sea as fast as they could go towards the islands, exactly as I have seen a crowd of ducklings rushing to avoid the charge of a voracious pike.

Enormous quantities of eggs are taken every year from

the islands, and yet there remain legions of birds to occupy them in company with the herds of sea-lions which inhabit the lower rocks, and roared a royal farewell to us across the ocean. These very interesting animals are a species of *Otaria*, or seals with external ears, the possession of which distinguishes them from common or true seals. There is a capital article in the 'Contemporary Review' for December 1875, which gives a very complete account of nine various species of sea-lions or *Otaria*, from which I conclude this Californian species is *Otaria Stelleri*.[1] The soft seal-skin of commerce comes entirely from some of the sea-lion family, and not from true seals; but this particular species has such scanty fur that it is useless for clothing. The head-quarters for the finest skins are in the Prybilov Islands off the coast of Siberia, in the Behring Sea, where the hunting is conducted in a very systematic fashion. At the Farallones the wild beating of the surf against the rocks, the screaming and whirling of multitudinous birds, and the solemn roar of the sea-lions booming across the water, make an *ensemble* which can never be forgotten by anyone who has seen them; and it is fortunate that a vessel bound for Japan goes so close to them that everything can be seen and heard to perfection. The birds hung about us till the evening, but on the following morning all were gone with the exception of about fifty or sixty huge brown gulls, very like small albatrosses, who were sweeping backwards and forwards across the waste of waters in our wake; and who, we were told, would go with us through all the 5,000 miles to Japan. Mr.

---

[1] Those at the Brighton Aquarium are of this species.

Rawson caught one of them with a hook; it proved to be a very powerful bird with a formidable beak, and measured seven feet six inches across the wings. They straddle awkwardly with their legs when they want to alight on the water, and fight with one another for scraps; and when they wish to rise again they are obliged to almost run along the water for some little way before they can fairly take wing and tuck up their long legs.

As to the 'China,' it was impossible to imagine a more comfortable ship, or one better managed. The food was luxurious, with salmon and other dainties kept fresh in ice for the greater part of the voyage, and for the first few days we had even strawberries in the same fashion. There was a large upper deck with a clear promenade of nearly 400 feet long, and abundance of room for the various games which prevail at sea; and there was a snug library in what goes by the name of the 'Social Hall.' The Chinese waiters were admirably drilled, and did their spiriting gently; there is a kind of delicacy and lightness in these China boys which makes them go about their work more in the manner of a 'neat-handed Phyllis' than in that of the sterner sex. They are very clean and painstaking, and their white dresses and long black pig-tails look exceedingly picturesque. One day, when a heavy north-west wind was rolling the ship a good deal and damaging the crockery, I saw a nice young pigtail struggling with a pile of about twenty plates, and having to resolve upon either dropping the plates or falling forward on the passengers at dinner: he preferred property to politeness, stuck to his plates with all his might, and saved them by throwing himself forward between the heads of two stout gentlemen, whose shoulders saved him from falling with his nose in a dish of stewed chicken.

On the second day of our voyage the first of our Chinese passengers died, and was followed by a few more before long. It is one of the duties of the ship's doctor to embalm them or preserve them by some corresponding process; they are then put into coffins and taken home comfortably to their friends. To throw one overboard would probably produce a mutiny, and as the crew are all Chinamen except the officers and quartermasters, it would perhaps be as well not to disregard their feelings in a matter which to them is one of sacred importance. A sick Chinaman will come on board quite happy and fully prepared to die in a day or two, knowing he will be taken back to home and heaven; but the Company would soon be deprived of their Celestial passengers if they thought that there was any chance of their being pitched into the sea. Most of them never show themselves for the whole voyage: if a few of them come up for a breath of fresh air on deck it is a certain sign that the wind has gone into a warmer quarter than usual. We had W.N.W. and N.N.W. winds for the greater part of the time, and it was generally cold enough for a thick jacket.

There were only about half a dozen English passengers besides ourselves, but most of them were capital companions; and we had the advantage of the society of an American Admiral going out to hoist his flag on board the 'Hartford,' accompanied by his wife and several officers of his staff, who were, as I have always found officers of the American Navy, exceedingly agreeable and intelligent men. The whole party of cabin-passengers was so small that everybody knew everybody else, and there was plenty of room for us all to have separate state-rooms.

When we had been four or five days at sea we were told that if we liked to write letters, a bag would be ready in the hope of our meeting the homeward-bound 'Japan' in a couple of days. The laudable custom of the Company's vessels was to try to steer so exactly the same course as to fall in with the returning ship, and effect an exchange of letters and news. On this occasion, however, to the great disappointment of everybody, we missed the 'Japan,' and had to finish our letters on arriving at Yokohama: we were told, however, that they generally succeeded in meeting, which, in a voyage of 5,000 miles, shows pretty accurate navigation. The 'Japan' has since then been burnt at sea between Yokohama and Hong Kong, when an awful loss of life took place among the Chinese passengers. Two years ago the 'America,' the finest of all the Company's ships, was burnt at Yokohama, and, though she was actually in harbour, she burnt so quickly that I believe eighty lives were lost before the people could be got out of the ship. Fire is the great danger to be dreaded in such vessels as these. They are built of pine-wood, and those who know this know also that when once alight they burn like a box of matches. Great precautions are doubtless taken, and the captains inspect every part of their ships every day; but, after all apparent care, ships will take fire sometimes, and woe to those who find themselves in a box of burning deal, thousands of miles from the nearest land!

Nothing, however, occurred to disturb our serenity as we went steadily on over purple seas flecked with white caps, and escorted by our great and faithful gulls, whose long knife-like wings were seen every morning with the dawn sweeping right and left over the surface of the sea, and continuing without rest till night closed in and hid them. But if we were not manifestly threatened with the immediate loss of the whole of our lives, it was clear that on passing the 180th degree of longitude we should at all events be deprived of one day. As we approached the fatal spot, many jokes were tried by the old hands, such as remarking that having gone up-hill so far, we should now begin to go down again; or saying that the place was marked by a magnificent buoy, always illuminated at night; but at last the reality came. May 17 was a Sunday, and the next day at noon was posted up as Tuesday, 19th. Monday had been thrown overboard and disappeared, and there was nothing left to represent it in our diaries but 'Perdidi diem' in a black border.

Most people of course know that this is only a conventional custom to set right a difficulty of time, and that we should have had *two* Mondays if we had been going in the opposite direction. I should hardly have mentioned the matter if I had not fallen in with a certain book in the ship's library. It contained an account of this same voyage by an American minister of unknown sect, who was greatly exercised when he came to reflect upon this loss of a day. The worthy man was enabled to realise for the first time the awful fact that 'the Sabbath' was not kept at the same time in all parts of the world; and he starts a number of delicate questions almost as absurd as the famous inquiry of 'how many millions of angels can dance on the point of a needle without jostling?' He appears to wonder what would have happened if his Sabbath had been taken away from him bodily as our Monday was. He learns with a kind of horror that in two neighbouring islands in the Pacific, one of which got its Christianity from the West and the other from the East, the Sunday is kept on different days; and he raises the question with great apparent gravity and seriousness as to whether the Almighty will be disposed to pardon His creatures for this want of unity in their worship of Him!

On May 24 we loyally kept Her Majesty's birthday, our little English party supplying champagne to the rest of the passengers. The American Admiral proposed the health of the Queen of England, and I had the honour of being asked to return thanks. On the 27th we found the great gulls had left us during the night. By some mental process of their own they knew that the voyage was over, and that they might rest somewhere quietly till the next steamer went back to San Francisco. At three o'clock in the afternoon that day we sighted land, and soon afterwards had a good view of the snow-capped summit of sacred Fujiyama at a distance of about 100 miles. At 9.30 we rounded the headland and lighthouse of Cape King, and, after mooring the good ship in the early morning, we went to sleep wondering what Yokohama would look like by the light of day.

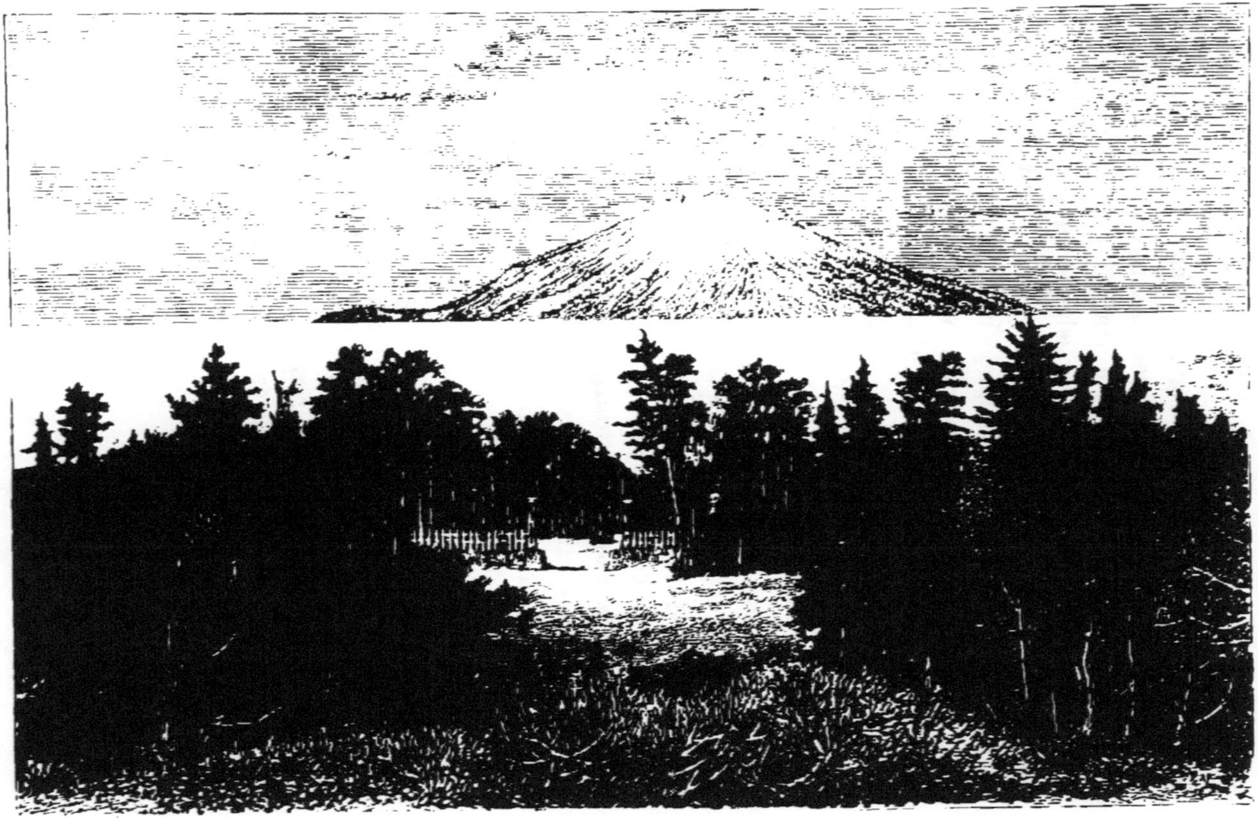

Fuji-Yama, Japan

CHAPTER XIV.

First view of Yokohama—Substitutes for Cabs—Lilium Aurntums—Start for the Interior—Our Head Coolie—Pelted with Blossoms—The 'Plains of Heaven'—Kanasawa—Kamakura, and the Temple of Hachimon—Daibootz—Disestablishment of Buddhism—What the Priests thought of it—Popular Religion—Will they break their toys?—The Holy Island of Inoshima—Race into Fuji-sawa—A break-down—The Treaty Limit—Town of Odawarra—Abundance of Ferns—Destruction of Hata—A Native Gentleman—View of Hakoni.

THERE WAS NO NEED of rousing to make us get up early in the morning for our first near view of mysterious Japan. From early dawn we had been surrounded as if by a swarm of marine bees. Boats of all descriptions were around us, from the smallest of sampans to the great cargo barges rowed by about a dozen brawny fellows naked to the skin with the exception of a strip of linen round the middle. The hubbub of the scene appeared, perhaps, more remarkable from the fact that we had been nearly a month without seeing anything but the barren ocean; for not even a distant sail had been observed since we left the coast of California. At Yokohama the water seemed alive with picturesque animation. Here we saw for the first time the wondrous forms of junks, which never ceased to astonish me. They appear like a gaily-painted medley of mats, ropes, sticks, poles, bamboos, tubs, wooden anchors, frames, sails, and boards, in hopeless confusion. They look as if the first heavy sea would knock them into a thousand pieces; but they are very buoyant, and are said to behave extremely well in bad weather. In striking contrast to them were the stately forms of the great European and American mail-steamers and the men-of-war at their anchorage.

The huge native town was seen covering the flat ground on our right; the foreign settlement, with its handsome houses built in European fashion and often ornamented with gardens; the luxurious abodes of wealthy merchants, and the white Consulates gay with the flags of all nations, occupied the front; while on the left were the green slopes of the 'Bluff,' coming down to the edge of the sea, studded with bright houses, beloved of Foreign Ministers and all who are fortunate enough to live there, and crowned with groves of trees in every shade of brilliant verdure mingling with the sombre shade and graceful forms of the firs and cedars for which Japan is justly famed. All around us was a gay scene, and an inviting prospect for the wanderers from the great Pacific.

Among the crowd of people who soon came on board the ship, we discerned an active little Englishman who had come off in the capacity of steward of the new Grand Hotel, and was prepared to convoy anybody who might intend going to that establishment. Until very lately, travellers to Japan, being few and far between, were generally accommodated at the 'Club,' which, under the kind and admirable management of Mr. Smith, offered every convenience to a visitor. When, however, we reached Yokohama we found a 'Grand Hotel' opened and in full operation, to say nothing of an 'International' in another part of the town. We followed the steward of the former, and in the course of the morning we received the whole of our baggage without having had a single article opened at the Custom-house. Here then was proof the first of the manifest civilisation of Japan. We found ourselves in a large comfortable house, built of stone, and supplied with European comforts added to the cane lounging-chairs and luxuries of a warm climate. There was a capital billiard-room with three or four tables, where we had the novelty of Japanese markers in their native costume; they were very good-tempered fellows, and did not at all mind being a little laughed at for errors in scoring and pronunciation. All the attendants in the hotel were natives, and the gay patterns of their long and ample dresses had a very pretty effect as they hurried about among the more sombre dresses of the Europeans. The hotel is managed by a company, and nothing can exceed the kindness and attention with which their manager and secretary exerted themselves on behalf of their visitors. The breakfast-room was a very pleasant institution, often visited by officers from the men-of-war, where plans were made for the day over beefsteaks and spatch-cocks of which I still retain a grateful remembrance.

In front of the hotel was our cab-stand, represented by a row of *ginrikishas*, which are, as far as I know, the drollest vehicles that ever were invented for the benefit of mankind. They are rather larger than a perambulator, and in shape something like a Hansom cab: only, instead of a horse, you have an active little Japanese who gets between the shafts and runs away with you at about six or seven miles an hour. But if you require a long journey, or wish to go up a steep hill like that which leads to the top of the Bluff, two men are required instead of one, the leader attaching himself by a short rope over his shoulder. In fine weather they are not much troubled with clothes, but when it rains they appear in a very remarkable garment, made of coarse dry grass with the ends sticking out like porcupine-quills, and standing out so stiffly from their shoulders as to make their stumpy figures look preternaturally broad. In this costume they have the appearance of something between a haycock and a thatched cottage, but it has the effect of keeping them partially warm and of throwing off a good deal of rain. With a mushroom-hat like a Macbeth-caldron turned topsy-turvy, and a pair of straw sandals, your Japanese cabman is fully prepared to 'rough it.'

These useful little vehicles are an invention of the last three or four years. Till then, people were carried only in *kangos*, a kind of basket suspended from the ends of a bamboo; or in the more dignified *norimon*, which corresponds rather more to the palanquin of India. From time to time the ear is aroused by the monotonous groaning of four or five coolies pushing and dragging a barbarous sort of cart with heavy goods. The words of their tune seemed to vary, though the burden was the same; and, listening to them carefully, I thought the most intelligible words to sound like 'Hi! Ho! Pish! Push! Ho! Ho! Carthy! Ho!' with variations. As long as they were pushing and pulling, they seemed to be suffering the extremity of human misery, and every syllable of their chant seemed to carry with it the last expression of their breath on earth; but the moment they stopped, which happened pretty frequently, they began to laugh and chaff again as if nothing had been the matter.

We had scarcely had time to land when we received a visit from Mr. Arthur Barnard, the son of the well-known Alpine artist; and this was quickly followed up by making the acquaintance of Mr. Charles Wirgman, who has long been the representative of the 'Illustrated News' at Yokohama, and is the author of 'The Japan Punch,' which is a source of perpetual amusement to the community of foreigners. Both these gentlemen have resided there for many years; and with them, and a few other friends well acquainted with the language and customs of the country, it may easily be imagined that we did not find time hang heavy on our hands.

We were soon introduced to the treasures of Curio Street, where the native shops, full of bronze and China ornaments in every kind of beauty, are always tempting the traveller to empty his purse. Equally attractive are the stores of silks, and embroidery as tasteful in design as it is brilliant in colours. It is customary to go to one of these places to buy a jacket or dressing-gown of their beautiful quilted silk, and I was much amused to find that the little tailors were so small of stature that I was obliged almost to kneel down before they could get at my collar to measure me, though I am not particularly tall. By far the greater part of the Japanese whom we saw either in town or country are exceedingly short, and the women especially so: many of them are pretty, but there is something doll-like in their prettiness. Of their national amiableness there can be no doubt, and we found them as agreeable as they must have been in the days of Xavier, who recorded his delight in associating with so gentle and kindly a people.

A good many of our friends lived on the Bluff, like Mr. Barnard, who could there enjoy the pleasure of a garden in which I found a fine crop of foxgloves and other home flowers grown from English seeds, and flourishing among the native beauties of Japan. We were too soon to see his *Lilium Auratums* in flower; but as this noble lily is now becoming pretty generally known to the English public, it may interest many to know what it is capable of in its own country. He assured me that in the previous year one of them opened sixty-nine blossoms, and about sixty more either fell from the stalk or were helped off by himself. Close by was the house of Sir Harry Parkes, to whose kindness we were much indebted; and not far off were the barracks of the English Marines, whose red coats and cheery bugle-calls used to delight our hearts. They and the French Marines have been lately withdrawn; and I only hope events may prove that their services can be safely dispensed with.

The charming glimpses of scenery in the immediate neighbourhood of Yokohama during the first few days of our stay there only made us long for an expedition into the interior, where we might see the natural simplicity of the country uncontaminated by the civilisation of the coast. Several important matters had to be considered with a view to this. In the first place, the question was whether we could go at all with comparative safety beyond the Treaty Limits of ten *ris*, or twenty-five English miles, from the port. Some of our friends declared that the authorities had been particularly strict of late in preventing travellers from crossing the boundaries, and that the feeling against foreigners was increasing; but, after consulting the highest authorities, we made up our minds to go. It appeared that the Japanese Government would not grant passes, and the Foreign Ministers would not condescend to risk refusal by asking for them; but that in all probability the worst that could happen to us would be our being arrested at the frontier and sent back under a Japanese escort, which might cost us about 200 dollars. It seemed to be a common custom to plead ill-health, as the Government allowed foreigners to go up to the hills on medical certificates which were easily attainable, but we agreed in detesting any such fraudulent practices, and preferred taking our chance in an honest fashion.

The next thing was to consult Mr. Smith, the kind adviser of the traveller in Japan, who never seems to think anything a trouble so long as there is a friend to be helped. We found him at the Club, where presently he sent for a head coolie, who was to do the best he could for us as 'guide, philosopher, and friend' in an expedition of about a week, to include Kamakura, Inoshima, Oda-warra, Hakoni, and Meanoshita. The arrangements with Màt, the coolie, were made in the language of the country, and interpreted by Mr. Smith; the route was fixed and the halting-places decided upon, together with the horses and men to be engaged, and the formidable amount of chow-chow, or provisions, to be taken for the whole time, as we should not anywhere find food adapted to European appetites. The handsome face and upright bearing of our intended guide promised well; and, being told that he could speak a little English, we trusted that we should make our way with tolerable success.

We went to bed full of hopes which were rudely dashed by a drenching rain when we awoke in the morning. As the baggage was to be reduced to the smallest possible dimensions, it was something beyond a joke to start in such weather with scarce a change of clothes. We waited dubiously, but about eight o'clock the weather-wise Mr. Smith delivered himself of an oracular note to the effect that matters were mending, and that we might depart in peace. Our horses, which by the way are always called ponies by the English in China and Japan, were soon waiting at the door in charge of the bare-headed and half-naked native bettows, or grooms, whose duty it is to keep up with the horses as best they can and whatever the pace may be, running by their side or taking short cuts, according to circumstances; but at all events compelled to be ready to take the bridle from the rider when he dismounts at his point of destination. A batch of coolies were sent in advance carrying bamboo poles on their shoulders, from each end of which was suspended a tray or basket of chow-chow of various kinds—beer, wine, preserved meats and vegetables, bread, and a great joint of cold beef, which unhappily came to an end long before we were prepared to dispense with it. We were soon in our saddles; Màt gave a final look round him to see if everything was all right; we turned a corner, and soon afterwards crossed the canal into the open country.

Màt would pass muster anywhere as a handsome man, and as he stripped to the work of running with the horses at a hand-gallop, I thought he was as neatly built a specimen of the light-weights as could well be imagined. He was one of the comparatively rare type of Japanese with long sharp aquiline nose and well-formed mouth which are much more common upon vases and tea-trays than in the actual life of Japan. By far the greater part of all the men and women that I saw were of the decidedly snub-nosed and somewhat simious section of humanity. Our guide was a marked exception to the general rule, and there was a certain appearance of natural nobility about him that made me at first feel ashamed of letting him run by our side under the blazing sun of a Japanese midsummer. However, it seemed to be the custom of the country; he made his own arrangements, and appeared to feel no kind of inconvenience. His style and action were simply perfect.

A considerable part of the first division of the journey was over narrow paths between the rice-fields, where we saw numbers of people setting out the young plants in that mixture of mud and water which is so congenial to them; but by degrees we began to rise, by winding paths and shady lanes, to a lovely region of trees and flowers among the hills. White cluster-roses and brilliant bushes of *Weigelia rosea* bloomed side by side; and *Deutzias*, ten or twelve feet high, clothed in sheets of snowy blossom, formed flowery arches across the path, often making it necessary to protect our eyes with an upraised arm as we forced our horses through festoons of overhanging flowers. Emerging from the 'pitiless pelting' of blossoms, we found ourselves upon high undulating ground, sprinkled with thickets and groves of oak and pine and cedar, between which were ever-varying views of range after range of hills in the interior with Oyama and the snowy summit of great Fujiyama over all. We were on the 'Plains of Heaven,' and made our horses walk as slowly as they could to enable us to enjoy the enchanting view as long as possible. Turning from the endless succession of sunny hills and dark clumps of fir and cedar on our right, we saw below us on our left the blue sea, stretching far away past headland after headland, with evergreens waving over the edges of the cliffs, and studded with islands which looked like green tufts of cedars growing out of the very ripples of the ocean.

I was indeed unwilling to leave this glorious spot, but we knew we had still a great deal to do before we could lie down to sleep in the sacred island of Inoshima. We pulled up at a solitary tea-house by the side of the road to give the coolies a chance of getting ahead again; here I had my first cup of Japanese tea, and formed a decided resolution never to have another if by any means I could without positive rudeness avoid it. I solemnly protest against being obliged to drink about two table-spoonfuls of primrose-coloured boiling water : and yet, what is to be done when, almost before your foot is out of the stirrup, a good-humoured laughing girl with a graceful bow offers you what she considers the 'greatest delicacy of the season?' I do not like having my head broken even with 'precious balms;' and the Japanese tea drove me as completely to despair as when years ago I used to suffer from the boiling maté-pots and *bombillas* of South America.

Towards noon we arrived at Kanasawa, about twelve or thirteen miles from Yokohama, and here we were to make the experiment of the first meal from our own resources. The bettows tied up the horses in a queer apology for a stable, while we ascended to the upper chamber of a small tea-house close to an arm of the sea which washed the wall of its little garden. We were requested to take off our boots, which is always an act of humiliation, and particularly disagreeable when you know that they have to be laced up again ; but we had to submit to it as a prelude to the customs of people who, like the Japanese, choose to live upon mats, with nothing but their bare heels to sit upon. The Kanasawa tea-house was so far Cockneyfied by the neighbourhood of Yokohama, that the proprietor was enabled to give us the rare luxury of a small table and a few chairs, where Màt with the aid of the family spread some tiffin in remarkably simple style. The mats are thick enough to be something softer than mere boards, but they are nevertheless fearfully uncomfortable for unaccustomed joints to lie upon, and it needs a considerable amount of education to enable people to eat their food comfortably while sitting on their heels ; so I don't mind saying that I was extremely grateful for the vulgar innovation of chairs and tables when we could get them, which was by no means generally the case.

When our humble feast was over, and while the horses were still engaged upon their own, we rambled into the ruins of an old temple, half overgrown with cedars and other evergreens, among which I found some broken walls ornamented with two sorts of ferns in high favour with English collectors—the *Cyrtomium falcatum*, and the *Onychium Japonicum*. Not far off, I also began to notice the abundance of *Camellias*, and the beauty of the *Cryptomeria Japonica*. This last plant, which may often be seen struggling for limited existence in an English garden, is one of the chief glories of Japan, where it grows in much the same form as the *Sequoia* or *Wellingtonia*, reaching the height of from 100 to 150 feet, with a trunk of eight or ten feet in diameter. They make superb avenues with their dense green crests forming a royal arch against the sky. The Camellias are everywhere, but very few flowers were left upon them at the time of our visit. Earlier in the year they must be magnificent : some near Odawarra were about forty feet high, with trunks eighteen inches in diameter. Our beautiful old friend, the lilac *Wisteria*, twines over everything it meets with ; but we were too late to see much of it in bloom, till we found it in perfection at a far greater height above the sea.

The weather-oracle had been right ; by noon the sun had entirely beaten the clouds, and it blazed upon us with undisputed glory when we re-mounted and rode away from Kanasawa. It would be difficult to imagine anything more charming than the day's ride with its varying views of sea and land, and its ever-winding hilly paths among luxuriant vegetation. Charming too were the alternations of light and shade, when every now and then, satiated with divine sunshine, we entered a deep and narrow defile between cool damp rocks, clothed with pendent masses of holly-green *Cyrtomiums*, clusters of *Primulas*, and many-coloured Iris in moist places at their feet. Then we again dashed out into the broad sunlight and gave the bettows a lively run into Kamakura, where we pulled up at the approach to the famous temple of Hachimon, who appears to have been the 'Mars' of Japan. Here we had to dismount, and put ourselves in the hands of a bowing old priest, who led us up a broad avenue, furnished at the upper end with what looked like two huge sentry-boxes, each containing an immense wooden figure, painted gorgeously, and frightful to behold. They gave me the idea of a sort of Japanese Gog and Magog; and their great red bodies were dotted all over with little white knobs, which proved to be pellets of chewed paper spit at them by the rustics in the anticipation of good luck if they stick to the uncanny idols.

Passing between these we went up a flight of broad stone steps to a terrace partly shaded by cedars and other evergreen trees, whence an upper flight of steps led to the shrine of Hachimon himself. Other priests here came upon the scene, and showed us the contents of various cupboard-like structures round the sides of the inner square, which consisted chiefly of wondrous suits of armour and weapons said to be relics of the ancient hero Yoritomo. When we came to the end of the show we asked Màt what would be considered an appropriate offering to the priests, and he replied 'quarter boo:' this is a slip of card representing 3*d*. sterling, which seemed to afford them great gratification. The old priest who first conducted us looked at parting as if he should like something too, and as he was very civil and seemed as if he might be something like an archdeacon, we gratified him hugely with a present of another 'quarter boo' for himself. The wonderful carving and brilliant colours of these Japanese temples, surrounded as they generally are by cedars and cryptomerias, have an immense attraction to the eye; and this temple of Hachimon was one of the most picturesquely situated of all that we saw in the country. Before leaving its precincts we asked to see the Omanko-Ishi, a large and very remarkable stone lying under a fir-tree, and much frequented by women who are anxious for an increase to their family; an old woman who was contemplating it seemed highly amused by the interest which we appeared to take in it.

This temple is said to have been founded about the end of the twelfth century by the renowned Shôgun, or Tycoon, Yoritomo, whose relics are so carefully preserved. With the exception of the great figure of Daibootz, which we were next going to see, there is now little more to be seen among the ruins of Kamakura, the former residence of the Tycoons. Its glory has departed. From the front of the temple we rode for a considerable distance down the long road which leads to the margin of the sea, and then turned to the right by a narrow path among fields of rice, barley, and vegetables, flanked by low hills studded with groves of trees in all imaginable beauty. We passed the spot where a few years ago Major Baldwin and Lieutenant Bird were cruelly massacred; and soon afterwards found ourselves face to face with great Daibootz, serenely seated amidst an exquisite surrounding of cedars and fir-trees extending up the slope of the rising ground behind. This is 'The Great' Buddha, a marvellous work in bronze, whose origin was also due to the great Yoritomo, though it was not completed till the middle of the thirteenth century. The figure is placed in a sitting position, and is fifty

DAIBOOTS AT KAMAKURA, JAPAN.

feet in height. The expression of the face is one of ineffably calm dignity, combined with what might be a scornful contemplation of the wondrous changes that have taken place during the 600 years since the days of Yoritomo.

It was formerly covered by a temple which has long perished in the general ruin of Kamakura; but the effect is probably still grander now that Daibootz sits in the open air surrounded by the beautiful works of Nature. In front of a small building by its side we found two or three disestablished Buddhist priests, who had nothing better to do than to sell refreshments and photographs to pilgrims and travellers. Reminded of a hint from my friend Mr. Simpson, who had preceded us by a year, we addressed ourselves to these gentlemen, who at once produced sundry bottles of pale ale from a cool retreat. Truly it was a strange sight to see these men in their long violet gowns, with heads shaved all over as smooth as billiard-balls, laughingly struggling with a British corkscrew in the neck of a bottle tightly clasped between their reverend knees. I imagine that Mr. Simpson had a better interpreter than was our friend Màt; at all events he got more out of the priest, who informed him that 'the priesthood was, as a line of business, not worth following; at least, to be a Buddhist priest was useless now since the State had thrown it off. The people did not seem to care for it, and a living could scarcely be made out of it. He blamed the foreigners as the cause, not that they had any direct hand in disestablishing Buddhism; that was only part of the great movement going on, which was all due to this foreign influence. He did not speak bitterly, for he explained that the sale of beer paid better than the religious services to the few Buddhist devotees who still came. He talked of ceasing to be a priest, and becoming a merchant.'[1]

Now, it is quite beyond the limits and the intentions of this book to enter into long discussions as to the religious and political transformation of such a country as Japan : it is a subject of mystery and uncertainty even to those who have had long time to watch and study it; and the changes are so rapid that it is particularly impossible to say what a day may bring forth. While, however, we are in the almost awful presence of 'The Great Buddha' looking serenely down upon 'the changes and chances of this mortal life,' as the generations roll away before him, it would be well to glance at a few salient points of this interesting question.

If an average foreigner in Yokohama is asked what he thinks about the religious system of Japan, he will probably say, 'Oh! they have got none: they have disestablished and disendowed Buddhism without putting anything in its place; they have allowed the temples to be sacked, and the gods sold at so much a pound for bronze; and they tell people that when they have finished their iron-clads and made a few more railways, and find a little time to think about other matters, they will try to invent a new religion for the people, if they want one!' This may seem rather a flippant way of treating the subject; but in all probability it is not very far from the truth. The pretence of the Government is that they are purifying religion by destroying Buddhism and restoring Shintooism, which was the ancient religion of the country, but

[1] 'Meeting the Sun.' By William Simpson. 1874.

which gave place to the Buddhism imported from China about the sixth century. The unfortunate thing, however, is that Buddhism, having been the popular religion for a thousand years, the principles of the older faith are only understood by a few of the more learned men, and the practical result is the abnegation of religion and forms of worship. The present Government is essentially revolutionary, and its maintenance of power may very likely be felt to depend upon continuing a crushing force upon the feudal interests that fell with the Tycoon. The Tycoons were all Buddhists, and their enemies may think it therefore a wise precaution to crush that form of religion; but we have yet to see whether it is possible, even among the submissive Japanese, to destroy a popular religion without giving some tangible substitute.

A people cannot easily adopt abstractions such as those of Shintooism, any more than it can satisfy itself with such a calm statement as that of Confucius, who, when asked by one of his disciples about the existence of another world, replied, 'I have never been there, so I know nothing about it.' It seems that in many places the two systems have gone on side by side, and that the Government have shown some discretion in not making any general edict against Buddhism in parts where the people seemed inveterately devoted to it; but they discourage it to the utmost. Whatever may be the prevailing custom in the temples, it will probably not affect the private religion of the people, who all have at home a shrine in which they worship their penates, the spirits of the dead, and the memory of their ancestors. There they offer little gifts of corn and rice and incense: there they whisper to the god of the winds to blow away all evil from their homes, and to bring them all that is good: there they pray to the gods of the sun to ripen their harvests and to fill their barns: there they ask the spirits of their ancestors to look down upon them favourably and to bring up their children in the ways which they themselves have been accustomed to follow.

Some may think that here is a promising field for the activity of Christianity, but apparently this would be a mistake; there are no indications of it at present. It has been tried, and failed under the auspices of greater men than are to be found in these times. The Japanese Government has been compelled by recent treaties and arrangements to tolerate the Christianity of foreign residents; but it is said that a native Christian has to suffer a most miserable existence. No one, however, can foretell the future of Japan: some of the best-informed people have assured me that the Japanese are children delighted with their toys. Civilisation has been their last toy; Christianity may possibly be their next; but who can say how soon they may break them, as they have broken them before?

Before leaving Daibootz to his contemplations, we entered by a small door into the shrine which is afforded by the hollow of his interior, where little offerings and burning joss-sticks testified to a surviving respect for 'The Great One;' and one of the party, a young American who had asked leave to join our expedition, marked the moment of our departure by sacrilegiously clambering into the sacred lap and measuring a thumb-nail, which he found to be eight inches in length! Daibootz sits calmly among the Buddhist ruins, or did sit there very lately; but can we say of him as of Theseus, *sedet eternumque sedebit* ? The six centuries have not made him 'look a day older;' and the *æstriplex*, or stout bronze of his constitution, seems to promise him eternal life if people will only consent to leave him alone. But alas! a report has gone forth that the Government will sell Daibootz as coolly as if he were a trumpery member of the *dii minores*; and, if it is true that they have found the presence of gold and silver in his head, there is only too much reason to tremble for his fate.

The next village that we came to presented the appearance of being paved with mats. The cottages were densely packed on both sides of the road, and nearly all the space between was covered with mats on which barley was spread out to dry in the sun, so that there was very little room for the horses to pass among them without scattering their contents. The coolies always insisted on 'putting the pace on' in a crowded street, and it was as difficult as dancing among eggs to gallop through the maze of mats and people without doing damage to life or property. We got more used to this state of things before long; but at first I was very glad to get to the end of a village safely. A sudden turn led us rather steeply down to a beautiful sandy beach, with the swell of a summer sea breaking idly upon it, and we followed close by its edge for the three or four miles that remained in our day's work. A number of men were hauling in a net upon the long sandy spit which connects the mainland with the island of Inoshima, and which, at low tides, as when we saw it, can be crossed dryshod.

We had hardly time to dismount before we found ourselves in the centre of an admiring crowd, in which the principal figure, clad in a long purple gown, was bowing profusely to us. He turned out to be the proprietor of the tea-house where we were to sleep; and after some conversation with Màt he conducted us through the village, the main street of which consists of a series of steep and narrow stone staircases, with nasty fishy little shops on both sides of the way. After mounting for some time by the crowded steps, our host turned to the left up some more steps into a courtyard in front of his house, where he renewed the bowing in a way that seemed to welcome us into the establishment, evidencing at the same time a manifest intention to bow our boots off before he let us enter his rooms. Having succeeded in this desire, he began to bestir himself about supper, and we were greatly amused in watching his treatment of two fish brought to him alive in a shallow bowl: he wanted to knock them on the head with a short stick, but he seemed afraid to hold them steady, and hopped round them, hitting in such a vague fashion that the operation lasted a cruelly long time. Fish, rice, and eggs seem abundant, but travellers who want anything else must bring it for themselves.

After waiting long enough to cook a Lord Mayor's feast, we got a humble supper, and began to contemplate the prospect of bed with no great satisfaction. A thin mattress was laid for each of us on the floor, with a great garment like a quilted dressing-gown with a huge velvet collar that was to be spread over us: there we lay out in two rows, and tossed and tumbled all night, devoured by mosquitoes which attacked every corner of us that emerged from these substitutes for bed-clothes. I was truly glad when at length a little daylight showed itself through the paper screens which serve the purposes of doors and windows in Japan, and I could get out into the fresh morning air among the azaleas of the garden.

If I had to make another expedition of the kind, I think I should prefer trusting to the light food of the natives: a man can live very well on fish and eggs and rice for a week or two at all events, and he would be saved an infinite loss of time and temper caused by unaccustomed coolies unpacking and handling things they do not understand. Only let the traveller see that he takes his own spoon and fork like a little boy going to school : it would take him some time to eat a sufficiency of rice and eggs with a pair of chopsticks.

Such was the delay in the morning that we were reluctantly compelled to curtail our visit to the caves and temples of the holy island. It is, however, well worth seeing even for a short time. Small in size, but rising abruptly from the sea on all sides, it contains every kind of picturesque combination of rock and cave and tree, with the ever-beautiful firs and cedars in clusters at the top. According to the custom of the country we were each presented with a fan on leaving the tea-house, and returned down the long staircases to the spit of sand where the horses were waiting for us. Then came another delightful ride for some hours through lanes and woods and villages, to the outskirts of a large and crowded town called Fujisawa. Here our friend Màt in his favourite fashion made the running at a tremendous pace, and we were obliged to follow him helter-skelter through the streets with our horses, scattering the people in a way which I did not at all like to see.

At last he pulled up at a large tea-house, where we were compelled to taste the tea, and went through a mixture of laughing, staring, and vain attempts at conversation which were all very amusing in their way among a crowd of merry girls. From this place a great change was prepared for us : we had struck the high road, and were to make use of wheels along the Tokaido to Odawarra. Accordingly, a large waggonette with three horses had been sent from Yokohama the day before, and there it stood in front of the tea-house, affording immense gratification to the native crowd. The driver was a little Europeanised Japanese, clad in black coat and trousers, with a sun-helmet on his head, and a pair of white Berlin gloves on his hands! The saddle-horses were sent back to Yokohama with the coolies, and Màt prepared to pack us and our goods into this vehicle. In vain we protested, and told him there was no room: in vain we asked him to hire a couple of ginrikishas which would carry some of our traps; he seemed to think his credit depended upon stuffing everything in, and at last we started, with our legs jammed at uncomfortable angles between carpet-bags, bottles, and parcels of bread and beef.

There was a great exchanging of *saionara*, or 'good-bye,' between us and the laughing crowd, and things went on very well for a few hours after we had shaken down a little. We crossed rather a large river, with carriage, horses and all, in a ferry-boat; soon after which, in the midst of a pretty village with a steep hill in it, one of our hind-wheels suddenly came off, and we had to make a hasty jump out. It was an amusing scene in spite of being very annoying. A crowd of natives came round us in a moment, looking full of curiosity at seeing how completely our demon-substitute for a *norimon* had come to grief, but they were exceedingly good-tempered and polite; and I can hardly help thinking that, if a carriage full of Orientals in full costume were to be upset in an English village, they would not meet with such merciful treatment at the hands of our small boys. Our little coachman came down from his perch, and drew off his Berlin gloves with great deliberation, while the people brought all sorts of wonderful but useless instruments to our assistance; I doubt, however, if the wheel would ever have been put on without the superior intelligence of some of our own party. The sun was blazing upon us, and everybody was pretty hot before we could start again. However, in the next village, off it came again, and we made up our minds to walk the four or five remaining miles to Odawarra, after patching up the vehicle to enable it to carry on our goods slowly.

Presently we passed the place which is announced in several languages to be the Treaty Limit. We had crossed the Rubicon, and we knew that if we got into a scrape in the course of the next few days we should have no remedy, and nobody to thank for it but ourselves. However, we did not expect much difficulty, and certainly we found none; *daimios* and two-sworded *samurais* are not so dangerous as they used to be; and, as to the ordinary people of the country, it would be impossible to find a more civil and good-tempered race. Our complaint against Odawarra was that there was too much of it; there seemed no end of the length of the streets to be walked through, and they were disposed vexatiously. A broad street seems terminated by trees, and you say, 'Behold, this must be the end of Odawarra;' and you push on in the conviction that your place of rest must be somewhere within that line of houses. Not a bit of it. At the extreme end the road turns at a right angle, and discovers another line of seemingly a mile of houses, and then another before the halting-place is reached.

The lame waggonette having arrived a little before us, there were plenty of people on the look-out for our arrival; and we soon found ourselves in a tea-house which, in trying to reconcile Japanese and European notions, had failed with regard to both. Instead of the beds scattered miscellaneously on the matting, there were some separate little rooms, but they were rather like dirty cupboards; and the ordinary cleanliness of Japan was wanting not only in the arrangements of the house but in the appearance of the young women, who were more amorous, but less attractive than usual. This is probably the same house as that which was described to Mr. Simpson as 'All same like Yokohama.'

In the morning, while preparations were being made for a fresh start, we had time to prowl about the streets and look at the curious shops and strange productions of an old-fashioned country town in Japan. Not a little amusing too were the arrangements making for ourselves. We were to trust to our feet from Odawarra, and enjoy a few days' walking-tour in the loveliest and most renowned hill-region in the country. Our very limited baggage was sent forward by a shorter route to Meanoshita on a baggage-horse which was a wondrous spectacle. His head-gear was gorgeous with red and yellow and fringes, his feet were carefully encased in large sandals of straw on the same principle as those of the coolies, and the crupper was a ponderous affair of gilt vermilion, of such proportions that I could not help buying one of them as a curio; it is a marvellous affair, and no European to whom I have shown it at home could venture a guess at its proper purpose.

Four neat-limbed naked coolies were standing by with two *kangos*, one of which was to carry *chow-chow* by the way, and the other was to be at the disposal of anyone who from fatigue or accident might want to be carried. We saw our bags and a few odds and ends safely packed on the lofty saddle of the horse, who with his huge mane and gaudy trappings, and his abundant tail hanging out of the vermilion crupper, might have been almost compared for dignity with the Prince of Wales's elephant at Baroda, if he had not been sadly vulgarised by his straw shoes. Then we looked at the *kangos*, and tried them with much suspicion. A *kango* is a kind of stuffed basket suspended from both ends of a short thick pole. A lissom little Japanese, accustomed to tie himself in knots and sit in marvellously compressed attitudes, is quite at home in his national perch; but for an ordinary long-limbed European the position is one of such torture that he would never willingly submit to it. The covering is so low that he must sit back to avoid bumping his head, and the machine is so short that he must double up his legs under him, or he will infallibly kick the naked and tattoed back of his front bearer. Before we had done with our cruise, one of the party, who was not very well, tried the *kango* for awhile, but he was soon glad to get out of it, to the great relief of the two coolies ; for he was exceedingly heavy.

Armed with Alpine boots, when all was ready, we started forth for a long day's walk in a heat which, though not exactly tropical, was by no means to be despised. There were some pretty gardens and gigantic camellias at the outskirts of Odawarra, and then presently we found ourselves in the real country with an exquisite region of hills immediately before us. The macadamised road ceased, and made way for one constructed of small blocks of stone, tolerably well laid but quite impracticable for anything on wheels. It began to rise gradually and tortuously, shaded for the most part with noble trees, combining the beauties of cedar and Scotch fir, a species of conifer characteristic of Japan, and one which I have never seen elsewhere in the world. The sun in all its glory threw broad lights among their dark and solemn boughs, and glanced among the shadows on the road, while between their ruddy stems we had changing views of the valley and the river beneath us on the left and the forest-covered hills which rose in all their beauty on the farther side of them. We passed through straggling villages with shops like stalls at a fair by the side of the road, full of quaint toys, fans, boxes, and small cabinets made of the delicious camphor-wood, one of which I keep always on my table for the sake of its refreshing perfume. The people always cheerily returned our greeting of 'Ohio,' and seemed highly delighted.

About an hour's walk from Odawarra we crossed the river by a bridge, and went steadily up-hill on the other side of it, the beauty of the forest scenery continually

VIEW ON THE WAY TO HAKONE, JAPAN

increasing as we advanced. The banks were rich in ferns and flowers, and exquisite butterflies danced in the broken lights and shadows of the overhanging Cryptomerias. Among the handsomest of the ferns that I knew were two species of *Cyrtomium,* an *Osmunda* almost identical with our own royal fern, *Adiantum pedatum, Lastræa Standishii, Onychium Japonicum,* and an abundance of *Lygodium scandens*; there was also an unknown *Adiantum* of peculiar beauty which I never saw before or since, and the conditions of our excursion left no room for drying materials. Many of the brilliant and many-coloured Irises of our gardens are among the natural ornaments of Japan, and the people are so fond of flowers that they often use these and many others to decorate the actual structure of their houses by planting them in a row of turf-sods, which are fixed like a cornice on the top of their thatched roofs. The effect, as may be supposed, is charming.

After two or three hours of a very hot walk up-hill in this beautiful part of the Tokaido, we stopped for a while at a queer little hut by the road-side, where an old bleareyed crone, who might have sat for a picture of the Witch of Endor, was peering over a boiling pot upon an open fire. The coolies entered at once, and their brown and polished naked figures were soon grouped over their tea-cups on a bench in the corner. Among the old woman's stores we discovered a basket of eggs, and made her boil them hard while we smoked our pipes and cooled ourselves on a rude little bench at the door. The payment of one boo, or a shilling, for eggs with tea *ad libitum* and cakes and lollipops for coolies and all, seemed to call down Japanese blessings on our heads, as we pushed up the hill to the village of Hata, a little way higher up. Hata was famous, up to a fortnight before our visit, for being perhaps the loveliest place in this most lovely district of Japan; but a fire had broken out at the windward end of the village and destroyed every house in it except two, which were, so to speak, behind the scene of the outbreak. In a crowded assemblage of buildings made entirely of wood and matting and flimsy screens, a conflagration must go right through till it has nothing more to feed upon. The whole place had burnt up like a bandbox, or an American wooden steamer. It was a piteous sight; but in the midst of their ruined gardens the light-hearted people were hard at work in rebuilding, and seemed as happy and careless as if nothing had occurred to disturb their prosperity.

The road now became much steeper, and the rounded paving-stones were rather slippery, but we began to see before us a hollow in the hills which was evidently the summit of the pass to Hakoni. Just before getting to the top I sat down to cool myself upon a ferny bank, when I saw a strange figure walking down the hill towards me, clothed in the usual Japanese gown-like dress and waistband, with a white English sun-helmet on its head, and side-spring boots with the tags projecting from otherwise bare shins! It proved to be a Europeanised young native gentleman out for a walking-tour like ourselves; and to my great surprise he stopped in front of me, raised his helmet, and remarked in very fair English that he had had the pleasure of seeing me in Yokohama. Not to be outdone in politeness, though I had not the slightest remembrance of him, I jumped up to shake hands with him and express my delight in walking about his charming country.

He seemed very much pleased, and presently said good-bye with another elevation of the helmet. The circumstance was to me very suggestive. Only a very few years ago, the traveller who met a native gentleman on the Tokaido would have found him in full state, with a crowd of armed retainers who, at a word from their chief, would think nothing of cutting the intruder into pieces and leaving him by the side of the road!

The top of the pass lies between green hills, which from a little distance looked covered with fresh pasturage, but the vegetation is a growth of coarse grass and dwarf bamboos of little use for domestic animals. We saw hardly any animal life, though there are plenty of pheasants in the thickets, and bears and deer among the hills. As far as I could judge from the time taken and the steepness of a great part of the way, I thought we had ascended about 4,500 feet from the level of the sea. Turning a corner, we had a sudden view of the beautiful lake of Hakoni, and a long steep descent soon led us down to its banks.

CHAPTER XV.

The Lake of Hakoni—Running Postmen—Sulphur Baths—Meanoshita—Apparition of Màt—The 'Good Gardener'—The Baths—Two-man Ginrikishas—Native curiosity—Tattooing—A touch of Earthquake—A dangerous Bridge—Excursion to Totska—Caves and Tumblers—Japanese Executions—The Tomb of Will Adams—His Story—A Tattoo-Professor—Railway to Yeddo—Temples of Shiba—The 'Hundred Steps'—New Fashions—The Invisible Prince—Tombs of the Shôguns—Temple at Asakusa—The merciful Kuanon—Binzuru—A Japanese Tussaud—Miracles of Kuanon.

The lake of Hakoni lies entirely among richly-wooded hills, which here and there run out into bold fir-clad promontories like some of the finest parts of Lucerne, while other points of view reminded me rather of the softness of Loch Katrine. The grandest feature of the scene is, however, the magnificent cone of the snow-capped Fujiyama, rising to a solitary height of about 13,000 feet above the sea, and calmly looking down upon the rich verdure of the surrounding country. This mountain is very sacred, and people make pilgrimages to the summit, stopping at different station-houses by the way. We were informed that it would be useless to make any attempt of the kind before August, as the melting snow was too deep.

We reached the edge of the lake at a point where the ruins of a recently spoliated Buddhist shrine afforded convenient seats for admiring the view, and one or two of the party had a swim in the lake whilst the others rested or wandered about. With my eye always open for plants, I was attracted by a particular shade of green which I thought I knew, and it proved to be a huge bed of that beautiful fern the *Struthiopteris Pennsylvanica*, spreading among the roots of trees and ornamenting the ruins with its graceful fronds. Here, by the road-side, I found for the first time the azaleas of our greenhouses in all the beauty of blossom in their wild state. It was a lovely sight to see bushes of white, red, and purple bloom amongst the stems of the noble trees which partly shaded the road, as we followed it close by the margin of the lake, till we came to the tea-house at Hakoni with its pretty garden by the water-side.

Preferring the open air, we discussed a cold fowl which we had brought with us, while the usual tea and rice proceedings were going on in the interior; and we were not a little amused to see a pretty girl come up with her lap full of young chickens which she placed carefully on the ground to pick up the scraps and clean the bones of their departed relation. The prudent lassie thought that it was too good a chance to be lost. On the hill-side at Hakoni is a temple, approached by long flights of stone steps, flanked on each side by a row of enormous *Cryptomerias* which unite their boughs into a lofty archway over a maze of flickering lights and shadows on the steps below.

Whilst waiting by the road-side we were fortunate enough to see two Government couriers pass. Their lithe bodies were stark naked except for their straw sandals and the narrow cloth about their middle; each carried a bamboo on the shoulder with a small packet attached to each end of it; and they ran swiftly past us like two silent yet beautiful machines. They did not look right or left; but with closed mouth, head up, chest expanded, and perfect action, they combined force and ease in a way which made me think that there was no apparent reason why they should ever stop.

We ought no doubt to have remained at Hakoni for the night, but the plan had been made for us to go on to Meanoshita, and we did not know how many miles farther we should have to walk. We had at first to retrace our steps by the side of the lake, and climb up again to the top of the pass which we had crossed in the middle of the day: thence we turned off the high road and followed a narrow path over the hills, nearly clear of trees, but varied by rocks with ferns and bushes, amongst which the red azaleas spread sheets of blossom in such abundance and perfection that they seemed all ready to take a first prize at the Horticultural Gardens. In the neighbourhood of an old burying-ground we passed by a cave in the rock, on the back of which was carved a figure of Buddha with a 'glory' round the head large enough to cast into the shade anything ever dreamt of by the school of Perugino. Presently we came to a large establishment of sulphur baths, where a few of the residents popped out of their tubs *in puris naturalibus* for a moment's peep at the strangers. The people in charge of the place were extremely polite and gave us a delicious draught of water, cold and pure as from an Alpine spring, and inconceivably welcome after a long and very hot walk. A little farther, some high ground gave us a complete change of scene, and disclosed, far away below and before us, the depths of the valley through which we were to walk to Meanoshita before night. On the left was Fujiyama in his glory, nearly clear of the clouds which had interfered with the view from Hakoni.

The descent from the high lands of grass and bushes was rather rapid, and we soon found ourselves once more among trees to complete the charm of everything around us. The path followed the course of a stream which leaped and sparkled among brown rocks and boulders; here and there the familiar *Pyrus japonica* displayed its scarlet flowers near some bank of ferns; brilliant azaleas of many colours seemed as it were to offer their bunches of blossom to the passing hand; the *Wisteria* waved its lilac tassels wherever it pleased to wander, and in one instance succeeded in outdoing even its own beautiful self. It had climbed the stem of a tree which overshadowed a rocky pool of the mountain torrent, and thrown itself out to the very ends of the branches, whence it hung down over the stream in festoon above festoon of drooping blossoms. Raising our eyes from the pleasant things within our immediate grasp, we saw the hills rising gradually on each side; and before us lay the depths of our beautiful valley folding itself already in the evening gloom.

At length the lights of Meanoshita began to sparkle in the distance, and presently a smiling and bowing individual came to meet us with a lantern, for 'all the paths were dim.' The previous arrival of our magnificent baggage horse had prepared the mind of Meanoshita for our approach; and the amiable demeanour of our lantern-bearer was only the forerunner of the abundant bows, salutations, and smiles that awaited us. As soon as we had been wheedled out of our boots we were ushered into a large and neat room with peculiarly clean matting, upon which we were invited to perch in any attitude that our limbs admitted of while the *neshans*, or young ladies of the house, took up the favourite position of sitting on their heels with both knees together on the ground. Some of them were very pretty, and they laughed merrily at our attempts to sit down properly and take the tea and cakes which they bowingly offered us on little trays. The chief old lady, the 'Mother of the Maids,' or whatever her proper title might be, was rather anxious to shampoo us, an honour which we respectfully but firmly declined. Another room was prepared for our supper, and was happily provided with a small table and chairs. Màt and the young ladies busied themselves with cooking eggs and fish and rice, to which were added a few trifles from our own stores, and at last we sat down to a very humble feast. It was, however, a very merry one with such laughing attendants, and there was a good deal of lively conversation, considering that none of us knew half a dozen words of the language, and Màt's interpretations were not always particularly intelligible.

Meanwhile the conventional blue mattrasses were being spread upon the matting in another apartment; and, as there is no furniture whatever in a Japanese bedroom, when we were ready for bed we had to roll up part of our clothes on the floor and sleep in our shirts and trowsers. The movable screen-substitutes for windows were closed round us, and, though very far from comfortable, we had had a sufficiently long day's work to make us sleep tolerably. We had no idea of hurrying ourselves in the

The 'Good Gardener' of Japan at Home.

morning, and after a final snooze we were aroused by a voice saying, 'I tink it eight o'clock.' There stood Màt, quietly contemplating us in an opening of the sliding screen. His half-shaved head alone emerged from a long white garment which reached the ground at his heels, and which we took for a vast night-gown, till we found it was an old white European waterproof that he must have picked up in the house as a becoming kind of costume in which to attend upon us in the morning. His appearance provoked an amount of laughter which roused us completely, and next moment the girls came into the room and made us get up by taking the mattrasses from us. The screens flew aside, and we were in the fresh air, with a bowl of water on the verandah, whence we could realise the position which it had been too dark to see in the evening.

The village of Meanoshita is very small, and principally exists for the sake of its baths and those who stay there to make use of them. It is embosomed among the hills, and stands on such steep ground that the houses are picturesquely arranged at very different levels. Under our little verandah was a small garden, bounded by a low stone wall, which made a high parapet on the other side down towards the sloping valley. Here were azaleas and other shrubs cropped into strange forms, some in imitation of animals; little ponds with gold fish, little bridges, and lilliputian waterfalls; with plenty of the tall blue Iris blooming by the water-side. The taste for flowers and gardens is universal in Japan: the garden given in the accompanying illustration is somewhat historical, which led to its being admirably photographed by Mr. Beato. It appears that the owner, though one of the labouring class, had devoted his spare time to his garden with such success that people went to see it; and at length the Tycoon himself paid it a visit, when he was so pleased with what he saw that he raised the happy owner to the honour of the two-sworded class as an encouragement to all 'good gardeners' for ever.

The shops of Meanoshita are not many, but correspond to what we see at watering-places all the world over, where visitors are tempted by collections of boxes, cabinets, camphor ornaments, and all sorts of pretty trifles: and we had hardly finished breakfast before we found several young lady emissaries from them established by our side, on their knees and heels, exhibiting their treasures on the floor, and now and then jumping to their feet and tripping back to the shop for something fresh. With their purple robes and beautifully dressed heads of jet-black hair fastened by elaborate pins and combs, they made very picturesque shopwomen. Some of the Meanoshita damsels were really very pretty, but as a general rule I should say, from what we could observe, that a pleasing amiability constitutes the great charm of the Japanese women much more often than absolute beauty. After a very amusing morning, in the course of which we descended by a narrow and steep path among ferns, azaleas, jasmines, &c., to a bathing establishment, about 200 feet lower than where we slept, and scrambled about the shady banks and huge boulders of the river, it was decided to start down the valley to Odawarra. There was a great amount of leave-taking and 'saionara'-saying as we parted from our lively little friends at Meanoshita, and the female president gave us each a porcelain cup, with a picture of Fujiyama inside it. When all was ready, and we were moving down the passage, it seemed to occur to Màt that he had forgotten something: he opened the door of the nearest bath-room, where we had a glimpse of two laughing girls already established in the water; that, however, was quite immaterial both to him and to them: he had a hasty wash, and, not being much encumbered with garments, he contrived to pick us up in about a hundred yards. Everybody knows that till very lately men, women, and children in Japan thought nothing of bathing together in the family tub within view of the public: in deference to the new civilisation this custom is prohibited, but it is evident that the people see no more impropriety in it than Adam and Eve did before the Fall.

We had a fine walk all the afternoon down through the wild scenery of the lower part of the valley, with the river dashing down on one side of us, and rocky places decked with ferns and flowers and crowned with fir-trees on the other side. Gradually the valley opened out from the gorge-like character which it had for many miles assumed; and at last we saw the bridge which we had crossed two days before where it spans a tranquil river among rice-fields instead of the wild torrent of its upper waters. We left the lovely hill-regions with infinite regret, and another hour's walking along the crowded Tokaido brought us back to the point where we had started from Odawarra.

The people of the 'same like Yokohama' tea-house were a sorry change after the brightness and cleanliness of Meanoshita and its charming inhabitants, but we had to make the best of them till the morrow. The little coachman with the Berlin gloves had been left behind with nothing to do but to get the waggonette mended if possible; he declared it was all right, and we hoped it might prove so. We started next morning, but in about an hour we found the old wheel coming off again, and another was nearly red-hot; we crawled into the first town, where we resolved to abandon it, and trust to two-man *ginrikishas* for the remaining twenty miles. The order for half a dozen of these vehicles created a great commotion in the village, and while Màt was settling who should go and who should not go, we sat patiently in the front of a tea-house submitting ourselves to the curiosity of the natives. The men for the most part were content with quietly staring at us, but the women and children were insatiable in their examinations. They were very anxious to find out what our clothes were made of, even to the buttons; they were delighted at the ticking and spring-open action of our watches, and they wanted to see all the contents of our pockets and play with our rings. One of my friends had a diamond ring worth fifty guineas, which they insisted on passing round, but everything was scrupulously restored with a merry laugh. What seemed to interest them more than anything, however, was a beard. A dear little Jap about three years old, his head shaved as usual with the exception of two little black tufts, stood for some time looking at me about a yard from where I was sitting; by degrees I coaxed him nearer till he came between my knees and softly put his little hands upon my beard to stroke it. Finding that no harm happened to him after this daring feat, he laughed and called up some of his small friends to follow his example. When they got over their first alarm, they seemed to enjoy the process immensely; they did their spiriting very gently, however, and did not attempt to indulge in that tugging operation which is so dear to the average British infant.

At last we managed to effect a start, amid a shower of bows and smiles, and 'saionaras.' It was evidently a treat to these simple people to see such a large party of foreigners rattle away with a procession of *ginrikishas*. Each of the droll little vehicles had one man in the shafts, and another in front of him attached by a short cord which he passed over his shoulder. We insisted on faithful Màt having a *ginrikisha* for himself, in which he brought up the rear triumphantly; the coolies all seemed to enter into the fun of the thing, and ran away with us at about seven miles an hour as merrily and laughingly as if they were out for a holiday. They were beautifully naked, and we had a good opportunity of studying various styles of tattooing which in some cases covered nearly the whole of their bodies with many-coloured pictures and wondrous works of art. They only stopped for a few minutes at intervals of about five miles for a cup of tea and a whiff of tobacco, after which they were soon rattling away with us again and laughing like a parcel of boys. Some of them gave up their places to fresh men at one or other of the tea-houses, but others ran the whole twenty miles to Yokohama. Among these was the prismatic-coloured 'leader' of my tandem, a wiry little fellow who seemed perfectly fresh at the end of the journey. Near Totska, towards sunset, we were almost startled by a sudden view of the summit of Fujiyama, looking even grander than when we were nearer to it. Darkness was coming on fast before we reached the outskirts of the city, where a short halt was called. It appeared that *ginrikishas* are not allowed to run about wildly in the streets at night without lanterns; so the coolies had to lay in a stock of the gay articles which are so familiar in illuminations at home. Then they put on their final dash through the apparently endless streets of Yokohama; the swinging of the lanterns, the shouting of the men, the rushing round corners and the flight of the natives, all combining to form a curious and exciting scene. It was about nine o'clock when we jumped out at the door of the hotel, eager for supper at the end of a long and hot day without having had anything substantial to eat in the course of it.

A few evenings after the end of this delightful journey, Mr. Wirgman had been chatting rather late in my room, and I was preparing to turn into bed a few minutes after he left me, when I heard a great growling noise and underground shaking like that which is caused by a Pickford's van going at a gallop over a paved street in London. Yokohama was wrapped in the calm of midnight, so I knew that this was the effect of an earthquake; at the same moment I saw the jug dancing a lively measure in my basin, and I quietly considered what would be the right thing to do under these circumstances. I knew that those who are most accustomed to earthquakes generally bolt immediately into the street, but as this was my first experience I thought I would take it coolly and see what would come next. I reflected that if it came to something serious I might perhaps be killed in the passage before the front door could be opened, in which case I should only have put myself in a flurry for nothing; and

I decided to sit still and finish my pipe peaceably. The jug relapsed into its customary position of rest; there were no more subterranean growls; so I went to bed very comfortably and slept till morning, when I found that some of the people in the house had got up in a terrible state of alarm. Fujiyama had only given a broad hint that though sleeping he was far from dead; and the inhabitants were on the whole gratified, because if he is long silent they fear that he is preparing for a worse style of mischief.

A couple of days later my friend Mr. Barnard offered to make a day's holiday, and ride with us to see some curious caves near Totska. His knowledge of the language as well as of the manners and customs of the country always made him an invaluable companion, so we ordered up horses and bettows and started at eight o'clock We followed the side of the wide and deep canal for some time, till he led the way across a high-pitched and very narrow wooden bridge to the other side. Mr. Austin followed him, and I was next. I had nearly reached the middle when I was conscious of that dangerous sway which is fatal to weak bridges. The whole affair tottered, and I instantly stopped my horse to call out to our two friends behind not to follow. In a moment afterwards I heard the sound of breaking wood, and saw that the horse in front of me had put his foot through the flimsy boards. My friend dismounted, and, as his horse was very luckily not frightened, he led him carefully to the other side. I knew that if I went after him we should be sure to smash the bridge, which seemed ready to break up; so I slipped off very quietly, though there was scarcely room to stand between my horse and the hand-rail, and backed him gently 'bock again' to the side we had come from. We united our forces further on by crossing a more solid structure, but we had the narrowest escape possible from being dashed, horses and men together, from a considerable height into a dangerous canal. It turned out that we had tried to cross on horseback a frail bridge that was only meant for foot passengers.

In due time we reached the tea-house at Totska and halted there; in the middle of the public room full of people was a nest of swallows built upon a pillar which supported the roof, and the old birds went in and out unconcernedly amongst us, while the young ones kept their heads out over the edge of the nest to receive anything that their parents brought them. Thence we rode a few miles further to the house of some peasants near the caves. The bettows ran in front of us, carrying bottles of beer from Totska in their hands; and an old man promised to cook us some eggs and rice, while one of the family gave us each a dirty little oil-lamp and led the way into the bowels of the earth. The caves are not very large, but decidedly curious, being rudely carved on the sides and roof with many sorts of birds and beasts; and the top of one of them is made to represent the Japanese signs of the Zodiac.

Everything inside was wet and dripping; and the stone was soft enough to enable Japanese Cockneys to cut their names in it. The old woman had a small garden with a tank containing strange fish of a kind which I afterwards saw in China. They were something like small gold fish, with a queer arrangement of fins which made them look as if they were blessed with half a dozen tails moving in different directions.

Remounting our horses in the afternoon we returned to Totska, whence Mr. Barnard led us home by a delightful cross-country track, among woods and hills, commanding a fine general view of Yokohama in the distance, backed up by the still more distant sea. I ought to have said that before leaving Totska, whilst seated at the entrance to the tea-house, we saw a curious outdoor exhibition of tumblers and contortionists. They were dressed in tight scarlet clothes, and had strange masks on their heads, representing wild beasts such as we see in a pantomime; in this ludicrous costume they tied themselves into knots in the most approved fashion; and two of them, joined together in the form of a wheel, rolled up and down the dusty road till they were tired of it.

Visitors to Japan are generally informed that they ought to go and see an execution, and there are plenty of opportunities to gratify such a taste. A person connected with the hotel used to get official information on the subject for the benefit of all whom it might concern. The executions generally took place in the morning, and I was naturally rather horrified at breakfast on being told that if we finished our meal soon we should be in good time to see seven men beheaded and one strangled. Fortunately, we had a counter-attraction in the promise of an expedition with Mr. Barnard to see the tomb of Will Adams at Yokoska, and we certainly did not regret the choice which we made, when we afterwards found from those who were present that, after the hideous sight of the head cutting, the operation of strangling the poor wretch was conducted in such a barbarous way that it lasted for seven minutes and a half! The victims have a very short shrift: the sentence is sent down from Yeddo and read aloud, after which the condemned ones are at once led off to the place of execution. The beheading process was described as a triumph of skill: each head fell like a slice of cucumber at a single blow delivered sharply from the elbow without any apparent force.

Meanwhile, we were mounting our horses and riding forth for a long day. Again we skirted the rice-fields, and passed through flowery lanes to enjoy once more the magnificent view from the 'Plains of Heaven.' Thence we reached the Kanasawa tea-house, close to the edge of the bay. The lowness of the tide caused some delay, and it was for some time uncertain if we could get a boat out of the bay, the water being very shallow, and the breeze very strong against us. At last, however, we got away in a boat rowed by three men, who with much labour and many groans succeeded in clearing the point of the bay and reaching Hemi-mura at the head of an adjoining inlet from the sea. We passed near Yokoska in another of these inlets, where, under the superintendence of foreigners, the Japanese Government have made docks and factories, with all the requirements of a naval station. We ran the boat into a quiet little creek and landed in a village, where we were shown in a temple several relics of the old Englishman whose fame is still preserved among the people.

Will Adams, a man of Kent, reached Japan as pilot of the first Dutch ship that arrived there in 1599, where his skill in mathematics and the art of ship-building procured him great favour from the Emperor, who carried his friendship to such an extent that he detained him in honourable captivity till his death, which took place in 1620. He was never allowed to return to his wife and children in England, but the Emperor gave him a Japanese wife instead, and made him lord of a village. He made a will, which is preserved in the East India Museum, leaving his property between his two wives. All this has been matter of history, but until two or three years ago nothing was known as to the burial-place of Angiu Sama, the Japanese name of this English worthy. A conversation between a Daibootz priest and an English resident, Mr. Walter, led to the discovery of the fact that Adams had lived at this village of Hemi-mura, where relics of him, including a letter in Japanese, were still preserved, and where the head man showed Mr. Walter the tombs of Adams and his wife on the top of an adjoining hill. Mr. Walter has at his own expense put the whole place in order and cleared it from an overgrowth of grass and bushes; and the people of the village were so delighted with the care and interest that he displayed, that they made him a present of Adams's Japanese letter, though they had previously refused any money for it.

A quarter of an hour's walk up a rather steep footpath took us to the spot. A flight of steps leads up to a little railed inclosure on the top of the hill, in which stand the two tombs only a few feet apart, and commanding an exquisite view of bays and islands, of bold headlands crowned with groves of oak and fir, and the snowy summit of Fujiyama in the distance. Pious hands had laid a bunch of white *Deutzia* blossom between the graves. We went back to the beach and found that our men were 'asleep in their boat on the bay:' however, they were soon ready, and we took advantage of a spanking breeze in our favour to set sail and race merrily over the waves till we landed again at the little garden of the Kanasawa tea-house. As soon as the horses were ready, we started to ride back to Yokohama, and by fast riding we succeeded in arriving just in time for a late dinner.

While at Yokohama we were rather urged by sundry friends to undergo the process of tattooing, which is carried to great perfection in Japan. Two of my friends succumbed to this temptation, and a leading man in the profession was sent for. He was a queer little old man, bearing books of patterns from which a customer might select any sort of device he pleased; and it was a mere question of time and money to decide between a few modest flowers upon the arm or the gradual covering of the whole body. One of the party chose the former alternative, and endured his sufferings without a word of complaint; the other ventured upon a huge blue eagle picked out with red, which covered nearly the whole inside of his fore-arm. This was a large undertaking, and the pain at last became so irritating that he was obliged to send a message requesting some of his unoccupied friends to come and sit with him during the rest of the operation, at the same time ordering a couple of bottles of champagne to keep up the spirits of himself and those who looked on at his sufferings. We found him looking very miserable in an armchair: the little man in his dark purple gown, and wearing a monstrous pair of spectacles, was squatted before him on his heels, laboriously prodding him with a many-pointed instrument of torture, and wiping away the drops of gore with a cloth. The work was completed in three hours, with every feather distinct; and it remains as a triumph of art, reflecting great credit not only on the artist, but on the patient endurance of the animated canvas.

We had no difficulty in seeing Yeddo, now called Tokio, the capital of the country. Until a very few years ago strangers were altogether excluded from this city: but already a railway of eighteen miles in length connects it with Yokohama, and sends trains in each direction at almost every hour in the day. The guards and officials are dressed in the European style of uniform, and bring round steel clippers to nick holes in the tickets, which are exactly like our own, except that they are printed in sundry tongues. They have adopted European clocks instead of measuring time in a way that I should be sorry to attempt the description of; and if it were not for the rather lilliputian proportions of the officials, it would be easy in the absence of native passengers to forget the fact that the railway is in Japan. At the Yeddo terminus the illusion disappears with the speed of lightning. Passing by clocks, offices, and doors in European fashion, we found ourselves instantly amongst a crowd of *ginrikishas* with half-naked tattooed coolies, upon whom we had to depend for locomotion till we should return to the railway in the evening.

We were armed with a piece of paper upon which a friend had written in Japanese characters a list of places to be seen; the coolies seemed to fully understand the plan, and to enter into the joke of taking a parcel of helpless foreigners over the capital. Yeddo is a vast and straggling city about eight miles by nine, containing many scattered districts; and the only parallel to our case that I can suggest, would be that of a foreigner not knowing a word of English, who, on arriving at Charing Cross, asks the first cabman to drive him to all the principal sights within five miles of St. Paul's!

With a good day's work before us we of course had two-man *ginrikishas*, in which we were dragged swiftly through the streets till the procession was brought to a halt by one of Mr. Austin's wheels flying to pieces; another vehicle was soon found, and away we went to see the Shiba Temples. The grandest had been burnt down a few months before, and the conflagration must have been a very great one if we might judge by the extent of ground cleared by it. The Japanese temples are gorgeous structures of wood brilliantly painted and gilded, with a variety of ornamentation in bronze. Their general form is that of a gigantic old-fashioned barn with broad overhanging eaves, which are gaily painted and decorated to their extremities. In the inner shrines there are splendid specimens of bronze and lacquer-work, gongs, incense vessels, &c. The priests allowed us to move about freely, but they seemed to stand aloof, and looked, as I thought, extremely sulky. It was pretty evident that they had no love for foreigners, by whose influence such unpalatable changes have been introduced into the country. The brilliant colour and exquisite workmanship displayed in many of these buildings afford a great treat to a visitor; for my own part, however, I think I was even more delighted with their situation and surroundings. They are generally accompanied with groves of noble firs, cryptomerias, and lofty hard-wood trees of intensely dark foliage; and it is but a step to pass through a wicket-gate from the sunshine playing brightly upon the gay colours and high-pitched roofs of the temples into a profundity of cool shade, with an undergrowth of camellias and other shrubs. The contrast afforded both to the eye and the feelings by these gay shrines intermingled with clumps of darkly overhanging trees, was a source of keen enjoyment.

We ascended Atago-yama by the famous 'Hundred Steps,' a broad staircase of stone, from the summit of which the view gives a general notion of the extent and appearance of the city, and the strange medley that is being created by the many novelties of civilisation. Yeddo was the capital of the Tycoons till their power was lately crushed and entirely subordinated to that of the Mikado, and the ancient Tycoon's castle is an inclosure of vast extent. Looking over roofs of temples, tops of trees, endless houses, and crowded streets, mingling with broad roads and gardens and parks, we could see that Yeddo is a huge conglomeration of town and country combined, the whole effect being one of exceeding beauty. But among the picturesque charms of old Yeddo a new and very different element is every day spreading around and doing its best to mar everything characteristic of beautiful Japan.

The new civilisation is raising large buildings in European fashion as barracks, schools, colleges, manufactories, and dwelling-places for the ever-increasing number of foreign residents who are required to teach everything in the shortest possible time. Adventurers of almost every kind and every profession have gone from Europe and America, and made themselves necessary to the Japanese, from whom they extract enormous salaries. How they are to go on paying for it all is the mystery. The heart of the sacred city has been actually penetrated by a new street of houses in European style, and over one of the shops, as we trotted by in our *ginrikishas*, I saw the inscription :

AN HAIRDRESSER GOOD FOR JAPANS AND ENGLIERS.

That is what the city of the Tycoon has come to ! Those who wish to see Japan had better go quickly : for, either the new notions will destroy its peculiar charms, or the civilisation which has sprung up like a mushroom will collapse with a crash. If it does, then woe to the foreigners!

There are people who think each of these alternatives about equally probable. Already there are some disagreeable symptoms. The *Cologne Gazette* a few weeks ago gave an interesting account of a split in the Mikado's Cabinet. Two powerful ministers, Itagaki and Schimadzu Sabouro, have been dismissed. The latter is the head of the Satsuma or feudal party, and they are both ' energetic men, full of dislike for foreigners, and rigidly adhering to the old Japanese customs and dress.' They are now the declared enemies of the Government ; and, though the reactionary movement may advance slowly, yet there are abundant materials to feed it in a country which contains a dispossessed priesthood, an insulted feudal aristocracy, and a people who will have to groan under continually increasing taxation.

The name of the Mikado is still so sacred and awe-inspiring that rebellion may be difficult for a time: but it must be remembered that every action of his new-fashioned career is cutting away the very foundations of the mysterious veneration that surrounded and supported him. A very dear old friend of mine in his young days had a passage given to him by the friendly captain of a French man-of-war. He enjoyed himself greatly, but one day he asked his host why he never showed himself on deck as an English officer would. '*Mon ami*,' replied the captain, '*il faut que le Capitaine d'un vaisseau de guerre soit comme le Bon Dieu—jamais vu.*'! This was precisely the former position of the invisible and inaccessible Mikado: but the people who adored an invisible Prince, and acted on the principle of '*omne ignotum pro magnifico*,' are not likely to approve of their mysterious being appearing in broad daylight to open a railway in a cocked hat and the uniform of a European General.

There can be no doubt of the natural ability of many of these innovators of the new school in Japan; and an extraordinary quickness of apprehension is, I believe, united with a great deal of amiable aspiration to be received upon equal terms with those who are blest by the civilisation of Europe. But the change has been so sudden, and at present so superficial, that many who are sufficiently well disposed towards them doubt if, in the face of a strong party in opposition, they can ever force their views upon a recalcitrant population. They order European clothes, and they have learnt the civilised art of borrowing money. The question is whether they can really develop the resources of the country sufficiently to pay for the comparatively extravagant cost of the new civilisation. I wish them success; for, if they are wrecked against superior forces, Japan will probably be closed once more by the '*Anciens partis*,' and that would be a great loss to the world, to say the least of it.

In their transition state they of course have to go through the ordeal of a little ridicule : European coats and hats do not yet seem to suit them ; and they have the disadvantage of having passed the greater part of their lives with half their heads shaved, the consequence of which is that the hair, when allowed to grow, is apt to assume the appearance of a black brush. However, that need not be the same with the rising generation. The unkindest thing I heard said against them was said by, it must be remembered, a disappointed man. We brought over from America an agreeable German gentleman who had spent many years upon engineering works in the United States and Central America. He was looking for employment in Japan, but when we had been there about a fortnight he called to say that he had come to say good-bye at once. 'Why, I thought you were going to remain here for a long time,' I said. 'My dear sir, no,' he replied, 'I will go back to Mexico, to Costa Rica, to Guatemala; at all events to some country where the monkeys have tails!' I suppose his interviews with the authorities had not been satisfactory.

We had some very good tiffin at a small hotel kept by civil Japanese in European fashion, after which we started the *ginrikishas* again to see I know not how many more miles of Tokio, including the district of Uyeno. Here we walked up a broad road between rows of fir-trees to a very handsome temple at the end ; passing behind which, we found a tortuous path leading to the Tombs of the Shôguns, whose burials took place at Uyeno alternately with Shiba. They are fine monuments in stone, and the retired situation among the fir-trees was suggestive of perfect peace. Thence our coolies ran away with us to the peculiarly sacred temple at Asakusa, where a service of some kind was being conducted by three or four priests and a boy, kneeling in a row with their backs towards us, facing a richly-adorned and lighted altar, and chanting to the accompaniment of sundry instruments of music. We had stood quietly and unobserved close behind them for a short time, when the merry-eyed urchin of a boy looked up from his tom-tom and evidently passed on the word that there were 'strangers in the gallery.' One of the priests immediately arose from his devotions and came forward to ask for money : the sum of half a boo, or sixpence, appeared to afford intense satisfaction, and the service went on with renewed vigour.

This temple was built in honour of Kuanon, the all-merciful one, who appears to be sometimes represented in male, and sometimes in female, character. Votive offerings, amulets, &c., are suspended here and there, and the ceiling and walls are covered with representations of legends in the Japanese Buddhistic style of art. On the right of the priests we observed a venerable image of Binzuru, worn out of all knowledge by the kissing and rubbing of centuries of believers who hope to cure themselves of local diseases by touching the corresponding portion of the idol. Poor Binzuru, however, seems to have suffered sadly from over-popularity, and the former situation of his principal features can now be only a matter of conjecture. In front of the temple were two colossal demons in niches behind iron gratings, very like the guardians of Hachimon at Kamakura. One of them is said by a little Guide-book for Tokio ' to be ever ready to welcome a man who repents and endeavours to reform; the other is pleased when children are born who will become good men.' These are certainly excellent sentiments on the part of the amiable demons, but anybody who had not been told their real character would certainly, from their expression and appearance, have predicted qualities of the very opposite description.

Straw sandals are hung in dozens on the railings in front as votive offerings from those who wish the deity to defend their steps: and around the neighbourhood of the temple is a scene of constant crowding and bustle as in a fair. Shops and stalls full of toys and pretty things to be carried off by the many pilgrims, combine with places where food is bought for sacred pigeons and for an Albino pony devoted to Kuanon; together with shows, amusements of all descriptions, a circus, a theatre, a pagoda, other smaller shrines, and places for bodily refreshment. The variety of colours and costumes, the bustling gaiety of the people, the banners, scrolls, music and laughter, all under a most brilliant and glorious sunshine, made one of the liveliest sights that can be imagined.

One of the shows we visited was a very remarkable exhibition. It is a collection of life-size figures representing thirty or forty of the most famous miracles of the merciful Kuanon. The execution is perfectly marvellous, and in form and expression far surpasses anything of the kind that I ever saw. The modelling of a hand, or the animation of a countenance, was so skilfully rendered that it was difficult to believe that some of the figures were not alive. The arrangement was curious: we had to follow a zigzag path among the various separate groups, so that only one or two could be seen at a time. There was ingenuity in this form of construction, for it enabled several successive showmen to appear suddenly from round unseen corners and demand more quarter-boos, though I believe we had paid on entrance the sum that entitled us to see the whole. They saw that we were too much interested in the affair to turn back upon a question of pennies; and, after all, they don't very often get such a good chance of spoiling the foreigner.

The first tableau represents the staying of a plague by drawing out the image of Kuanon; and I must mention two or three of the remainder as samples of this curious collection. In one, a pious damsel, who worshipped Kuanon, never killed any animals, and saved the life of a crab which a man was going to kill; afterwards a snake, transformed into human shape, came to seize her; but a multitude of grateful crabs appeared and rescued her, by order of Kuanon. One of the drollest groups represented a man suffering grievously from headache, who is directed to the spot where the skull which belonged to his body in a previous state of existence is being split open by the root of a tree growing through the socket of the eye. On removing it, he is relieved from his headache. In another, a holy man buys and sets free a tortoise which was going to be killed and eaten. Three days afterwards his child falls overboard, and is apparently lost, but after awhile returns safely on the back of the grateful creature. Another represents a worshipper of Kuanon who is wounded by robbers, thrown into the river, and accidently brought up in a fisherman's net. Having an image of the good Kuanon in his bosom, he is resuscitated, and lives to bless his preserver. Wonderful escapes are provided for holy women, pious woodcutters, and other devotees of Kuanon, but I hope I have said enough to prove that there is a very admirable and curious exhibition awaiting a visitor to Asakusa, which, being interpreted, is the 'Morning Grass.'

CHAPTER XVI.

Departure from Yokohama—Waterfall at Hiogo—The Inland Sea—Countless Fishing-boats—Straits of Simonosaki—The Cathedral Rock—Nagasaki—Cruel method of Coaling a Ship—Farewell to Japan—A Japanese Pilot—His Powers of Drinking—Arrival at Shanghae—Chinese Heat at Midsummer—A Boat at Midnight—Voyage to Hong Kong, and View of Formosa—Flora of Hong Kong—The 'Happy Valley'—Fresh Ferns—Crossing the Island to Little Hong Kong—A Hot Beach—Wild Pine-apples—Lychees and Mangosteens—Expected Typhoon—Visit to Canton—Chinese Gardens—Catastrophe of 'The Spark.'

AT LENGTH THE DAY CAME when it was necessary to pack up our baggage and prepare to say farewell to the pleasant life of Japan and to the good friends who had made it doubly delightful. On June 18 we started in the American steamer 'Costa Rica' to go through the Inland Sea of Japan to Shanghae in China. The so-called Inland Sea is, in fact, a long and tortuous strait, separating the main island of Niphon from the smaller southern islands of Sikok and Kinsin, much in the same way as the Straits of Magellan separate Patagonia from Tierra del Fuego, and extending for about the same distance of, roughly speaking, 300 miles.

We started with a very fresh breeze against us, and, when fairly outside the Bay of Yeddo, we encountered half a gale of wind and a heavy head sea, which made the great hull of the 'Costa Rica' dance in a lively manner. The wind continued all the next day, accompanied by a hot and steamy vapour, which obscured the land and made things in general very uncomfortable. We reached Hiogo at night, seventeen hours behind time in a voyage which ought only to require thirty-six hours in all. Torrents of rain were falling, but next morning after breakfast the weather mended, and we went on shore to see what could be seen in a few hours.

The appearance of Hiogo from the sea is far more attractive than that of Yokohama. It is backed by beautiful hills, rising one above the other, and looking like rich green velvet. The town has the advantage of irregularity in form, and is immensely beautified by clumps of ancient fir-trees and cedars scattered about among the best quarters. A very strong sea-wall had been lately completed, a typhoon having carried away everything before it about three years previously. We at once took *ginrikishas* and rode about a mile to the base of the hills, whence we walked by pretty winding paths to see a very interesting and beautifully-situated waterfall of about 100 feet in height. The heavy rains had filled it to perfection, but had also done great mischief, breaking up the paths and washing away a small tea-house near the bottom of the fall. Here we found singularly perfect specimens of the Maidenhair fern, in conjunction with *Onychium japonicum*, in great abundance, near to a pond which was exquisitely ornamented with many kinds of blue and white Iris. An upper path led to near the top of the fall, in front of which we enjoyed an hour's contemplation of the scene from the shade of a comfortable tea-house placed so as to command the best view. The water plunging down over rocks, among which dark fir-trees clung to every available holding-place, produced a charming effect.

At the bottom of the steep path we found the coolies waiting patiently with their *ginrikishas* near some buildings, one of which we entered, attracted by the sound of machinery in motion. We found ourselves in a watermill worked by the rushing stream, and pounding rice with a machine made on exactly the same principle as the quartz-crushers we had seen in California, except that in Japan they were entirely made of wood. As we re-entered the town the coolies stopped at the door of a native photographer's shop, and signified that we had better look in there. We went in accordingly and made some purchases, our bare-backed coolies coming in with us and evidently making amusing comments to one another concerning the comparative charms of the young ladies represented. When we explained that we did not want any more, and were ready to start, each of them took up one of the photographs and appropriated it without paying: the artist laughed, and I perceived that London is not the only place where servants get tipped by tradesmen for introducing a good customer.

This was the last of our many transactions with the coolies of Japan, both in town and country; and I feel bound to say that they seemed to be a very merry and amusing set of fellows. They behaved extremely well, and I doubt if we ever had any wrangling or altercation with them. Very likely we sometimes gave them rather more than a native would, but, as far as I remember, they never took advantage of it to clamour for more. They seemed naturally to enjoy a laugh much more than a squabble, and they worked with a will when going. Now and then, when we came back to them after a temporary halt, I found myself remembering some particularly wondrous tattoo-mark more than the facial appearance of the man to whom I was attached for the time. If I pointed with my finger to a flying dragon or other strange device, which I recognised in brilliant colours upon his breast, making signs that I knew him only in that way, he seemed immensely amused. So we said 'saionara' to the last of them, and returned on board the ship.

We passed a good deal of the night in battles with mosquitos, who, as usual, got the best of it; and at 4 A.M. the ship sailed for Nagasaki. We were all day running through the Inland Sea and threading among countless islands, so varied in form and appearance that the scene was continually changing its character. The weather was delightful, the air having been cooled by the abundance of rain. Some of the islands were like pyramids of brilliant green, standing out against others which presented nothing but a bare mountain-side of rough reddish rock, looking as burnt-up as St. Vincent. Some were cultivated in terraces one above the other, like the vineyards on the Rhine; and some were crowned with dense masses of fir-trees stretching their gaunt limbs across the sky-line. Junks with white and fluted sails were continually passing us, sometimes so close that we could see the queer collections on their decks. Every village seemed to have sent out its own fleet of fishing-boats in such swarms that we were frequently at close quarters with them, and the animation of the scene increased the pleasure of the day. It was difficult to believe that we were not sailing upon a real lake studded with never-ending islands of every form and colour that can be imagined.

Broken clouds in the west were the means of showing us a superb effect at sunset. Bars of bright red shone through every gap, their reflections stretching across a perfectly glassy sea, and varying in intensity of colour in proportion to the height of the cloud-openings above the horizon. We turned out at four o'clock next morning to see the ship pass through the famous Strait of Simonosaki, which is so narrow and precipitous that a telegraph-wire was lately stretched over it, till the mast-head of an American man-of-war unfortunately carried it away. Emerging from this singular gorge, we were in the Corean Channel; and soon afterwards passed a remarkable-looking island of black basalt which the chief officer very aptly compared to the hull of an old wreck, showing its ribs. It is only accessible at one point, and it is so dangerously situated that the Japanese Government were making great efforts to establish a lighthouse upon it. An Englishman was in charge of the works, and the difficulties must have been very great; the huts for men and materials were with difficulty fastened to the rocks; they seemed piled one above the other in such dangerous positions that a typhoon could hardly fail to blow some of them into the sea. In this matter of lighthouses the Japanese have come out very strong and shown great enterprise: they have a department for it something like our Trinity House, with a distinctive flag of its own.

In the afternoon we passed the Cathedral Rock, an island Matterhorn on a small scale, with a perfect Gothic arch, apparently about 250 feet high, right through the middle of it; the effect was enhanced by seeing through it a large junk on the other side, which had all the appearance of passing under the arch. Towards sunset we rounded the lovely island of Pappenborg, where beautiful groups of trees wave over the rocks from which it is said that many thousands of Christians were, some two hundred years ago, cast headlong into the sea for refusing to trample upon the Cross. We were entering the Bay of Nagasaki, surrounded by hills and woods. We anchored about sunset, delighting our eyes with the freshness of the vegetation and the noble firs which, as at Hiogo, spread their broad shadows in the heart of the city.

Junks laden with coal came alongside soon after our arrival, together with a large number of both sexes, who at once began to fill up our huge bunkers with native coal, which appeared little better than dust, and is said to do scarcely fifty per cent. of the work done by good coal. The plan adopted was a new one to me, and the system eminently cruel. Boys and men on one side of the ship, and chiefly women and girls on the other, standing on frail stages raised one above the other, pitch the coals up from hand to hand in baskets holding twelve pounds each, the last one shooting out the contents into a tub which stands upon a weighing-machine on deck. The work began at 8 P.M.; and, though many of these poor people were mere boys and girls, they were all—men, women, and children—kept to it without rest for the whole of the night and the next day till 4 P.M. During these twenty hours of continual labour in a smothering coal-dust they were only allowed a few minutes to eat some food for breakfast which was brought off to them from the shore. In the midst of this wretched work I was interested at seeing a young man who, looking worn to death himself, contrived to make a rude seat for a pretty girl on the stage where he was standing, and with natural smiling politeness took nearly all the burden of her work for the rest of the day. It was cruel labour for so many hours in the heat of a Nagasaki midsummer; and it made me feel ashamed of the civilisation that could degrade the delicately clean women and pretty girls of Japan to such a picture of dirt and exhaustion as that which they presented at the end of their filthy task.

We had a few hours' rambling about the curious and crowded streets of the native town, prying at our leisure into queer shops and stalls, and buying a good many curious and strange odds and ends, including a telescope consisting of a singe joint of bamboo with a piece of glass at each end of it! We also saw the process of embroidering cushions, scarves, and shawls with exquisite representations of birds, beasts, and flowers; and we looked at Dessima, the only place in Japan where the Dutch alone of foreigners had been allowed to reside in a sort of captivity for about 200 years till other ports were opened by recent treaties. In the afternoon we sailed for Shanghae; and with most sincere regret watched the disappearance of the last fir-crowned headland of beautiful Japan, a country in which every charm of natural scenery, together with ceaseless interest attaching to the simple and amiable people, their quaint costumes and amusing manners, all unite to make it one of the most enjoyable regions of the world.

We had on board a little Japanese pilot in European costume to take the ship out of Nagasaki, after which he would have nothing to do till the return from Shanghae. One evening we saw him hanging about on deck near the smoking-room: he was invited to come in, and we offered him a glass of brandy-and-water. To our utter astonishment, he filled his tumbler more than half full of raw brandy, and then made a rush to the saloon, from which he quickly returned with a bottle of Cayenne pepper. This he shook over the brandy till it made a thick crust, and he swallowed the whole at a gulp. It appeared rather a remarkable performance, but it only made him sputter a little; after which he took a mouthful of cold water, and seemed gratified at having given the Englishman a proof of his powers in one department of his new civilisation.

We crossed the well-named Yellow Sea in about two days, passing within sight of the Saddle Islands and Parker Islands; stopped near a light-ship to pick up a powerful Anglo-American pilot who could have put our little Japanese friend in his pocket; and late at night we reached the wharf at Shanghae. Here we had our first taste of Chinese midsummer heat and mosquitos. In winter and spring it is said to be a delightful place: the foreign quarter is full of handsome houses with plenty of good streets and shops, and the English church and Chaplain's house would be an object of envy to hundreds, or perhaps thousands, of clergymen at home. Horse-racing is carried on in a grand style; and those that go up the river for shooting excursions often come back with many hundreds of wild pheasants and deer. The neighbourhood of Nanking was depopulated in the Taeping rebellion, and the best possible coverts for game are now provided by the vegetation which has grown over the ruined villages.

But the heat at midsummer is a very different affair; and there is a peculiar oppressiveness in the damp heat of China which makes it much more hard to bear at about 88° than that of many other countries with a higher thermometer: and it seemed to me to have the very disagreeable quality of being rather worse by night than by day, till a change for the better generally began about two o'clock in the morning. I complained one day that my boots turned mouldy a few hours after they were cleaned. 'Ah!' said a friend, 'you will be lucky if you don't wake up some morning with your forehead turned mouldy, and mushrooms growing in your beard.' The Peninsular and Oriental Company's ship 'Venetia' was going to sail next day for Hong Kong, and we determined to go in her, after spending a few hours on shore with some kind friends under the protection of a punkah.

The 'Venetia' was lying a couple of miles down the river, and we had sent our baggage on board in the afternoon; the question was how to get ourselves there at a late hour on a pitch-dark night, with a thunderstorm flashing and roaring in the distance. We contrived, however, to make a bargain with some Chinese boatmen, and effected a start about 10.30 P.M. The tide was running so strong against us that they were obliged to keep close to the side of the river; and we found ourselves creeping along past posts and piles, and dark little wharves worthy of a Chinese 'Quilp.' It was too dark to distinguish the forms of the ships lying at anchor, or to see anything of them but their lights, and these looked remarkably like one another : but the Chinamen were very clever, and behaved extremely well. If they had wanted to rob us in conjunction with any piratical friends on shore, we should have been in a rather helpless situation : as it was, they kept the boat near the bank for a quarter of a mile beyond what they declared to be the lights of the 'Venetia,' and then, shoving out into the stream, made use of the tide, and very quietly and skilfully brought us to the ladder of the ship we wanted.

It was past midnight : the cabin lights had been long put out, and it was some time before we could find a steward to show us our cabins. Being in darkness, I asked him to get the quartermaster to light the lamp for a few minutes. This he did, and opened my port at the same time : but I little thought of the consequences. The light attracted a swarm of mosquitos through the open port, and they made the rest of the ' night hideous ' for me. Early next morning we joyfully escaped from the hot and swampy level of the Shanghae river. With a good ship and a pleasant captain the voyage was a very agreeable one ; and about midnight on the fourth day we anchored at Hong Kong, the most striking feature on the way being the island of Formosa, which appeared from the sea like a beautiful chain of mountains, the highest point of which, Mount Morrison, is about 11,000 feet above the sea.

Hong Kong presented a very brilliant effect by night, caused by the innumerable lights of the shipping added to those of the town, and those which are scattered over the irregular hill-sides of the island. When the morning came I saw a view very different from what I had expected. This useful little possession of England is a hilly island which, though scarce a quarter the size of the Isle of Wight, rises at its highest point to very nearly 2,000 feet above the sea. We also hold Kowloong, a projecting peninsula of the mainland opposite, which secures our keeping the Chinese at a respectful distance in the event of war. From the busy town of Victoria on the shore, the land rises immediately behind, scattered over with substantial houses, flourishing gardens, and a great variety of native and exotic trees; above which again a good zigzag path leads up the open grassy slopes to the top of the Peak, where the Governor, Sir Arthur Kennedy, has placed a cool and airy residence. The barracks and cathedral are handsome buildings, and the dockyard contains everything necessary for the repair of our ships on the station. The general appearance of the island at the season of our visit was green and refreshing, though not so promising to a botanist as he afterwards finds it to be. Bentham's 'Flora Hongkongensis' states that 'there are probably few islands, if any, of equal area on the surface of the globe with so varied and extensive a Flora.' He enumerates upwards of 1,000 species and 550 *genera*, to which several more have since been added.

Here I was transferred to the hospitality of my cousin, Commodore Parish, who had a snug berth for me on board H.M.S. 'Princess Charlotte;' and, as some years ago he had taken care of me in a voyage up the Paraná, in South America, we now could amuse ourselves by comparing the doings of the East and the West. Every day we went on shore; and, when business was done, we made expeditions about the island. Very few people indulge in walking much during the hot season, and there are swarms of coolies in the streets with covered seats like what used to be called sedan-chairs, ready to carry people even if only from shop to shop; while those who are not so much afraid of the sun sometimes use light uncovered chairs like the Swiss *chaise-à-porteur*. The Commodore had a neat team of four bearers, who looked very smart in their uniform of white linen, edged with blue. The same may be said of the coxswain and crew of his gig, who always turned the boat out in admirable style. By the aid of boats and chairs, and a steam launch, we managed to see Hong Kong pretty completely; going round it, up and down it, ascending it to the Peak, and crossing the backbone of hills down to the beach on the other side of the island.

The favourite part of Hong Kong is known as the 'Happy Valley,' and is situated in a hollow among the hills at a short distance from the town. There is a good road to it, and the base is large enough to be used as a racecourse. Immediately behind it the hill-sides rise rapidly, and the path winds up among woods of several kinds of oak and pine, mixed with a jungle of evergreen shrubs and bushes, and varied with masses of the climbing *Lygodium japonicum* and other ferns. Among these may be mentioned especially the *Asplenium nidus*, *Cibotium glaucescens*, *Gleichenia dichotoma*, *Adiantum flabellatum*, *Aspidium molle*, several *Davalliæ*, together with an abundance of *Lycopodia*. Wild pine-apples, too, in the lower parts of the island, form very large plants, the growth of several years, often branching out with four or five fruits ripe at the same time.

Taking chairs to the farther side of the Happy Valley, we then set to work to walk up the hill, letting the bearers follow at their leisure. It was a very hot, but very interesting, excursion, the path becoming a regular mountain route in the upper regions, winding among rough and irregular rocks, beloved of brilliant rhododendrons and azaleas, from which we had constantly varying views of the surrounding sea and its legion of islands. The upper air was tolerably fresh, though the sun was blazing; but, when we descended to what is called Little Hong Kong, on the other side, and found ourselves at the bottom of a damp and steaming valley, covered with rank vegetation, the heat was very oppressive and made one of the party unwell. We rejoined the coast at a kind of creek used as a dock, and known by the name of Aberdeen, whence the coolies had to carry us a good many miles along the road before we came to the point where a boat was waiting for us at the Sailors' Home. The island is volcanic, and the rocks are mainly composed of granite, the upper surface of which, under the influence of great heat and moisture, easily disintegrates into a soil of argillaceous loam, resembling that of the hill regions of Brazil, which are under very similar conditions.

Making the tour of the island in the steam-launch, a round of about twenty-eight miles, was another very interesting expedition for us with the Commodore and one or two other officers of the Navy. He had taken care to have a sufficient supply of good things put on board for a long day, with a stock of ice which proved useful in more ways than one before the day was over. We first steamed round by the north, past Cape d'Aguilar and Stanley;

after which we ran into a sheltered little bay with a beach of pure white sand and wild pine-apples growing on the edge of it. We had previously extemporised a tiffin on board, and now we were to land in the hottest part of the afternoon. Moving through the water we did not feel the heat excessive, but the moment we set foot on the white sand, sheltered from every breeze, we felt transported to a burning, fiery furnace. Instinctively we all, I think, rushed for a few minutes' shelter among some huge rocks, till, recovering from the effects of the first blast, we came out by degrees and began to look about us. I went in one direction to examine some dwarf palms in full fruit, while some of the party, getting familiarised with the heat, thought it a good opportunity to make a bonfire by piling dead bamboos and flotsam and jetsam from the sea into a heap round the nearest clump of pine-apples, which were soon blazing in a way that would bring tears into the eyes of a gardener at home.

While I was roasting myself in a search for plants, one of the officers had gone off alone to look for a fern which he very kindly wanted to get for me. He had crossed some higher ground, and when we went to look for him he was nowhere to be seen. After in vain taking the boat round the next headland, we returned, and found him coming back to the first point looking very ill, but carrying in his hands some fine plants of the *Cyrtomium falcatum*, the dark holly-like fern of China and Japan which is now well known in English ferneries as one of the handsomest among the half-hardy species. We had hardly time to get on board the launch before we found that he was very sick and seriously ill with a touch of sunstroke. Then it was that the ice came into play; lumps of it were held upon his head and rubbed backwards and forwards; he got better by degrees, but was still very unwell when we left the island. It was evidently unsafe to play tricks with Chinese sunshine at midsummer. We completed the cruise all round the island, but anxiety about our sick friend was a serious damper to the latter part of the expedition.

The ordinary daily routine on board was very enjoyable. A delightfully neat and handy Chinese boy brought in an early bath of salt water. At 8 A.M. we had a light meal, consisting of a cup of tea with a sardine or poached egg, followed by the exquisite delicacy of fresh lychees cool from the ice. No one who has only seen them as dried fruit in Covent Garden can have any idea of what they are in a natural state, when the broken crimson case reveals a snow-white fruit inside about the size of a plover's egg, with the consistency of cream-ice and a flavour of indescribable delicacy. Then generally came business, reading, or letter-writing, till the genuine tiffin at about one, which, with punkahs going, is perhaps the most enjoyable meal in the East. In the afternoon there were sundry excursions to be made or shopping expeditions among the treasures of the Chinese stores, where it is easy to feel lost among the endless beauty and variety of vases and bronzes, silks and embroidery. Not unfrequent was a good game of croquet with some of the officers and ladies in the comparatively cool hours—between five and seven o'clock—as a prelude to dressing for a late dinner. The midnight heat was to me the most objectionable feature of the twenty-four hours, and I often sat half-dozing in a cane chair, with my bare feet on another chair, in the open gallery of the ship, wearing only the thinnest of *pyjamas*, and not venturing to turn into bed till towards two o'clock in the morning. That, to my fancy, constitutes a really trying climate.

One morning early, the 'boy,' as Chinese servants are always called, brought me a message from the Commodore to get up and look at a curious sight on the water. A furious wind was blowing and driving dense torrents of rain before it. The people thought that the typhoon was upon them, and all the swarms of natives that live in boats and barges were in full flight to the most sheltered nooks upon the coast. We had a good view of them from the upper gallery of the three-decker as they passed in a continual stream for several hours. The sea seemed covered with them, and the poor creatures—men, women, and children—all wet to the skin, were urging their boats as fast as possible before the howling storm. The shipping in harbour took due precautions, but the typhoon did not come then; about six weeks later, however, it came with almost unexampled fury in the middle of the night, and inflicted fearful ruin and misery. Ships of all sizes were driven on shore or sunk at their anchorage; solid walls and roofs disappeared as if made of pebbles; and, in the confusion and horrors of the night, the boat population perished in hundreds and thousands. It appears impossible to conceive the power of one of these typhoons. The captain of a P. and O. ship assured me that he had seen his boats cracked like walnut-shells by the mere force of the wind pressing them against the strong iron davits, and that at other times the davits themselves were bent as if they had been mere scraps of copper-wire.

In the evening of that day's flight of sampans and barges we were to have dined with the Governor in his house upon the Peak. It was perfectly out of the question, however, in such weather, and the pleasure was deferred for a few days, when Sir Arthur introduced me to my first mangosteens, as he had received a present of them from Singapore. This most precious fruit is peculiar to the neighbourhood of Sumatra, and will not bear any long journey thence. It is the fruit of the purple-blossomed *Garcinia mangostana,* and has about the size and external appearance of a pomegranate; but when the outside case is broken a soft juicy pulp is found, divided into segments like an orange, and possessed of a delicious flavour which, as usual, is described differently by different people. One of the best notions of it that I have heard is 'a mixture of strawberries and grapes.' It is said to be the only fruit that may be eaten in any quantity with impunity, which is a hard saying for the vast majority of the human race who can never have a chance of seeing or tasting it. I have read that the famous Dr. Solander, when in the last stage of putrid fever in Batavia, found himself gradually recovering by sucking this delicious and refreshing fruit.

As we were being carried down the hill at night under a sky alive with stars, the effect was charming. The lighted Chinese lanterns swinging from the poles of our chairs illuminated the forms of the bearers; while the stars above were almost rivalled in number and brilliancy by the lights of the city far below, and of the vast variety of ships that were spread over the broad anchorage beyond. The illusion was complete, the appearance being exactly that of a reflection of the heavens.

During our stay in Hong Kong we received a kind invitation to spend a few days at Messrs. Deacon's house in Canton, and we went there gladly. A very comfortable American steamboat took us up the river, a distance of ninety miles, in eight hours; giving us excellent provisions, including wine, for eight dollars each. We passed close to the ruins of the once famous Bogue Forts, still remaining as they were left after being battered by the British guns. They consisted of a loop-holed stone wall at the edge of the water, at the bottom of a steep incline, and protected on the rear and flanks by a somewhat semicircular wall connected with both the ends. Nothing could be more rude than the design, and they now present exactly the appearance of a stone-walled inclosure for sheep in Cumberland. Here and there were grand pagodas which must have been neglected for centuries; for self-sown plants and even trees are growing out of every stage of the lofty edifices.

Nothing probably astonishes a stranger more than the incredible swarms of boats and vessels of every description, from junks to sampans, which seem to cover the water in the Canton river, unless perhaps it may be the marvellous skill by which the light boats save themselves from being run over by the huge paddles of the steamboat. In the midst of the crowd that settled on all sides of the ship like bees swarming, we were found by a capital old Chinaman who explained that he was in charge of our host's own house-boat, with which he had been sent to take us ashore. By dint of pushing and shoving through a crowd of disappointed sampan-owners, we got fairly off under the old man's leadership, and were deposited before long at one of the stone landing-places of the Shamien quarter, which contains the English Church and Consulate, together with the residences of the chief merchants.

No one, looking at the handsome stone houses and gardens of this district, and walking under the rich shadow of the trees which line the Bund, would imagine that at the capture of Canton, in 1857, the site was entirely occupied by a filthy mud-flat. It was, however, after that event decided upon as the situation for the new British settlement. It was made into an artificial island by building a massive granite embankment upon piles driven into the bed of the river, the interior of which was filled up with mud and sand, and made as substantial as the embankment of the Thames; it is connected with the city by a bridge and gateway, where a sentry prevents natives from entering without authority. The whole place is rather more than half a mile long and about a quarter of a mile wide; and, though the community is very small, they contrive to keep up a Club with billiard-rooms, a bowling-alley, a cricket-ground, and a croquet-ground. The different houses keep their boats always ready when wanted at the different steps leading to the river, and others promenade the Bund on foot or on horseback, if it so pleases them.

Peace, quiet, luxury, and hospitality reign supreme here in Shamien. Cross the bridge, receive the salute of the police-sentry as you pass him, and in one moment you are transported into the midst of the bustling hubbub, the crowds, the filth, and the ancient fish-like smells of a Chinese water-side population. On the other face of the settlement is the broad river and the perpetual motion of every kind of vessel, among which appear at their moorings the smarter boats and yachts of the foreign residents.

One of the residents in the house, only a few months out from England, was Mr. W. W. Mundy, who, being fond of boating, kept a small boat for his own use, and he proposed to take us to the other side of the river to see some of the famous flower-gardens at Fa-ti, a village near the mouth of the creek by which the waters of the north and west rivers reach Canton, falling into the main channel opposite Shamien. To ascend this creek was a work of extreme care and patience, so dense was the crowd of boats of all sizes passing in both directions, but we had by the way many opportunities of seeing the strange modes of life adopted by an amphibious population. At length we got alongside some stone steps and landed, leaving the boat's crew to wait for us. Our friend was well known there, and we were very politely ushered into a Chinese 'nursery-garden.' The Chinese, like the Japanese, curiously combine an intense natural love of flowers with a strange taste for artificially dwarfed and distorted plants and shrubs. Thus, in the gardens which we visited on that day, we found beautiful plants of azaleas, althæas, lilies, and the splendid crimson hibiscus. The camellias were out of season, but jasmines, ixoras, chrysanthemums, balsams, and alamandas were, with many other flowers, in full beauty; and these gardeners are all through the year in the habit of sending constant supplies of bouquets and pot-flowers for a few dollars a month.

But, amidst all these beauties, the grotesque element was made to predominate. Potted shrubs and plants of all descriptions, twisted and trained into strange forms, were all around us. There was a bamboo grown in the shape of a moving serpent, and close by was an evergreen bush trained into the similitude of a stag, horns and all. Dolphins seemed rather fashionable, standing on their heads, with curved tails on high, and fitted with huge artificial eyes staring over the edge of the flower-pot. Other shrubs were trained into all kinds of strange figures of men and women, partly helped out by comical heads, arms, and legs, of terra-cotta, forming exquisitely ludicrous effects. Others again were in their natural shapes, but excessively dwarfed; it is said that one of the Foreign Ministers in Japan was favoured with the sight of three trees of different kinds, all grown in perfect form, and entirely enclosed in a single box of about six inches in diameter! I examined some of the Chinese dwarfs pretty closely, and it seemed to me that an important element in producing them is the constant worrying of the plant by disturbing its roots, and pulling the crown rather out of the ground, so as to keep it with as little vitality as possible.

We had a long ramble in several of these gardens, and as our kind companion and guide steered the boat back again, we little thought that in another month he was to be the victim of Chinese pirates. He went down the river in the American steamer 'Spark,' and was peacefully dozing over a cigar, when the ship was seized by a gang of miscreants who had come on board, secretly armed, but in the guise of common country-people. The captain and officers were killed, and Mr. Mundy was stabbed in nearly every part of his body: they tore off his watch and rings, and left him on the deck for dead. Then, finding that he was not quite dead, they laughed at his agonies while smoking his cigars: they lifted him up, pretending to throw him overboard, but disappointed him by dropping him on the deck again; and they tore out the handkerchief which he had stuffed into his ripped-up side. After some hours of this horror, the pirates were taken off in a confederate junk which was looking out for the fellow-conspirators: the survivors then crawled out of their hiding-places, and the pilot, whose life had been spared, took the vessel into Macao, where Mr. Mundy was ultimately healed of nearly a score of wounds, several of which had actually touched both heart and lungs. It is supposed that his miraculous cure was aided by the fact of his having so nearly bled to death that there was nothing left for fever to lay hold of. He came home soon afterwards, and, though greatly shaken in nerve, he seemed a great credit to the Portuguese surgeons at Macao.

CHAPTER THE LAST.

Sights in Canton—Temple of the Five Genii—Temple of the Five Hundred Gods—Chinese Shopkeepers — Goldsmiths—' Dogmeat' and ' Oatmeat '— A Broken Bottle—The City Walls—Chinese Cleverness—Farewell to Hong Kong—Thoughts of Cambodia—Singapore—Divers—Botanical Gardens— A Mixed Crew—Penang—Myriads of Cocoa-nuts—The Atchinese—The Monsoon—Ceylon—The Cinnamon-Gardens—Great Rascals—Homeward-bound—The Milky Sea—Heat in the Red Sea—The Suez Canal—Alexandria—Home Again.

To ENABLE US to see some of the lions of Canton, our hosts sent for a first-rate Chinese guide, who gave us his card in English fashion, with the name A Cum upon it. He spoke English intelligibly, and in every way behaved so extremely well that I have great pleasure in recommending him to anyone who may follow in our steps to China. Sedan-chairs were produced, and away we started through a wondrous labyrinth of narrow streets lined with shops, and reminding me of the Bazaars at Stamboul more than anything else I can think of. The extreme heat of summer compels people to keep the sun out as much as possible from the streets, which are therefore in many parts of the town so narrow that it is difficult for two sedans to pass one another. The eternally bustling crowd of a Chinese city is peculiarly noticeable under these circumstances; and all day long the bearers with frequent shouts seemed forcing us through an interminable swarm of ants.

A Cum showed great discretion in not dragging us through too many of the endless temples, which with their fish-ponds and shrines are somewhat monotonous; while in their services, 'the alternate risings and genuflections, the droning hum of the chanters, the silvery interruption of the bell, the vestments, incense, decorations, flowers, and images combine to invest the scene with a striking resemblance to the ceremonies of the Romish Church, and the mummeries of the so-called "Anglican" imitators of Romanism.'[1] He took us, however, to the very curious and interesting Temple of the Five Genii.

The strange legend connected with the foundation of this temple is that, some two thousand years ago, five shepherds appeared on the site where it stands, who were suddenly transformed into rams, which again changed instantly into stone, while a voice was heard proclaiming that the prosperity of the adjoining city should endure as long as these objects were worshipped on this spot. From this legend Canton derived its sobriquet of the City of Rams; but the rude stone images were destroyed some years ago in a conflagration. In front of the building in which these mystic stones were so long preserved, we were shown a huge bell suspended from an archway, concerning which there is another legend. It is said to have been cast and hung up about two centuries ago; but, in consequence of a prophecy that calamity would fall upon Canton whenever this bell should sound, it was deprived of a clapper, and access to it was prevented. During the bombardment of Canton, in 1857, it

[1] 'Treaty Ports of China and Japan,' p. 161.

is said to have been 'suggested to one of H.M.'s ships to aim a shot at this bell, and the result was that, while calamity was indeed befalling the haughty city, the bell, struck by a cannon-ball, boomed forth its unwonted sound.' The effects of the shot were pointed out very frankly by A Cum; and, in a censer underneath it, incense is still continually burnt as an offering to the spirit of the bell.

We also saw the temple which is called by Europeans the Temple of the Five Hundred Gods, because an important feature of it is a vast Hall of Saints, containing about five hundred richly gilded images representing deified worthies of the Buddhist faith. Many of the figures are extremely curious; and in one case a Buddhist version of the history of Elijah is represented in the person of a saint, who in his banishment is being nourished by wild monkeys! The Temple of Longevity also deserves a word, for in it we were delighted with the image of a very fat man placed in the most prominent position: the expression of irrepressible laughter was admirably given to the features; and the moral of the whole affair appeared to me to be, ' Laugh and get fat, if you would fain live for ever.'

There was, however, no end to the amusement and interest involved in going through the marvellous variety of shops, and seeing the people engaged in various handicrafts, surrounded by the brilliant scrolls which describe the nature of their business. The stores of the leading vendors of vases, bronzes, lacquer-work, China bowls, ivory-carvings, &c., were bewildering from the quantity as well as the variety of beautiful things. The proprietors were gentle and polite, showing no disposition to press visitors to buy the lovely things which they displayed to them: they seemed to content themselves with stating a very high price and standing on their dignity in refusing to reduce it, till the last moment of trial arrived, when, seeing the customer actually leaving the shop, they would quietly offer to let him have the pair of vases upon which he has set his heart for fifty dollars, instead of the eighty which had been firmly demanded.

Everywhere was the moving crowd, good-naturedly pushing its way along, 'giving and taking in the squeeze,' and perfectly civil to those who are civil to them. We went into jade-shops and ivory-shops; saw the process of Chinese glass-blowing with a large pair of bellows; paid a visit to a maker of strange locks such as are brought to Europe as puzzles; and, what delighted me perhaps more than anything, we went into the shop of a jeweller who was making earrings of silver-gilt ornamented with small points from the deep blue wing of a species of kingfisher. So exquisitely small were the feather particles, and so wonderful was the skill with which he worked them into the pattern of the metal, that the effect of an enamel was produced, and the intense loveliness of the colour made them seem to me the prettiest earrings I had ever seen in my life. They were not at all expensive, so we secured specimens which have been treated as genuine novelties by friends at home.

The streets appeared on the whole to be neat and clean; and, in spite of intense heat, there was no large amount of evil odours: but in the midst of gay and amusing sights to arrest the eye at every moment, there was one class of institutions which now and then made me almost sick to look at. These were the butchers' shops; and I never could understand how such decent people as the Chinese can consent to eat such garbage as they do. The most loathsome-looking scraps were hung up or otherwise displayed among a variety of skinned animals with heads and limbs sticking out in all kinds of irregular positions, and looking so disgusting that I turned my head the other way. But A Cum was not going to let me off so easily. He pulled me up suddenly at one of the first of these places; and, pointing to some ghastly little carcases, he said, 'What you tink dat? Dat a catmeat. And what you tink dat? Dat a dogmeat.' 'Move on for heaven's sake,' I replied, for I saw that he did not mean cats'-meat and dogs'-meat, as I thought at the first moment, but that they were dogs and cats to be eaten by men.

We had been out for several hours on a very hot day without any apparent chance of anything fit to eat or drink in the city; but, in reply to a suggestion on this head, A Cum sent off one of the chair-bearers on a cruise while we were examining the stores of a dealer in embroidered silks. In about ten minutes the coolie returned with a bottle of pale ale which he had discovered somewhere. By this time there was a small crowd of good-tempered people at the entrance to the shop, watching with great curiosity all the doings of the foreigners. A Cum, with all his intelligence, could not produce a corkscrew, nor was such a thing to be found. My companion tried to knock the neck off, but carried away more than he intended, so that much of the beer was lost, and a good deal of glass was broken. The merchant was extremely polite about the mess which we had made upon his floor; and the crowd appeared quite as much delighted with the whole scene as if it had been an entertainment provided for their special benefit.

After getting through a great deal of shopping and sight-seeing on foot, we took to the chairs again, and were gradually conveyed completely through the city to the outer walls on the north, where they are carried over rather low and undulating hills, ornamented by handsome trees and crowned by what is called the Five-storied Pagoda. Climbing up this, we had a complete view of every part of Canton and its suburbs, the many-branched river, and the distant pagodas which marked the points which we had passed on the latter part of the journey from Hong Kong. Close by, are forts known to Europeans as Gough's Fort and Blue-jacket Fort, names which speak for themselves in connection with former English doings at Canton. In the low grounds outside the city the emerald green of the rice-fields had a charming effect; and the vegetation scattered here and there among the many strange and fanciful buildings assisted in making a beautiful as well as a highly interesting bird's-eye view.

Our friends loaded us with kindness during the few days of our visit, and we then returned to Hong Kong, from which we were soon to start on our way home to England. A few farewell festivities and pleasant parties increased the regret of leaving this distant English colony: but the Peninsular and Oriental 'Cathay' anchored one morning in the harbour, and gave us a hint to pack up and prepare for our departure. I was truly sorry to say good-bye to the old 'Princess Charlotte,' where I had enjoyed a happy home; and it was not without regret that I prepared to see the last of the 'pigtails.'

The Chinese are a wonderfully clever and interesting race of people, capable of great things if they ever free themselves from the thraldom of a grasping Government. I was told that an average Chinaman is afraid to build himself a better house or show signs of increasing wealth, as he would be instantly seized upon as a subject for extortionate taxation. There is no reason to suppose that the bulk of the nation would remain insensible to progress, if it were not for the Mandarins, who know that their power would melt away before the incursion of European ways. Hence they have steadily opposed every form of change. The only thing in which they were compelled to make changes has been the art of war. It had become abundantly clear to them by sad experience that, however superior their wisdom and philosophy might be to those of the European races, European weapons were at all events unanswerable arguments. They have therefore been building frigates, buying big guns, and training soldiers and sailors in a way which will make them far more formidable if we have ever the misfortune of another Chinese war. The telegraph is dawning upon them as a possibly useful appliance, and there was a good story at Hong Kong in connection with it. There were two Chinese brothers in business together, one at Hong Kong and the other at Shanghae. When the telegraphic communication was established, the Hong Kong brother thought he would venture to send a message to the one at Shanghae, who duly received it. Finding, however, that it was dated only about a couple of hours before, he indignantly tore it up, and found on the arrival of the mail that he had lost the chance of doing a magnificent stroke of business.

I was frequently told that their quickness at figures was something astonishing even to the sharpest of Europeans; and, as they do not live with any great expense or extravagance, their merchants can easily afford to undersell the foreigners. With this in their favour, in addition to their great natural acuteness and close attention to business, they appear to be becoming rather serious commercial rivals. The Chinese have far more dignity and solidity than their neighbours in Japan; but it will be a matter of great interest to the world at large to watch the progress of events amongst them for the next few years, and to see if the Celestials continue to succeed in resisting the force of modern inventions. Already some people may think they see the 'handwriting on the wall,' when we now read that 120 Chinese youths have been sent over to be educated for fifteen years in America, after which they are to return to Chinese dress, manners, and customs. After fifteen years of American education, with all its concomitants, will they do so? I trow not.

Towards the end of July the 'Cathay' weighed anchor, and picked her way out of the harbour crowded with vessels from all parts of the world, besides the swarms of junks with huge eyes painted on their bows, upon the Chinese principle of 'Ship have no eye! Ship no see where go!' and in a few hours the green hills of Hong Kong disappeared in the glowing distance. We passed within sight of the coast of Cochin China, and tried in imagination to go up the river Meikong in Cambodia, by recalling to memory the intensely interesting account in which Captain Garnier of the French Navy has recorded the explorations of his expedition up that river.

There they saw the mysterious ruins of Angcor and its temples, the largest and probably most highly ornamented in the world. No one knows accurately whence came the race of men that built them, and no one knows what has become of them. They had perished even before their works were known to civilised man; and the Tropical forest has grown through the ancient floors of stone, and thrown its dense shade over the gigantic statues which now startle a visitor by their presence in the midst of it; but the towers and causeways and miles of bas-reliefs remain to testify to the former vastness and magnificence of this wonderful place.

On the sixth day from Hong Kong we passed several beautiful islands covered with rich green woods full of monkeys, which, the sailors say, come down to the beach to 'trade' with the Malays for cocoa-nuts. We reached Singapore before sunset, and were made fast to the Company's wharf, which was said to have 60,000 tons of coal upon it. I had always imagined that Singapore, being within about one degree of the Equator, must be a very oppressive place, and was glad to find that the heat is greatly tempered by the breezes for which it is indebted to its insular position. We found the thermometer only 87° Fah. in the shade, and the sailors of H.M.S. 'Cadmus' were playing a cricket-match throughout the whole of the next day, just as unconcernedly as if they had been in England.

We got up early next morning to see the sunrise from the flagstaff-hill, under the escort of a passenger well acquainted with the ways of Singapore. The main road to the town runs at first under the shade of trees with peculiarly magnificent foliage; but our conductor presently led us aside through what was called the Rajah's Garden, whence he took us right up a hill-side covered with pine-apples that were dripping with morning dew. Pine-apples are remarkably prickly things amongst which to force a way, and, being clad in the thinnest possible raiment, I was not sorry to emerge upon a good path which sloped upwards for the rest of the walk. We found a little staff of men established in a building near the signal-station, under the charge of an old soldier, who from his lofty perch can give long notice of vessels approaching from any direction.

The sunrise was a lovely sight over the whole scene of highlands and islands rich with the glories of Equatorial vegetation, and the surrounding sea just ruffled by the monsoon. We saw the golden glow upon the distant jungles, and could not but think of the tigers that come across the Strait, and were estimated only a few years ago to kill two rustics on an average every day in the year. We returned for a bath and early breakfast by a more roundabout way, between lovely trees and ferns, conspicuous among which latter were masses of the climbing *Lygodium* hanging on everything by the road-side, as the clematis and briony drape the hedges in England.

We found that the ship was already the focus of a lively scene. Boats full of divers were clustering round her sides, their occupants shouting to attract attention; and, at the first glimpse of a promised coin, diving to the bottom and coming up with pieces of stone and coral, or passing directly under the ship's keel. All about the quay were vendors of monkeys and cockatoos, cocoa-nuts and mangosteens, beautiful nautilus shells, Malacca canes, and the famous sticks which are known by the name of 'Penang lawyers.' The constant clatter of bargaining, and the eager boys climbing out of the water by a rope's end, with their red and white corals and shells, made a very amusing *entourage* of the long black hull of the 'Cathay.'

Soon after breakfast three or four of us took a 'gharry,' something like a four-wheeled cab, with a diminutive horse, and drove into the town of Singapore along a good road lined with palms, and, in many places, dark-foliaged overhanging trees. We then drove on to the Botanical Garden, a very large and well-kept institution, where, amongst broad lawns and paths, a vast collection of heat-loving trees and plants have been brought together. Here were palms and ferns, bread-fruit trees, mangos and mangosteens, spice-trees, red and yellow *Hibiscus*, *Begonias*, and *Gardenias*, splendid creepers, and wondrous *Amaryllis*, all flourishing in that luxuriance which is attained in the Equatorial regions, where every leaf and every shoot seem to revel in the utter happiness of vegetable life; nursed by abundant heat and moisture, and never touched by the breath of evil winds or anything to check their development into a state of absolute perfection. Here, too, amidst other treasures, we found a small lake covered with the huge leaves and splendid blossoms of the *Victoria Regia*; and, seeing it thus growing in a natural condition, I could easily imagine the intense astonishment and admiration of its first discoverer.

We drove back to tiffin at the hotel, and looked on for awhile at the sailors playing cricket, which at two o'clock in the afternoon, and close to the Equator, was really rather a remarkable performance. The ground was large and spacious, green and fresh, though the grass was of that rough and coarse nature which within the Tropics is the only substitute for the smooth lawns at home. At one end of the ground is the English Church, a large and handsome Gothic building. Government House is another large affair; and, altogether, the general appearance of Singapore induced me to believe that it must be a far pleasanter place than I had any idea of. The mixture of races there is very remarkable. The majority of the people are Chinese and Malays, but there are African negroes and Sidi men; and the duties of policemen and post-office people were being discharged by Sikhs! Under these circumstances it is natural to expect a good deal of mongrel language; and 'Horse Doctory Shop,' which I saw painted over a house, may be taken as a favourable sample of the forms assumed by the English tongue in the chief place of the Straits Settlement

I was rather surprised to see another very motley collection in the ship's company of the 'Cathay.' It appears that the ordinary British sailor has made himself so unmanageable and so expensive that the Peninsular and Oriental Company prefer utilising the populations of the East. We had some picked Englishmen for quartermasters: next in rank came a few Manilla men, who were entrusted with the task of helping to steer: the main part of the crew were Lascars; and a batch of Chinamen had the special task of keeping the boats in good order. Last of all in the social scale came the luckless children of Ham, the only men in the world probably who can stand the work of stokers and drudges in the depths of a steamer on the Red Sea and the Indian Ocean: and I was told by the officers that these poor fellows never aspire to anything better than their present lot.

We sailed at 5 P.M. for Penang, or Prince of Wales's Island; and for the two following nights we suffered a good deal of inconvenience from the heat until after midnight, and I was reduced to remaining on deck for some hours in the lightest possible raiment and with bare feet encased in Malay slippers. About one o'clock in the morning a perfectly fresh breeze came up, and I could then venture to turn into bed and sleep comfortably under a sheet and counterpane.

Drawing within sight of the flag-staff which crowns the forest-covered hill of Penang, we took on board a native pilot, gorgeous to behold in his gay skull-cap and flowing crimson garments. He threaded a way for us between an immense quantity of extraordinary arrangements for fishing. They appeared like square corrals, or inclosures, made of bamboos driven in near together: a net covered the interior, and was so arranged that it could be bodily lowered like a vast dish, and raised again by a windlass, with all the fish that happened to be above it.

Wooded hills of marvellous greenness rise above the sea round Penang, but amongst all the varieties of vegetation spread before us, it seemed to me that this place was pre-eminently the head-quarters of cocoa-nuts. Their productiveness appears to be astonishing. The fruit is picked from the trees, as I was told, about five or six times a year; and a lady passenger who joined us there informed me afterwards that, on what her family considered one of their small plantations, 108,000 cocoa-nuts had been picked after a rest of only two months. The scenery is lovely, and Penang seemed generally considered a very healthy station: we found the thermometer at only 82° in the shade, and some of our passengers reported that it never rose above 90°.

All next day we were within sight of the great and beautiful island of Sumatra, which is altogether nearly a thousand miles in length, and appears from the sea like one vast chain of blue mountains, till on getting nearer to the coast it becomes evident that they are for the most part clothed with richly verdant forest Some of these are evidently very lofty, and one summit is said to be about 13,000 feet above the sea. We passed near enough to the Atchinese territory at the extreme north of the island to get a very fair notion of the style of country; and we wondered if we should see the smoke, or any other symptom of the Dutch war. Naturally it was a subject of great interest to us when so near the spot, and it became the general matter of conversation, in the course of which I heard some of those who well knew that part of the world giving vent to very strong expressions about the dishonourable conduct of the British Government in abandoning the Atchinese to the Dutchmen, whom they detest with undying hatred.

Meanwhile the war goes on, and seems likely to go on for ever, according to what we heard about the determination of the natives. Seeing the country for the first time, I could observe in a moment that they have an immense advantage in being dwellers in a hill-country, which they will probably continue to defend with the same resolution as the Swiss would display in the presence of an invader. It seemed to be a common opinion that the Dutch would be bled in men and money till they find that '*Le jeu ne vaut pas la chandelle.*'

Clearing the northern end of Sumatra, we almost immediately began to feel the influence of the south-west monsoon. For the remaining days of the voyage to Ceylon we enjoyed the infinite luxury of refreshing wind and a cool ship, even though the sea was heavy enough to justify the carpenter in closing a great many of the ports. We passed immense numbers of flying-fish, some of which we calculated must have travelled at least 200 yards without touching the water; and I particularly marked one of them change its course at a sharp angle twice in a single flight; a clear proof of control over the so-called wings. The morning-baths were deliciously cool, and the monsoon made everything so comfortable for us, that it was hard to believe that we were actually moving day by day on the parallel of only 5° from the Equator.

After several days of strong wind against us, we entered the anchorage of Point de Galle in Ceylon, which is dangerous to go into, dangerous to stay in, and dangerous to get out of. It is liable to tremendous seas, and is full of peril from reefs and sunken rocks. We let go two anchors immediately, and two more were prepared for use at a moment's notice: and this was hardly done when the ship was boarded by scores of long-robed men with white turbans who, in spite of their imposing appearance, had merely come to compete for the honour of washing our linen in the three days during which the ship would stop there. The boats that come off from the shore are probably the most uncomfortable vessels in the known world. The hollow trunk of a small tree is surmounted by two vertical sides so near to one another that the narrowness of the boat scarcely gives space for a man's legs to enter, and passengers have to sit sideways on little boards overhanging the water. It is easy to imagine the difficulty and danger of getting into a boat only a few inches wide, which is dancing up and down the side of a ship under the influence of a heavy swell, and which is only prevented from upsetting instantly by a huge projecting outrigger of wood.

We had intended spending two or three weeks upon a visit to Kandy and the interior of Ceylon; but I found letters awaiting me which made me feel that it was my duty to give up that pleasure and to go straight home in the 'Cathay.' At the same time it seemed a very great pity that my companions should leave the beautiful island without completing the last act in the programme of our journeyings on shore. Somehow or other, after the various and immense distances which we had traversed, I felt in Ceylon quite close to England, and I remarked that it was just as if two men arrived at the Waterloo Station and raised the trifling question of whether they should take one cab or two to convey them to their respective homes. The rest of the voyage seemed nothing at all. It was agreed, therefore, that I should go home at once as pioneer for my companion, who would follow in a fortnight. Looking at the state of my wardrobe, I prudently wrote *viâ* Brindisi to my tailor and bootmaker, so as to give them nearly a week to prepare

THE CINNAMON-GARDENS IN CEYLON

some respectable garments in time for my arrival at Southampton.

This decision having been arrived at, I prepared to enjoy a couple of days in the neighbourhood of Galle. The Oriental Hotel provided us with every comfort and luxury; and, the place being the point of contact for all travellers to and from every part of the East, there is constant activity and daily change of more or less amusing society. The *table d'hôte* dinner was served in admirable style, and I have never seen such splendid table-decorations as were provided by vases full of the grand crimson and yellow blossoms of the Hibiscus. A short drive took us to the famous cinnamon-gardens, where may always be had a ramble under the delicious shade of evergreen trees, and among the exquisite vegetation on the banks of the little river. Boys were on the look-out to sell walking-sticks of cinnamon-wood, which at the touch of a finger-nail give forth the fragrant perfume of the spice.

Hence an easy walk up gently-rising ground took us to a conspicuous point commanding a wide view of green hills and valleys of rice away to the distant blue mountain-tops of the interior. Here we were amused by the ingenuity of some native boys who climbed up to the tops of palm-trees to bring down some of the young leaves, which they then split with penknives into strips, working them quickly into the form of bird-cages with birds in them, and many other curious devices. On this hill we found 'sensitive plants' and some magnificent acacias drooping brilliant blossoms over our heads; and the climbing *Lygodiums* reached, if possible, a greater perfection than those of Singapore and China. Sweet breezes tempered the heat, which, even according to the thermometer, was not excessive: the road towards Colombo by which we returned, passing close to the sea, with dark woods on one side, and the surf gently breaking on the other side where groves of cocoa-nut palms waved over the pure white sand of the beach, was lovely in the extreme ; and my short glimpses of Ceylon scenery were eminently suggestive of Paradise.

Never, however, have I seen such a set of unblushing rascals as the men who hung about the hotel all day, selling sham jewellery, lace, embroidery, and ornaments in ivory and tortoiseshell. The police tried to keep them off, but some of them were continually intruding and trying to fleece new-comers with an unsparing hand. When a friend of ours who knew their ways came up and openly said to one of them in the midst of a bargain, 'Why, you are the greatest liar and rascal of them all,' the fellow only smiled as if he were rather proud than otherwise of the distinction. A purchaser, thoroughly obstinate in refusal, would ultimately get things for a sum which was in ludicrous disproportion to the price originally demanded.

One of the most useful works that the Prince of Wales has inaugurated in his Indian tour will be the new breakwater at Colombo, which will soon be made into a safe and commodious harbour. The steamboat traffic will be removed to it, and Point de Galle, with all the manifold dangers which have been fatal to so many noble ships, will be abandoned. The rogues will have to migrate also, if they wish to continue their tricks upon travellers.

We were delayed for a day or two by waiting for the concurrent steamers. Then came the 'Baroda' from Australia, bringing about 700,000*l*. in gold, which, added to a cargo of tea and silk worth about 1,000,000*l*. and divers sundries, raised the insurable value of the 'Cathay' to about 2,000,000*l*. The next day brought us the 'Peshawur' from Calcutta and Madras, bringing us some very agreeable passengers; but there was a sadly striking contrast between the evident delicacy of health of many of them and the robust condition of those who had just before arrived from Australia.

My companions left for Colombo and Kandy on the day when I started homeward in the 'Cathay.' Across the Indian Ocean we encountered a very strong south-west monsoon, which promoted a good deal of sea-sickness among the ladies; and the only event worth noting was the rather rare and extraordinary phenomenon which is called the 'Milky Sea.' One night the sea was an entire sheet of phosphorescence, illuminating everything, and making the horizon visible. The huge waves rose up like mountains of milk driven before the wind, producing one of the most astonishing sights in the world. It is totally different from the ordinary phosphorescence of broken water, and is, I believe, peculiar to that part of the Ocean.

Ten days brought us to Aden, which reminded me of the rocky, burnt-up appearance of St. Vincent in the Cape de Verde Islands. Then we entered upon our week in the Red Sea, the first half of which was something too dreadful to think of. The temperature of the sea-water pumped up for 'cold' baths about six o'clock in the morning was 92° Fah. for three consecutive days. The feeling of fatigue and languor was oppressive: the evaporation from the sea appeared to have destroyed all wholesome atmosphere, and the sun shone down in a cloudless blaze of heat like fire. The limbs seemed almost to lose their power, and we spent the greater part of the twenty-four hours stretched at full length upon cane lounging-chairs, and impatiently waiting for a breath of fresh air. At length we met the North-West breeze, which once more made life endurable, and we reached Suez in a state of comparative freshness.

We only remained there for a few hours, during which the consumption of grapes was something astonishing to behold; and then we entered the Suez Canal, and stopped for the night at the entrance to the Bitter Lakes. The colouring of the neighbourhood of Suez was superb: the sea was graduated from emerald green to deepest blue, and the long ranges of reddish brown hills were softened to cobalt in the distance. In the Canal, however, there was nothing to see but desolate sands giving off a glare which was rather painful to the eyes, and induced many of the passengers to wear dark spectacles.

The only picturesque element in the scene was furnished by the occasional ferries which are placed where the caravan-routes go across the line of the Canal. There we saw wild groups of Arabs with their camels, waiting to enter the ferry-boats as soon as we had passed, and staring at us silently: I could almost fancy the sulky-looking camels were thinking, 'We are the ships of the desert; how dares this black monster intrude upon us here?' We stopped at a siding of the Canal to allow the magnificent steamer 'Ava' of the French Messageries to pass us, and when we saw her lofty decks and her ports high out of the water, we could not but think of how we had been half-stifled with ports closed for a trifling sea, in the hot latitudes, on board what ought to be considered a cargo-boat of the Peninsular and Oriental Company.

We passed by Port Said into the dirty water of the Nile basin, and ran on to Alexandria, which, with the aid of its splendid breakwater, seems worthy to recover some of its ancient glories : and we spent the greater part of a day on shore in seeing most of its principal sights and amusing ourselves with shopping among one of the most motley populations in the world. We spent another day at Malta, which might have appeared hot to anyone who had not, like ourselves, been lately delivered from a veritable furnace. From Alexandria to Gibraltar the voyage appeared like sailing over a sea of warm blue glass, though it must be remembered that the boasted colour of the Mediterranean is vastly inferior to the sublime violet-blue of the Atlantic and Pacific Oceans.

As we approached Gibraltar I pointed out to the chief officer a wild white cloud hanging about the summit of the Rock, which I felt sure was indicative of rough weather, though we were still in perfect calm. The wind came down to us presently as I had predicted; and the last four days of our run home were the most miserable that we had experienced since leaving England nearly a year before. A cold north-westerly wind, with almost constant drizzling rain, called out pilot-coats and seal-skin jackets to cover the flimsy garments that we had so long been wearing; and our comfort was not improved by the addition of Gibraltar passengers. Our first glimpses of England were seen through howling wind and cold rain, which descended in torrents; and, as we went up the Southampton river, the very engines testified their disgust at our reception by partially breaking down. When at last we discovered that the barbarous stinginess of the Company prevented the Captain from taking the ship into the Docks, and compelled delicate women and children, and invalids, returning from India, to be huddled into an open tug, under a deluge of bitter rain, we felt that the cup of wrath was overflowing.

But let me not conclude with a growl. Most of the passengers went to London by an evening train, whilst I and an officer of the Artillery resolved to sleep at Radley's Hotel, after enjoying a good English dinner with a solemn bottle of port. And, as I thought of all that we had seen and done in the past twelvemonth, by land and by sea, without the smallest accident, sickness, or misadventure, I felt that there was no room for any feeling but that of extreme thankfulness and satisfaction.

www.ingramcontent.com/pod-product-compliance
Lightning Source LLC
Chambersburg PA
CBHW032001300426
44117CB00008B/858